Poverty, Ethnicity, and Gender in Eastern Europe During the Market Transition

Edited by Rebecca Jean Emigh
and Iván Szelényi

Westport, Connecticut
London

Library of Congress Cataloging-in-Publication Data

Poverty, ethnicity, and gender in Eastern Europe during the market transition / edited by Rebecca Jean Emigh and Iván Szelényi.
     p.   cm.
   Includes bibliographical references and index.
   ISBN 0–275–96881–2 (alk. paper)
    1. Poverty—Europe, Eastern. 2. Europe, Eastern—Social conditions—1989– I. Emigh, Rebecca Jean, 1962– II. Szelényi, Iván.
   HC244.Z9P6175 2001
   305.5′6′094709049—dc21   00–029839

British Library Cataloguing in Publication Data is available.

Library of Congress Catalog Card Number: 00–029839
ISBN: 0–275–96881–2

First published in 2001

Praeger Publishers, 88 Post Road West, Westport, CT 06881
An imprint of Greenwood Publishing Group, Inc.
www.praeger.com

Printed in the United States of America

The paper used in this book complies with the Permanent Paper Standard issued by the National Information Standards Organization (Z39.48–1984).

10 9 8 7 6 5 4 3 2 1

Contents

Preface

In April 1998 we organized a two-day workshop in Budapest, Hungary, with funding from the Ford Foundation. At that time, we were just embarking on a multiyear project to study poverty in Central, Eastern, and Southern Europe. We asked experts from these countries to participate in, and to write papers for, this workshop. This volume is an outgrowth of this work. Included in this book are chapters discussing poverty in Bulgaria, Hungary, Poland, Romania, and Slovakia. As we explain in the volume, we purposefully selected these countries because they varied with respect to variables of theoretical interest. We would like to thank the Ford Foundation for their generous support of our project and Rachel Cohen for her editorial assistance.

1

The Racialization and Feminization of Poverty?

Rebecca Jean Emigh, Eva Fodor, and Iván Szelényi

Quite understandably—and quite correctly—poverty is usually studied as a persistent, unchanging social problem that, hopefully, can be ameliorated through specific social policies. Indeed, the biblical saying that, "the poor are always with us" has withstood the test of time. The present volume, however, tackles poverty from a different angle. We ask how poverty changes during an epochal transformation, in this case, the transition from economies based on socialist redistribution to those based on capitalist markets. We use this major transformation as an epistemological lever to provide insight into the causes and nature of poverty. In the same spirit of drawing on difference as an analytic tool, our approach is also explicitly comparative. We compare and contrast poverty—and what we argue are associated social processes of racialization and feminization—in different countries during this transition. We hope that this approach not only provides sociological insight but also illuminates policy debates.

During the past decade, there have been dramatic and sweeping changes in the countries of the former East European communist bloc; all have moved toward a market economy. In some places, marketization has been very rapid. At the same time, however, poverty has increased in all the countries. In this chapter, we offer some hypotheses about the relationship between poverty, markets, and ethnicity in this region and suggest how the evidence from these countries, as reported in the later chapters, addresses these hypotheses.

POVERTY, MARKETS, AND REDISTRIBUTION

To define our theoretical puzzle, we draw on the distinction between neo-classical economists and traditional institutionalists. These two positions provide opposing views concerning the origins of poverty. They also recommend strikingly different policies to eliminate poverty. For decades—during the ideological hegemony of traditional institutionalism—the received wisdom among social scientists was that unregulated markets were the primary sources of poverty. Welfare redistribution by governments was necessary to reduce poverty (Polanyi 1944; Townsend 1970) whether it was defined in either relative or absolute terms. Recent evidence suggests that welfare states (in particular, the encompassing "social-democratic" welfare states, in contrast to their more minimalist "liberal" counterparts) have been remarkably successful in alleviating poverty—especially long-term poverty—and minimizing inequality while maintaining growth (Headey, Goodin, Muffels, and Dirven 1997; Kenworthy 1999; Korpi and Palme 1998).

Neo-classical economists, on the other hand, have a dismal view of the welfare state. They argue that unconstrained markets generate rapid economic growth that eventually benefits the bottom of the social hierarchy. Neo-classical economists believe that welfare redistribution offers no cure for poverty; it only suppresses the symptoms and prolongs the disease. Governmental welfare redistribution locks the poor into welfare dependence and usually supports the middle class because it does not reach those in extreme poverty anyway. Thus, poverty will be reproduced indefinitely unless the poor take responsibility for their own welfare (Friedman and Friedman 1980; Hayek 1944; 1960; Stigler 1970). Over time, the social-democratic model of the welfare state has also lost ground ideologically to the neoliberal model of the limited welfare state (especially in terms of its poverty-reducing effect), and the more limited model is being instituted in Central and Eastern Europe (Esping-Andersen 1996; Standing 1996). At the same time, however, the ability of welfare states to reduce poverty has been weakened by capital flight that has undermined some of states' key economic-planning institutions (Stephens 1996) and by an increasingly globalized labor and skill market, which has undermined labor–market policies (Esping-Andersen 1996).

Kuznets (1955) offered a theory that was consistent with this neo-classical position but posed the relationship between economic growth and social inequality in a more complex way. He analyzed income distribution data over a long period of time using countries with different levels of economic development. He concluded that income inequality increased during an economic takeoff but that inequality declined after economic growth reached a certain level. Thus, the relationship between economic growth and social inequality can be well described by an inverted U-shaped curve. Assuming that free markets produce the fastest possible economic growth, especially in highly developed economies, Kuznets' theory suggests that the expansion of markets may initially increase inequality. By implication, poverty, at least in relative terms, will also increase. Even an increase in absolute poverty is not unimaginable from this theoretical perspective. Eventually, however, free markets will correct the socially undesirable effects of economic growth. Markets will reduce inequality, thereby reducing not only absolute, but also relative, poverty.

In a recent comparative study of inequality and poverty, Lal and Myint (1996) formulated the question of the relationship between equality, poverty, and economic growth in a particularly clear and provocative way. They found that income distributions in the core capitalist countries of the world during the past quarter century did not follow the pattern observed by Kuznets. In particular, inequalities in Western Europe and North America increased during the last decades of the twentieth century. Similarly, Li, Squire, and Zou (1998) found little relationship between development and inequality in their cross-country time-series analysis. Nevertheless, though Lal and Myint (1996) find little evidence that economic growth reduced inequality (relative poverty), they did find evidence that economic growth reduced absolute poverty. Thus, free markets and economic growth may produce greater inequality, but they may reduce absolute poverty.

POVERTY AND THE UNDERCLASS

Whether economic growth and marketization eliminate absolute poverty is our central analytic question. We realize that social inequality is a serious problem, but here we focus on underclass formation and, therefore, on absolute poverty. Thus, we arrive at the problem of the tricky and often debated definition of the underclass. Unfortunately, this term has been recently adopted by ideologues of the political Right, who combined it with the "culture of poverty" tradition (Lewis 1966). They define the underclass in behavioral terms, as the "welfare dependent," the subset of poor mired in crime and blamed for its own condition (Levy 1977; Russell 1977). However, we prefer to return to the concept as it was originally used in the 1960s and early 1970s. As far as we can tell, the term "underclass" was coined by Myrdal (1963; 1964), who used it to designate the unique position of the long-term poor who were not benefiting from the postwar economic boom. These individuals were locked into long-term structural unemployment because they did not have, and could not acquire, the education and skills demanded in a diversified economy. We believe that William Julius Wilson (1978) intended to use the term this way (Aponte 1990), though he may not have been entirely clear, as he sometimes shifted between an economic and behavioral definition of the term "underclass." Here, we simply highlight that Wilson expanded Myrdal's notion of underclass in useful ways, by moving away from an economically deterministic understanding of the underclass and by bringing the issue of racism into his analysis.

Thus, although the concept of the underclass has been surrounded by numerous debates, we argue that much of the conceptual unclarity can be resolved. We distance ourselves from attempts to define the term in behavioral terms (Ricketts and Sawhill 1988), which unfortunately only point out the social problems resulting from persistent poverty, and return to its original, structural definition. While recognizing that structural definitions may also have slightly different variants (Aponte 1990), we make use of a three-part definition of the underclass, drawing from Myrdal (1963:14, 38–39), Wilson (1978:156–157; 1987:10–12, 60), and Massey and Denton (1993:3–9): (1) extreme poverty (2) that is persistent and thus tends to be lifelong and intergenerationally transmitted, and (3) spatial segregation. We also follow Myrdal (1963:14–16) and Wilson (1978:1–23; 1987:20–62) in hypothesizing that an underclass forms during economic transformations that adversely affect some segment of the population. In the last 50 years, this transformation has been the decline in highly paid, low-skill work brought about by deindustrialization, leaving an entire segment of the population unemployed and unemployable, thus creating persistent poverty. Thus, we define the underclass in terms of the objective life chances of its members. These individuals are separated from the rest of society by a castelike cleavage; members of the underclass become the "untouchables," the "undeserving poor," or the "no-hopers." In the next section, we argue that an underclass is likely to form in conjunction with the presence of certain social characteristics, and in particular, ethnicity or gender.

UNDERCLASS FORMATION AROUND ETHNICITY AND GENDER?

All evidence at our disposal indicates that during the transition from socialist redistribution to capitalist markets, both absolute and relative poverty increased. Within this empirical context, we formulate our hypotheses by drawing on the neo-classical and institutionalist perspectives. As market institutions become consolidated in former postcommunist countries, will absolute poverty decline, following a "Lal and Myint" curve, as neo-classical theory predicts, or will the poor reproduce themselves unless the government intervenes, as institutionalists predict? Of course, many factors impinge on this relationship. For example, Blank (1997a; 1997b) argues that economic growth in and of itself does not bring an end to poverty. Instead, the effects of growth on poverty are mediated by other factors, primarily the labor market and wage rates (see also Ayres and Clark 1998; Cornia and Danziger 1997).

Here, we consider another factor. In particular, we hypothesize that whether poverty will be reproduced under the conditions of well-functioning markets depends on the social characteristics of the cleavages that separate the poor from the not-so-poor and on the social characteristics of markets. We focus on two sets of socially achieved distinctions, ethnicity and gender, which can be used to mark differences in economic status.

Although Myrdal (1963:45) originally explicitly included other groups, including whites, as candidates for the underclass, we note that this process of underclass formation has been generally associated with urban blacks and, to a lesser extent, with Puerto Ricans (Tienda 1989). This empirical focus on racial and ethnic minorities, we argue, is linked to a fourth component of the underclass that suggests quasi-behavioral aspects to the underclass. Myrdal (1963:37) argued that members of the underclass are viewed as "outcasts," as socially unnecessary individuals who cannot participate in social life. Underclass formation is accompanied by an act of exclusion by the rest of society. Thus, although neither race nor ethnicity is by definition required for underclass formation, these minorities are more likely to be its members. Because underclass formation has this element of social exclusion, we draw on theories of social classification that explain this process. As Weber (1978:387–393) noted, ethnicity is one way to mark and exclude others. Thus, we argue, following Bourdieu (1991:221), that ethnicity is an outcome of classificatory struggles. Ethnic groups are categories of ascription and identification constructed by social actors (Barth 1969:10).

This link between poverty and ethnic and racial categories is a classic social science problem. Weber (1978) described ethnicity and class as two separate bases of social stratification. Yet, the two systems of classification not only overlap and reinforce each other (Jenkins 1994:206; McAll 1990:222; Williams 1989:410) but also tend to become each other. Those who are poor become "ethnic," while members of this ethnicity are more likely to be called "poor."

We make a stronger claim, however, that underclass formation is linked to the process of racialization. We use the term "racialization" in contrast to "ethnicization." While there are multiple definitions of these terms, we use "race" to refer to social actors' cultural distinctions based on physical or biological differences and "ethnicity" to their cultural distinctions based on social differences. Thus, while there may be a link between poverty and ethnicity (Caplan 1996; McAll 1990:173, 221–222; Ward 1989), we also link the process of underclass with race. We argue that the process of racialization, the process of turning cultural distinctions based on social differences into cultural distinctions based on physical differences, may be the exclusionary classificatory process linked to underclass formation. Thus, the process of racialization, the presentation of a social phenomenon such as poverty as if it were biologically determined, may lock certain groups into underclass positions. When an ethnic minority is concentrated in poverty, there may be a tendency toward the formation of an underclass if poverty is racialized. Ethnic labels, such as Roma, create social boundaries (Barth 1969:9–10; Jenkins 1994:202; McAll 1990:66–67; Weber 1978:388). Once the ethnic difference is created, it may be racialized; that is, social differences may be labeled as biological. For example, British and Irish ethnic differences became increasingly racialized between the fifteenth and the nineteenth centuries (Smedley 1993:52–61; Williams 1989:431). This process of racialization may create a Roma underclass.

Thus, we argue that the racialization of poverty is the outcome of a classificatory struggle. If this classificatory struggle is successful, a social phenomenon—poverty—is presented as if it were racial, not social, and therefore, as if it were genetically and biologically determined. From this perspective, racialization arises from a strategy used by the positively privileged ethnic group to keep themselves out of the category "poor" and/or to blame the poor for their own poverty at the same time. ("I cannot be poor, since I am not African American or Gypsy" or "They are poor since they are African Americans or Gypsies. It is their biological heritage or culture that makes them poor.") Our conceptualization of racialization is similar to Miles' position (1982). He argues that social actors in structurally similar social, economic, or geographic positions to ethnic minorities are likely to use race to separate themselves from these minorities. Understood this way, racialization implies a classificatory struggle: the social actors who are involved in struggles to define poverty as a racial issue pursue a specific agenda.

As actors pursue this agenda, of course, they construct reality. Nevertheless, they do so in reference to reality. In the absence of an ethnicity that is amenable to racialization, attempts to racialize a cleavage will fail. There are, indeed, some dispositions that increase the likelihood of successful racialization. These dispositions are historically variable: at one time they may be sufficient to create a sharp cleavage between the poor and the not-so-poor; at another time, they may not serve this purpose. For example, being Jewish may have been an ethnicity around which to racialize poverty 100 years ago in Eastern Europe, but it may no longer be possible to do so. Today, being Jewish may be an ethnicity from which a privileged status can be constructed. Thus, in the social construction of reality there must be some objective point of reference that can be used, though how this objective reality is used is a product of struggles between classifiers and classified.

In many ways, the Jews and Roma of Europe are examples of racialized ethnicities. There are, or were, sizable groups of ethnic minorities, and, thus, they could be targets of exclusionary classificatory practices. Historically, though Jews were a religious group, they were often separated out as a separate race (Rogger 1986:37). Even highly assimilated Jews were often distinguished from their neighbors by virtue of their complexions, facial features, and other physical characteristics (Pinchuk 1990:17). Similarly, Roma are distinguished from ethnic majorities on the basis of skin color or facial features and assumed to be descendants of some biologically inferior, non-European people from the East (Crowe 1991:151; Fraser 1992:249). Roma were slaves in Romania for nearly 500 years (Beck 1989; Crowe 1991:151). In fact, there is little evidence for a common Roma ancestry and no genetic basis for Roma ethnicity. The Roma are highly heterogeneous, viewed as a singular group, as "Gypsies," only by outsiders. An ethnic category is thus turned into a racial category by a hostile, outside world. Who is Roma is a result of an interaction between both the classifiers and the classified. In addition, we argue that those who are poor are more likely to be classified as Roma.

In this volume, we focus on Roma ethnicity. It is the largest cross-national group in Central, Eastern, and Southern Europe that is concentrated in poverty and, therefore, likely to be candidates for the underclass. Of course, there are other poor ethnic groups in these countries, but the Roma allow us to examine the link between poverty and ethnicity, racialization and underclass formation, using a cross-national, comparative perspective.

We believe that race is the product of classificatory struggles, thus, (1) no assumptions should be made about common ancestry; (2) empirically, it is untenable that race (or ethnicity) can be determined with certainty by anthropological characteristics (like darkness of the skin, facial characteristics, color of the hair, or eyes), and (3) therefore, the assumption made even by many nonracist researchers (Kemény 1976), namely, that all members of the society can agree with absolute certainty about who is a member of any particular racial or ethnic group (e.g., the Roma) is untenable. Who is Roma, Jewish, Hungarian, or Romanian is a result of classificatory struggles that involve both those who are classified this way and those who try to classify them. Thus, we argue that the object of our study should be the varieties of classificatory systems, not the "correct" way to determine who belongs to which group. This understanding of Roma ethnicity is closest to Okely's work (1983) and also similar to the positions of Stewart (1997), Lucassen (1991), and Pronai (1995).

Empirical research conducted in Central, Eastern, and Southern Europe makes it very clear that estimates of the size of the Roma population depend on how the classifiers define ethnicity. Different systems of classifications have been used in different countries and in different studies: (1) respondents were classified as Roma if they spoke the Romany language (this is what most censuses did before 1980); (2) respondents were asked to identify themselves as belonging to Gypsy "nationality" (most censuses asked this question after the fall of communism); (3) respondents were asked to identify the ethnic background of their ancestors (Szelényi and Treiman 1992); (4) experts or jurors (schoolteachers, headmasters, social workers, doctors, the police) were asked to identify Gypsies in particular communities (Kemény 1976; Kemény, Havas, and Kertesi 1995; Tomova 1995; Zamfir and Zamfir 1995); (5) interviewers were asked whether they believed that respondents were definitely or possibly Roma (Hungarian Central Statistical Office 1993; Szelényi and Treiman 1992; Szonda Ipsos 1997).

The size and composition of the Roma population in Bulgaria, Hungary, Romania, and Slovakia vary depending on how the Roma population is estimated. If individuals who self-identify as Roma are used as the benchmark, other estimates of the Roma population can be compared to the estimate obtained by using self-identification in the following way (these are rough figures, since estimates of the size and proportion of Roma population vary across countries). If the number of individuals who self-identify as Roma equals 1, then the number of individuals whose native language is Romany is 0.5, the number of individuals reporting Roma ancestors is 3, the number of Roma reported by expert judges is 5, the number that interviewers identify as definitely Roma is 6 or 7, and the number that interviewers identify as definitely or probably Roma is 10. Thus, estimates of the Roma population vary between 0.5 and 10, or about 20-fold (Kemény, Havas, and Kertesi 1995; Szelényi and Treiman 1992; Szonda Ipsos 1997), depending on the classificatory scheme used to define the population.

Drawing on this understanding of the racialization of poverty, we develop an analogous concept of the feminization of poverty, that is, a classificatory struggle around gender. Thus, the feminization of poverty occurs when women are concentrated in poverty and when biological, not social, causes are proposed as the explanation of this concentration. When poverty is feminized, it becomes viewed as inherent: young women with low intelligence and high fertility have many children, thereby creating a cycle of poverty. This image is often linked to what is assumed to be women's natural role in child-raising activities. Becker (1991:37–48), for example, argues that child-raising activities are biologically easier for women than for men. As a consequence, he argues that it is rational for women to specialize in such activities. Indeed, in popular parlance, poor women with many children are often viewed as victims of biological processes of fertility and childbearing. Thus, the "welfare" mother is treated as a quasi-biological construction. In a process analogous to racialization, when poverty is feminized, it is presented as if it were a naturally occurring attribute of sex, that is, women's biological capacities, instead of as a social construction.

While there are some objective, biological bases for women's role in reproduction, much of women's concentration in poverty is related to women's inferior market position with respect to men and to women's greater social responsibilities for child raising. There is some indication that in the United States, some women, in particular, some female ethnic minorities, form an underclass (Casper, McLanahan, and Garfinkel 1994; Rodgers 1996; Stack

1974). Such women tend to become single mothers at a young age, and for them poverty is not merely a life-cycle phenomenon. They do not cease to be poor when their children reach adulthood, and their children are also more likely to be poor and remain poor. For our purposes, Central and Southern Europe is again a strategic research site—this time because poverty appears not to be feminized, at least not in the same way as in the United States.

During the transition from socialist redistribution to capitalist markets, the racialization and feminization of poverty followed different trajectories. Under socialism, Roma experienced discrimination. Still, however, they did not constitute an underclass—though they were the most underprivileged group in these societies—because the socialist economy operated with full employment. Kornai (1980), with great accuracy, called the socialist redistributive economy an "economy of shortage." While economies based on market capitalism suffer from cyclical crises of overproduction—they have a chronic problem of excessive supply—socialist, redistributive economies represent their mirror images. They suffer from chronic shortages, even with respect to the allocation of labor. Threatened with chronic labor shortages, socialist societies institute laws that require individuals to be employed. Under these circumstances, there was sufficient demand for labor to draw Roma into the labor market, in addition to the legal compulsion requiring Roma to be employed. Thus, under socialism, Roma had access to a steady cash inflow for the first time in their history. Gypsies were employed where labor was in the most demand—precisely in the most privileged sectors of the economy, steel, mining, and construction, though racial prejudice slotted them into the most underprivileged positions. When socialism crumbled, these privileged bastions of the socialist economy were the hardest hit: what used to be the most privileged sectors of the economy became the least privileged ones. Thus, with the transition to capitalist markets, the Gypsies became the poorest of the poor. With the collapse of the mining, steel, and construction industries, Roma were the first to lose their jobs and had no hope for finding new employment (Barany 1994; Gheorghe 1991). This process is similar to the effect of deindustrialization in creating poor, black ghettos in major American cities. Deindustrialization in former socialist countries, however, has a much greater impact on the creation of a Roma underclass, because socialist ideology idealized those sectors in which the genuine proletariat, "the workers with hammers in hand," labored! Socialist planners were obsessed with "department one" and with the "production of the means of production" in a way that was unprecedented in market economies. As a result, when socialism collapsed, the Roma population moved out of the underprivileged stratum of the privileged economic sectors and into the underclass of postcommunist society.

The Roma have become geographically isolated as well. One unusual pattern of geographic isolation in Central and Southern Europe is rural, ethnic ghettos. Although African American ghettos in the United States are urban phenomena, Roma ghettos are found in villages. Not only are rural ghettos unique in comparison to the United States, but they are also novel historical developments in Central and Southern Europe. Traditionally, the Roma minority—if settled, and in the successor states of the Austro-Hungarian empire it tended to be settled—lived in Gypsy settlements next to villages inhabited by ethnic majorities. During the past several decades, there was a dramatic ecological change in rural social spaces. The ethnic majority population began to escape small, isolated villages and moved into centers of rural growth or cities. The vacated spaces were filled by Roma, who were able to move out of the Roma settlements and into the villages. The housing conditions of Roma improved dramatically when they relocated, as they often moved out of mud huts in the settlements. Nevertheless, the flight of the peasant population from these isolated villages was disastrous for the Roma. Peasants in the villages mediated between the rural Roma poor and the rest of society. Peasants consumed the services and products of the Roma. Rural Gypsies were hired as entertainers, as musicians at weddings and funerals, and as seasonal laborers. Peasants also bought goods that Gypsies produced. The out-migration of the peasants was, in many ways, analogous to the out-migration of the black middle class from urban black neighborhoods in the United States. Historically, rural Roma lived in an asymmetrical, but symbiotic, relationship with the peasants who belonged to the ethnic majority. When they lost these social ties, they were turned into a ghetto poor. Though the ethnic dimension is different, this process of the creation of a ghetto is similar to the way in which poor African Americans were turned into an underclass because of the loss of their middle class.

Nevertheless, the overlap between rural residence, poverty, and ethnicity is not complete. Gypsy ghettos are also visible in the cities of Central and Southern Europe. These ghettos of urban Roma are created by a similar process, when those who are doing better economically escape the Roma neighborhoods. In addition, as Tarkowska (Chapter 4 in this volume) indicates, poverty is prevalent in rural regions among the population of ethnic majorities in postcommunist societies, because these regions experience little economic growth and suffer from the collapse of socialist state farms. Tarkowska argues that an underclass is formed if its members are socially, economically, and geographically isolated from the rest of the society. By her criteria, the Roma qualify as an underclass.

Like the social condition of the Roma, women's position has been changing during the transition to capitalist markets. Their trajectories, however, differ dramatically. Women were also discriminated against under socialism. Unlike Gypsies, who ended up at the bottom of the privileged economic sectors, however, women were locked into the underprivileged sectors of the socialist economy, though they were allowed to climb the social ladder in these sectors. Women were therefore substantially overrepresented in the tertiary sector, the orphan of the socialist redistributive economy. They were also excluded from the royal path to power and privilege: Communist Party membership. Thus, they frequently compensated for their underrepresentation in the party, for their shortage of political capital, with higher levels of education. Indeed, by the end of the socialist epoch, women tended to be better educated than men. Though well-educated women often held relatively poorly paid and low-prestige jobs in the tertiary sector, they were also employed in reasonably high positions in banking, insurance, advertising, tourism, and similar industries. In this respect, the market transition affected women in very different ways than it affected Roma. When the transition to market capitalism occurred, women were concentrated in the sector that experienced the most growth. Furthermore,

Communist Party membership lost its prestige, so this form of political capital in which men were privileged lost its value, while education became more important. Well-educated women were not threatened by unemployment, and often they found themselves in good jobs with highly desired skills (Fodor 1997). As a result, at least in the early stages of market transition, there is little evidence of the feminization of poverty. In fact, the transition from socialist redistribution to capitalist markets benefits women, at least temporarily. As marketization proceeds, however, women's relative advantage may be eroded. Young men are rapidly entering the tertiary sector. It may take less than a generation for women to lose this relative advantage that accrued to them virtually by accident as a result of market transition.

While in the advanced, Western capitalist economies, racialization and feminization are two reinforcing processes that accentuate the boundaries between the poor and the not-so-poor, during the epochal transition from socialism to capitalism, we hypothesize that racialization, but not feminization, creates an underclass. Thus, while racialization may prevent a long-term reduction in absolute poverty and may be apparent in the early stages of transition, feminization may not have the same effect or may take place at a much later stage in the transition.

This difference between the dynamics of feminization and racialization highlights two crucial issues. First, the feminization of poverty is not inevitable and is a social, not a biological, construction. Second, it illustrates that both the institutionalist and the neo-classical theories suggest that markets have a singular effect, though the theories differ in the way that they characterize this effect. The institutionalist theorists argue that markets create a permanent underclass, while neo-classical theorists argue that they eliminate this type of poverty. Neither position, however, incorporates the historical trajectories of markets, and, therefore, neither position captures the relative advantages of the socialist legacy for women that are specific to a transition from socialist redistribution to capitalist markets.

Thus, drawing on Myrdal and Wilson's use of the term, "underclass," our own perspective, inspired by Bourdieu, combines a focus on the objective problems of structural unemployment with an analysis of the subjective classificatory struggles of ethnicity and gender to predict when sharp distinctions are drawn between the "hopelessly poor" and the "deserving poor." Thus, we focus on two mechanisms—racialization and feminization—that can reproduce poverty. Poverty may become racialized or feminized when ethnic minorities or women are overrepresented among the poor. This over-representation is a necessary, but insufficient, condition. Racialization and feminization occur when a social phenomenon—here, poverty—is attributed to supposedly ascribed characteristics of actors. If the racialization or feminization of poverty is successful, the cleavage between the poor and the not-so-poor becomes rigid, and social actors perceive this cleavage as natural, created by the "laws of nature." The outcome is that the resultant poverty is durable and long-term. It is likely to be transmitted to the next generation.

In drawing attention to these processes, we try to navigate between the Scylla of "objectivism" and the Charybdis of "subjectivism." Objectivism in this context would mean that a particular ethnicity or gender is locked into poverty because of certain objective, unalterable attributes of that group. Subjectivism, on the other hand, would imply that ethnicity and gender have nothing to do with poverty; the fact that the poor are ethnic minorities or women is purely a subjective assessment by social actors. Instead, our conceptualization lies between these two positions, because we call attention to the ways in which actors draw on differences to make social classifications.

TRANSITION TO MARKET ECONOMY: THE "LABORATORY" TO EXAMINE THE EFFECTS OF MARKETIZATION ON POVERTY

Societies in transition from socialist redistribution to capitalist markets provide an ideal site to consider hypotheses about the relationship between markets, inequality, and poverty. In these postcommunist countries of Central and Southern Europe, there is an ideal, almost "laboratory"-like situation. Comparisons between these countries are a powerful tool to examine our hypotheses concerning the interactive effects of marketization, ethnicity, and poverty, because these countries vary along these dimensions. Table 1.1 presents some of the major characteristics of these countries. In terms of economic development and degree of market penetration, Hungary, Poland, and Slovakia are more advanced than Romania and Bulgaria. Poland is a relatively homogeneous society with respect to ethnicity, while Hungary is a country with a substantial Roma minority. Thus, the comparison of these two countries will show whether the presence of an ethnic minority that is concentrated in poverty creates an underclass. The comparison of Hungary with Slovakia, Romania, and Bulgaria (all of which have at least one ethnic minority) will suggest how much impact marketization has on the creation of an underclass. If neo-classical theory is correct, there should be no underclass in Hungary. If Roma poverty is similar in these four countries, our "revisionist" institutionalist theory will be supported.

There is another interesting comparison between the ethnically heterogeneous countries. Hungary has a single ethnic minority, while Romania and Slovakia have two minorities: Roma, who are concentrated in poverty, and Hungarians, who are not. Thus, a comparison between Slovakia, Romania, and Hungary will help to explain how the presence of a second minority, which apparently has no elective affinity with poverty, affects the growth of a Roma underclass. Bulgaria falls into a unique third category. It is a multiethnic society, in which more than one ethnicity is overrepresented among the poor (Roma, Pomaks [they were not presented as a separate ethnicity in the data used for Table 1.1], and Turks are concentrated in poverty). With respect to our hypothesis about racialization, we expect to find little evidence of an underclass in Poland because the Roma population is small.

Thus, we hypothesize that there will be differences in the degree of underclass formation depending on how many ethnicities exist in a country and how many ethnicities have an elective affinity with poverty (see Table 1.2). We hypothesize that (1) if there is one ethnic group that is overrepresented among the poor, underclass development will be strong; (2) if there are multiple groups overrepresented among the poor, underclass formation may be weaker, since classificatory struggles using race to separate the poor and the not-so-poor cannot focus on a single group; (3) if there are two ethnic groups, one that is concentrated in poverty and one that is not, the racialization of poverty may be especially strong. The ethnic group that is concentrated in poverty will be blamed, with particular force, for its own poverty, since the nonpoor ethnic group will be cited as an example that ethnic minorities are not necessarily poor. If our hypotheses are correct, the racialization of poverty will be especially strong in Hungary, Slovakia, and Romania.

The comparisons between these countries also address our hypotheses about the feminization of poverty (see Table 1.2). Feminization may be more advanced when (1) a racially defined underclass is less developed, because classificatory struggles can use only gender, not race, to mark poverty; and (2) if marketization is more advanced, it may overcome the temporary advantage that women had in the early stages of market transition. Thus, the feminization of poverty in these countries may increase with marketization. Consequently, the feminization of poverty will be strongest in Poland, which is relatively homogeneous ethnically and where marketization is the furthest under way, followed by Hungary, where marketization is also well under way, but which has a sizable Roma minority.

THE EVIDENCE FROM CENTRAL AND SOUTHERN EUROPE

Poverty

The comparison of poverty and inequality under socialism and post-communism is a complex task. Examining poverty was a taboo in communist societies (Chapters 3, 4 in this volume; Warzywoda-Kruszynska and Grotowka-Leder 1996:68). In the reform-oriented countries, such as Hungary and Poland, data were collected on low-income groups during the socialist epoch, but this evidence is fragmentary (Bokor 1987; Ferge 1969; Frackiewicz 1983; Jarosz 1984; Kemény 1972; Tulli 1978; Tymowski 1973). Despite these incomplete data, scholars agree that both absolute and relative poverty increased substantially after the breakdown of state socialism (Cornia 1994; Kornai 1996; Milanovic 1994)

The causes of the increase in poverty and prospects for its amelioration are less obvious. Is an increase in poverty the price of transition? Is it the price that societies pay for radical, but delayed, economic transformation (Chapter 2 in this volume)? Or, stated more theoretically, is there an inverted U-shaped curve describing the relationship between poverty and marketization during the postcommunist transition? If so, then absolute poverty may increase during the early stages of marketization but may decline as the economy grows and as fully. developed market institutions restructure the economy. The existence of an inverted U-shaped curve of poverty during postcommunist market transition would be consistent with Lal and Myint's theory of the relationship between economic growth and poverty. So far, there is no evidence of a Kuznets' curve of income distribution in postcommunist transitional economies. As the economies of Hungary and Poland grow, inequality remains high and may even

Table 1.1
Selected Country and Population Characteristics—Bulgaria, Hungary, Poland, Slovakia, and Romania

	Population (July 1998 estimate) [a]	Urban population, % of total (1992) [b]	Secondary school enrollment, % of possible [cd]	Higher education enrollment, % of possible [cd]	Ethnic groups, each accounting for more than 1% of population [af]	% population of this ethnicity [a]	% GDP produced in the private sector (1998) [e]
Bulgaria	8,240,426	68.9	78.0	39.4 Male: 29.3 Female: 49.9	Bulgarian Turk Roma Macedonian	85.3 8.5 2.6 2.5	38
Hungary	10,208,127	63.1	73.0 Male: 71.0 Female: 76.0	19.1 Male: 17.6 Female: 20.7	Hungarian Roma German Serb	89.9 4.0 2.6 2.0	80
Poland	38,606,922	63.4	87.1	-	Polish German Roma	97.6 1.3 -	70
Romania	22,395,848	54.1	73.0 Male: 72.0 Female: 74.0	-	Romanian Hungarian	89.1 8.9	54 (end 1996)
Slovakia	5,392,982	57.4	94.0 Male: 92.0 Female: 96.0	-	Slovak Hungarian Roma Czech	85.7 10.7 1.5 1.0	82

a: *CIA World Factbook.* (Washington, DC: Central Intelligence Agency, 1998).

Table 1.1 continued

b: *World Tables 1995.* (Washington, DC: World Bank, 1995).

c: *Europa World Year Book 1999.* (London: Europa Publications Limited, 1999).

d: Dates for education data vary by country: Bulgaria, 1995; Hungary, 1994; Poland, 1997/1998; Romania and Slovakia, 1996.

e: Country Commercial Guides 1998/1999. Produced by American Embassy staff (in relevant countries). Distributed on-line by the Central and Eastern Europe Business Information Center (http://www.mac.doc.gov/eebic/ceebic.html). (Central and Eastern Europe Business Information Center 1998/1999).

f: A figure for the Roma population in Romania is unclear but is around 1% of total population (see Table 1.5). The Slovak Roma may be significantly undercounted here.

Table 1.2
Hypotheses for a Comparative Study of Racialization and Feminization of Poverty

Marketization	Ethnically homogeneous	Ethnic group(s) likely to be poor:		One group in poverty, others not in poverty
		One group	Several groups	
High	**Poland**: no racialization, but feminization	**Hungary**: strong racialization; medium feminization		
Medium				**Slovakia**: strong racialization, some feminization
Low			**Bulgaria**: medium racialization, little feminization	**Romania**: strong racialization; little feminization

increase. Still, it is possible that there is a "Lal and Myint" curve: absolute poverty may be declining despite high inequality. Thus, the top income decile may earn an increasingly larger percentage of the total income, while the bottom decile may earn an increasingly smaller percentage of the total income, though those in the bottom income decile may still increase their absolute income. For example, Polish researchers report what appears to be a decline in the proportion of population under the poverty line, the turning point being somewhere around 1994–1995 (Beskid 1997; Chapter 4 in this volume).

Although most scholars agree that poverty increased during the first five years of postcommunism, estimates of poverty vary substantially depending on how poverty is defined. One approach is to define poverty using a preestablished per capita income as a threshold level. Those who use this approach tend to produce a lower estimate of poverty, though the growth of the population falling below the poverty line is substantial. Kornai (1996), for example, defines as "poor" those who earn four dollars a day or less; his estimates of poor in some of these countries are given in Table 1.3.

Milanovic (1994) arrives at similar conclusions by using the monthly per capita income of $120 as the poverty line. He argues that the number of poor people in the region climbed from 8 million to 58 million between 1989 and 1993. The rate of poverty has increased in Poland and the Balkans from 5% to 17%, in the Baltic states from 1% to 30%, and in Central Europe (Czech Republic, Slovakia, and Hungary) from .5% to 1%.

Cornia (1994), on the other hand, measures poverty in relative terms as those earning less than a certain percentage of the median income of the given country. Using such measures, the rate of growth of the population under the poverty line may seem less dramatic, but the actual proportion of poor is higher. His estimates are given in Table 1.4.

Table 1.3
Percent of Population Below the Poverty Line (Poverty Measured by Absolute Income [$4.00 per day])

Country	1987–88	1993–94
Bulgaria	2	33
Hungary	<1	3
Poland	6	19
Romania	6	39
Slovakia	0	<1

Source: Kornai 1996.

Table 1.4
Estimates of Poverty (% of the Population)

	1989	1990	1991	1992	1993
Bulgaria (45% of 1989 average wage)	.	13.8	52.1	53.6	57.0
Hungary (40% of 1989 average wage)	14.5	.	19.4	.	.
Poland (40% of 1989 average wage)	24.7	43.1	41.2	43.7	.
Romania (45% of 1989 average wage)	33.9	21.4	29.7	51.5	.
Slovakia (40% of 1989 average wage)	5.8	9.4	27.7	34.1	.

Source: Cornia 1994.

As far as we know, the only survey with data for most of the Central and Southern European countries that used the same methodology on a large, random sample of the population is the study "Social Stratification in Eastern Europe after 1989," conducted by Szelényi and Treiman (1992). Because of the methodology, it provides the most comparable data for these countries. Following the conventions of the literature and for reasons of comparability, they defined "poor" as those whose per capita household income was below 50% of the national median. This poverty line is a relative measure, because its monetary value differs in each country depending on the national income level. We present detailed data on poverty in 1992 in Table 1.5. The results are consistent with Cornia's findings: the differences among the countries lie, by and large, in the same direction in Tables 1.4 and 1.5, although the degree of difference among the countries is smaller in Table 1.5. Thus, Bulgaria and Poland have the highest rates of poverty, followed by Slovakia and Hungary. Since the base here is 1992, not 1989, income, the poverty rate is lower. (In all countries, real incomes declined substantially between 1989 and 1992, and the decline may have been the sharpest in Bulgaria and Romania. This may account for the astonishingly high poverty rate found by Cornia in these two countries.)

Ethnicity

In this volume, we focus on the Roma, because they are the single largest ethnic group found in the countries of Central and Southern Europe that is likely to be concentrated in poverty. According to Davidova (1995), the Roma population of Europe during the mid-1990s was about 8 million; perhaps over 5.5 million lived in the Czech Republic, Slovakia, Hungary, Poland, Romania, Serbia, Macedonia, and Bulgaria. An additional 700,000 Roma lived in the other countries of the Central, Southern, and East European region (Albania, other successor states of Yugoslavia, Russia, and the Ukraine). Thus, almost 80% of Europe's Roma population can be found in the former socialist states of Europe. Aside from these countries, Spain and France are the only European countries with a substantial Roma population (750,000 and 340,000, respectively.) Davidova's estimates are rather conservative, so her figures may actually understate the size of the Roma population in the region (Table 1.6).

While the estimates for the 1950s and 1960s for Yugoslavia and Romania are highly dubious, it is reasonable to argue that the Roma population increased about threefold over the past three to four decades. This population growth can be attributed solely to high levels of fertility and declining rates of mortality, because international migration was not a major factor in the growth of the Roma population.

Although it is likely that Roma are concentrated in poverty, there is very little statistical evidence to support this assertion. Szelényi and Treiman's study (1992) again provides one of the few sources. Table 1.7 displays their findings for Bulgaria, Hungary, and Slovakia for individuals reporting Roma ancestors (about 2.5–3.0%of the respondents). These data show that the Roma tend to have larger families, less education, and higher rates of unemployment than the general population and the poor. Since Szelényi and Treiman used a nonstratified, proportional random sample of the population, the N for the Gypsy minorities is small, which makes the relatively consistent results across these countries even more remarkable.

Table 1.5
Poverty Rates for Women and Men, Bulgaria, Hungary, Poland, and Slovakia, 1992
(Population Between 20 and 69 Years Old [Percentages, with Ns in Parentheses])

The extent of poverty within:	Bulgaria	Hungary	Poland	Slovakia
Whole Population	**12.6%**	**9.0%**	**13.5%**	**10.9%**
	(567)	**(422)**	**(421)**	**(500)**
Men	11.0	7.8	12.9	9.2
	(237)	(150)	(205)	(202)
Women	14.1	10.1	14.1	12.6
	(330)	(208)	(216)	(298)
Economically Active*	**10.9**	**7.5**	**12.7**	**9.8**
	(361)	**(205)**	**(309)**	**(343)**
Men	9.5	7.0	12.6	9.2
	(162)	(106)	(168)	(175)
Women	12.3	8.0	12.8	10.3
	(199)	(99)	(141)	(168)
Retired**	**15.6**	**8.2**	**13.8**	**8.7**
	(137)	**(76)**	**(62)**	**(63)**
Men	15.5	10.2	14.6	7.6
	(57)	(38)	(28)	(19)
Women	15.6	6.8	13.6	9.4
	(80)	(38)	(34)	(44)
On Maternity leave/ at home (Women only)	**25.5**	**27.1**	**26.2**	**32.3**
	(49)	**(67)**	**(39)**	**(81)**
Ratio - Female to Male poverty (Whole population)	**1.28**	**1.29**	**1.09**	**1.37**

Notes: N for the whole sample population of Bulgaria = 4,485; Hungary = 3,987; Poland = 3,120; Slovakia = 4,577. The "poor" are defined as those whose per capita household income does not exceed 50% of the median national per capita income. * Economically active includes those working and looking for work. ** The retired also includes those on long-term sick leave.

Source: Szelényi and Treiman 1992.

Table 1.6
Estimates of the Size of the Roma Population in Central and Southern Europe

Country	1950s-1960s	Minimum, 1990s	Maximum 1990s
Czech Republic	(Czechoslovakia) 200-224,000	250,000	300,000
Slovakia		480,000	520,000
Bulgaria	230,000	600,000	700,000
Hungary	190,000	550,000	600,000
Poland	30,000	50,000	60,000
Macedonia	(all Yugoslavia) 85,000	220,000	260,000
Serbia		400,000	450,000
Romania	104,216	1,800,000	2,500,000

Source: Davidova 1995.

Gender

We can use Szelényi and Treiman's survey to consider the extent to which women are concentrated in poverty as well. As discussed earlier, their measure of poverty is a relative one. They defined the poor as those whose per capita household income did not exceed 50% of the median national per capita household income in 1992. Since they use per capita household income, as opposed to individual earnings and benefits, the gender gap reflects differential poverty rates among single people. This not only is the conventional definition but meshes well with social reality in Central and Southern Europe, because approximately 40% of the population over 15 years of age is single at any one time (Central Statistical Office 1991). Table 1.5 presents the gender difference in poverty, using this measure. Table 1.8 presents another measure of poverty, "potential poverty rates," which we define as less than 50% of the national median individual income. This indicator shows how poverty would be gendered if all adults had to make ends meet on their own income—a real threat for many people, given the high rates of divorce. The two measures together, we believe provide a more differentiated picture of gendered poverty in the region than either measure alone. The last lines in Tables 1.5 and 1.8 present the ratio of female to male poverty.

Table 1.7
Selected Social Characteristics of the Roma, Poor and General Population of Bulgaria, Hungary, and Slovakia, Adults 20–65[a] Years Old, 1992

	Bulgaria			Hungary			Slovakia		
	Roma	The poor	All respondents	Roma	The poor	All respondents	Roma	The poor	All respondents
Number of children under 18	2.5	1.8	0.8	2.4	1.8	0.7	2.3	2.1	0.9
Percent rural residents	53.3	45.9	37.2	43.2	41.4	32.4	43.9	53.8	47.5
Percent with less than primary education	46.9	20.4	15.0	37.9	18.6	14.1	30.5	8.1	8.9
N (men and women)	167	1,54	4,902	113	1,260	4,210	128	1,363	4,793
Percent male unemployment	46.0	19.9	12.1	44.2	20.0	13.3	27.6	10.6	6.11
N (men)	94	682	2,288	47	541	1,995	66	557	2,215

a. The ages were 20–70 in Hungary.
Notes: The Szelényi and Treiman survey grossly underestimates the percentage of unemployed—at the time of the survey other sources found it to be twice as large as this study indicated. We assume that Gypsy unemployment is underestimated to a similar extent. The definition of "poor" used here is: those whose household income per head is in the bottom three deciles of the national distribution.

Sources: János Ladányi, "Romák Közép-Kelet-Európában" (Roma in Central-Eastern Europe), *Táradlmi Szemle* 51(4). (1996). The data were from Szelényi and Treiman 1992.

Tables 1.5 and 1.8 illustrate that both the level of poverty and the gender gap differ across countries. In Poland there is a high poverty rate but little gender difference. In contrast, in Slovakia, the poverty rate is smaller, but the gender gap is larger. The poverty rate is higher in Bulgaria than in Hungary, but they have about the same-size gender gap. A poverty ratio of 1.25 would rank around the middle of the distribution in Casper, McLanahan, and Garfinkel's (1994:594) eight-country study, about the same as in Germany and Canada, lower than in the United States and Australia but higher than in Sweden, the Netherlands, or Italy.

Table 1.8
Potential Poverty Rates for Men and Women in Five Countries, 1992 (Population Between 20–69 Years of Age)

	Bulgaria		Hungary		Poland		Slovakia	
	M	W	M	W	M	W	M	W
Whole Population	6.1	8.1	3.3	9.4	6.7	14.8	1.6	10.8
Gender Ratio	1.32		2.8		2.2		6.75	

Notes: M=men and W=women; N for whole populations of Bulgaria = 4,485; Czech Republic = 5,054; Hungary = 3,987; Poland = 3,121; Slovakia = 4,577.

Source: Szelényi and Treiman 1992.

As Table 1.5 shows, the gender gap in poverty is not limited to either the economically active or the retired: rates are quite similar in both categories. Poverty, even feminized poverty, does not have an "elderly" face in Central and Southern Europe; the retired are generally not worse off than those who are active in the labor force. Rather, the typical poor family consists of a wage-earner father and a mother on maternity leave (or, less often, keeping house), as indicated by the high rates of homemakers living in poor households.

Women's plight is particularly apparent when we examine "potential poverty" rates in Table 1.8, which reflect differences in earning capacities in the labor market and illustrate women's dependence on a male breadwinner. The potential poverty rates in Table 1.8 are all higher than the actual poverty rates in Table 1.5, dramatically so in Slovakia.

In sum, then, these figures show that the gender gap in poverty exists in Central and Southern Europe, even though levels of state welfare spending as well as women's labor force participation rates are particularly high. This suggests that to understand gendered poverty, we must go beyond mere labor force participation rates and must examine, as Smith (1984) suggested, women's integration into the changing economy. The sizable gender gap in poverty also suggests that women living alone or with children, even when they are working and receiving social benefits, are perhaps the most vulnerable group in postcommunist societies. In general, women's poverty in Central and Southern Europe has few of the "welfare mother" or "state-dependence" associations; instead it is related to the social organization of a system of production where women's wages are insufficient to support themselves and/or a family. Thus, as we suggested, the concentration of women in poverty may not be as noticeable in some of these countries in Central and Southern Europe as elsewhere, because of the socialist legacy that provided women with some comparative advantages, though poverty does seem to be gendered. Our more specific hypothesis, that women are more likely to be concentrated in poverty in the more marketized countries, seems to hold, at least in general. Taken together, Tables 1.5 and 1.8 suggest that women may be less concentrated in poverty in Bulgaria, as we predicted. The small gender difference in poverty in Poland, however, is somewhat anomalous in terms of our hypotheses.

The Interaction between Ethnicity and Gender

Furthermore, not all women benefit from the legacies of communist "exploitative" emancipation. We argue that a significant bifurcation is emerging not only between the genders but also among women themselves. We expect this dual opportunity structure to be strongly associated with ethnicity, especially among the Roma. The interaction between gender and race creates a double disadvantage for Roma women. Table 1.9 presents our evidence. Almost half of the Roma, while only around 10% of the non-Roma population of the three countries for which data on ethnicity are available, live in poverty. But Roma women are even more likely than Roma men to be poor—by less than only 10% in Hungary but by almost 40% in Bulgaria. Thus, we argue that one of the characteristics of the newly emerging poverty in Central and Southern Europe is that important differences are created among women. This bifurcation, we propose, is structured along racial lines: women at the very bottom of the social hierarchy are minority women, in particular, of Roma ethnicity.

Table 1.9
Poverty Rates among the Roma Population in Three Countries, 1992 (Population 20–57 Years Old)

	Bulgaria		Hungary		Slovakia	
	Men	Women	Men	Women	Men	Women
ROMA	40.4	55.3	41.4	44.3	32.1	35.8
NON-ROMA	10.0	12.5	7.0	10.6	9.4	13.3
RATIO FOR ROMA	1.37		1.07		1.11	
N (ROMA)	61	46	42	49	57	48

Source: Szelényi and Treiman 1992.

Even before the collapse of the communist regimes, state authorities attempted to push Roma women out of the labor force. As the demand for labor tightened, Roma women were considered to be the most easily dispensable workers, particularly because their fertility rates were higher than those of the average population. In 1979 at a Politburo meeting discussing the lack of work opportunities available for the Gypsy, retired prime minister Jenö Fock argued, "We should seek employment for the [Gypsy] youth, not for the women, particularly not women with a lot of children. The fact that fewer Gypsy than non-gypsy women work is essentially related to the particular situation of the Gypsy population. . . . At times when employment opportunities are tight, we should give preference to the youth over women. . . . Gypsy women's problem can be best treated as a welfare question" (From the minutes of the meeting of the Politburo of the Hungarian Communist Party 288.5.770, April 18, 1979). This quote demonstrates that starting very early, the state made no efforts to provide Roma women with the means to fend for themselves in a non-state-centered economy. They avoided utter destitution because of state paternalism, but once the safety net crumbled, they were left to their own devices and sank into deep poverty.

Thus, we argue that while most women collected significant resources during the state socialist era, minority women could not do this, because they had been treated as a "welfare problem" even during the communist regime. To summarize our propositions, we argued that (1) feminized poverty in Central and Southern Europe is not primarily the result of the growth in the rate of single mothers or the insufficiency of welfare checks; rather it is due to women's inferior position in the labor markets. However, (2) we added that women's poverty, on average, is not the kind of hopeless destitution experienced by women on welfare in the United States, because Central and Southern European women had gained some resources in the communist era, which turned out to be marketable during the transition to a market economy. But not all women can do this: (3) minority women, devoid of these resources, are the most vulnerable social group; they are thrust to the fringes of society and experience downward mobility as does no other segment of the society.

CHAPTERS IN THIS VOLUME

The contributors to this volume also addressed the hypotheses about the formation of an underclass through the processes of racialization and feminization of poverty. These chapters address our hypotheses in two ways. First, we draw on these chapters to provide evidence for our argument. Second, more importantly—and more interestingly—is that the authors themselves consider these hypotheses. They often disagree with us in fascinating and fruitful ways. We provide here some hints about the outlines of the debate and hope that readers will draw their own conclusions about the veracity of our hypotheses.

The transition to a market economy in Poland has been more rapid than in the other countries we examine, as the popular term for the Polish transformation, "shock therapy," implies. Tarkowska in Chapter 4 examines the changing nature of poverty in this context. In doing so, however, she stresses the multidimensionality of poverty; deprivation is not just an economic matter of few resources but also a personal, social, and cultural phenomenon. Poverty, according to Tarkowska, is a many-faceted disadvantage that excludes individuals from full participation in society. Not surprisingly, Tarkowska advocates using the term "underclass" and adopts a broad definition of it that includes social, economic, and cultural correlates of poverty; spatial and social isolation; and the transmission of these attributes to the next generation. She also points to the changing nature of this multidimensional poverty. During socialism (the study of poverty was taboo, so accurate accounts are scarce), poverty was generally temporary, linked to a phase in an individual's life cycle. It was also dispersed throughout many groups in society. It tended to be, as Tarkowska points out, "private, invisible, unofficial, and uninstitutionalized." In contrast, Tarkowska argues that poverty during the market transition is much more likely to be a long-term condition that is concentrated regionally, not dispersed throughout society. It stems from unemployment and low levels of education, not from the stages of an individual's life.

As is already clear from the preceding tables, poverty is widespread in Poland. Furthermore, Tarkowska's chapter clearly illustrates that poverty began to increase during the 1980s, before the fall of communism, and continued to increase until 1994. Despite the decrease in poverty after 1994, however, Tarkowska provides some evidence that long-term poverty is increasing. She also argues that women are overrepresented among the poor and points to several indicators of the feminization of poverty. Most telling, perhaps is the evidence that long-term unemployment is more common among women than men. Tarkowska's assessment about the feminization of poverty is consistent with our hypothesis that this process should be relatively advanced in Poland, because of the degree of marketization and the absence of an ethnic minority.

In fact, Tarkowska makes the strong claim that in Poland the formation of an underclass is in progress, though it is not being created around classificatory struggles over ethnicity. In fact, Poland is a relatively homogeneous country with respect to ethnicity. Tarkowska cites workers from former state farms as an example of an emergent underclass or "new poverty" in Poland. This is an interesting argument and has some parallels in Hungarian historiography. During the interwar years, Hungarian ethnographers (in particular, Erdei [(1943) 1983] and Illyés [(1936) 1955] defined the laborers working on latifundia (*majorsági cselédek)* for an annual contract as a "society below society." According to Erdei and Illyés, these laborers tended to be ethnic Hungarians, but they were separated from the rest of the society by a castelike cleavage. They were likely to reproduce their living conditions of extreme poverty across several generations. Typically, state farms were created from land previously cultivated as latifundia. Thus, Tarkowska may see the resurgence of an underclass comprising the ethnic majority, which was partially integrated into society under state socialism, just to be shunned again with the collapse of communism. Tarkowska argues, therefore, that underclass formation is possible without racialization. Her analysis provides the strongest evidence against neo-classical theory: markets do not erase absolute poverty even in ethnically homogeneous countries.

Like Tarkowska, Radicová and Vašecka in Chapter 6 point to the changing nature of poverty during the market transition and also note the shift in poverty from being a life-cycle phenomenon under socialism to a long-term condition under capitalism. However, the context is quite different because Slovakia is a highly heterogeneous country, and the transition to a market economy has been slower than in Poland. They argue that the transition has been hindered by the retention of socialist-style redistribution and that the payment of welfare benefits has even increased over the past few years. This large welfare state stifles the growth of the market economy because it reduces individuals' incentives to work. Because of the strength of redistribution, which provides resources to all segments of society, they argue that poverty is not linked either to gender or to ethnicity. They note that the Roma are exceptional in this respect, as they tend to be concentrated in poverty. They also point out that other Slovaks tend to discriminate against the Roma and that they are socially isolated, though they also suggest that some of the difficulties of the Roma lie in their poor educational attainment.

In Slovakia real wages decreased between 1989 and 1994, after poverty had declined between 1958 and 1988. Unlike the other countries where poverty seemed to have decreased after the mid-1990s, in Slovakia, poverty continued to increase, according to Radicová and Vašecka's figures from 1992 and 1996. There is also some indication that poverty is deepening as well: Radicová and Vašecka argue that long-term unemployment rose between 1993 and 1995. They also point out that some segments of the Roma population, in particular, those who live in camps, are desperately poor and highly isolated from the rest of society.

Yet, despite some indicators of increased and deepening poverty, Radicová and Vašecka hesitate to label any particular portion of Slovak society as an underclass. Instead, they offer a different interpretation by pointing to the continued role of the state in redistributing income, which maintains a minimum standard of living for all Slovaks. According to them, no underclass is being formed in Slovakia around Roma ethnicity, because redistribution from the middle class to the poor by the Slovak welfare state prevents the creation of extreme poverty. Similarly, they argue that poverty is not feminized, because it is not linked to intrinsic biological characteristics of women. Although they note women's disadvantages in the labor market and the greater likelihood that they, instead of men, head single-parent households, they downplay the link between gender and poverty. Radicová and Vašecka argue that in Slovakia the patriotic, central right, populist government maintains an overgrown welfare system. Since they adopt a neoliberal perspective, they view the welfare state negatively. Analytically, however, their position suggests that the dismantling of the welfare state, along with increased marketization, may lead to the creation of an underclass. Their position may be consistent with the argument that the Roma did not constitute an underclass during socialism and that the development of the underclass would result from the expansion of the market and the decay of redistributive mechanisms. Such an argument parallels what we have called the traditional institutional perspective.

We hypothesized that there would be strong underclass formation and some feminization of poverty in Slovakia, given the large Roma minority population and the overall level of marketization. Some of Radicová and Vašecka's evidence supports this conclusion, though they would disagree about our use of the term "underclass." Nevertheless, it is quite plausible that income redistribution by the Slovak state prevents the formation of an underclass, contrary to our hypotheses.

Mitev, Tomova, and Konstantinova in Chapter 2 address the role of the state in a different way. They argue that the market transition itself did not increase poverty. Instead, they argue that poverty increased because of the delay in implementing market reforms and because of the way in which privatization and restitution became divisive political issues. They argue that maintaining unprofitable, state-owned enterprises leads to economic decline. Privatization, however, must not concentrate ownership among the incompetent. Thus, their argument suggests that economically sound and timely market reforms could alleviate poverty, which has increased dramatically since 1989.

Their chapter shows that Roma are more likely to be chronically poor than other ethnic groups. They also argue that the social distance between Roma and other Bulgarians and the stigmatization of Roma have been increasing recently, supporting our argument that an underclass is forming around Roma ethnicity in Bulgaria. Mitev, Tomova, and Konstantinova's argument also points to another important element of Roma ethnicity that has obvious implications for arguments about racialization. Like the other authors in this volume, they note that Roma ethnicity is highly heterogeneous and is perceived as an ethnicity only by the non-Roma. Subgroups of Roma differ by religion, language, and lifestyle. Thus, Mitev, Tomova, and Konstantinova argue that the only element common to all Roma is the experience of discrimination. Rephrased in the language of our hypotheses, we suggest that in Bulgaria, classificatory struggles successfully racialize Roma ethnicity. Similarly, as our hypothesis that there would be relatively little feminization of poverty in Bulgaria would predict, the poverty rates for men and women are nearly the same. Mitev, Tomova, and Konstantinova, however, would add a precautionary note: there are indicators that women's social and economic position is considerably worse than men's and that it is declining. The unemployment rate is higher for women than for men. They also note that women suffer most during the market transition, as the growth of the informal sector and of production for own use places a larger burden on women than men. At the same time, the overall loss of income tends to reduce women's share of the family budget more than that of the men.

Ladányi's argument in Chapter 3 neatly complements the chapters of Mitev, Tomova, and Konstantinova and Radicová and Vašecka. While Mitev, Tomova, and Konstantinova argue that the state should implement more market reforms to eliminate poverty, and Radicová and Vašecka argue that underclass formation has been prevented by the continuation of redistributive policies, Ladányi argues that the rapid market reforms and the rise of the neoliberal state in Hungary, combined with social processes that classify individuals by ethnicity, are creating a highly racialized underclass. He argues that poverty became a much more serious and chronic problem after the fall of communism, especially among the Roma. While state socialist programs to combat poverty often reduced inequality, they were also counterproductive because special programs for the "disadvantaged" were disguised forms of discrimination. With the decline in welfare state spending, the programs are too expensive to maintain. His chapter also provides insight into these social processes of classification by showing that estimates and social characteristics of Roma vary depending on the method used to identify them. As he aptly notes, racialization occurs through classificatory struggles: those who are poor are more likely to be called Roma and are more likely to be treated as Roma by those around them.

As in Poland, the economic crisis in Romania started in the 1980s, before the fall of communism. Poverty grew dramatically after the market transition. As Magyari, Magyari-Vincze, Popescu, and Rotariu note in Chapter 5, the transition to market capitalism in Romania has been relatively slow, and the state sector continues to be a large employer and owner. There is still a relatively large agricultural sector, and production for own use is important. Magyari et al. argue that poverty is both racialized and feminized because of classificatory struggles around ethnicity and gender. They point to the numerous ways that Roma and women are socially and culturally marginalized and disadvantaged in Romanian society. Though they distance themselves from the underclass terminology in some ways, they make a strong argument about the depth and breadth of Roma poverty, which in their view is linked to a "culture of poverty" that is intergenerationally transmitted through socialization. They also emphasize that the status of Roma as ethnic minorities is not isolated from the more general issue of multiculturalism in Romania and, in particular, is linked to the status of Hungarians.

While our hypotheses also suggest that poverty will be racialized around Roma ethnicity in Romania, Magyari et al. take issue with our suggestion that women may be advantaged during the transition to a market economy because of their advantageous position in the labor market. They point out that poverty entails more than labor market position and that what we consider advantages may be, in fact, the double burdens of femininity. Thus, by arguing that poverty is feminized in Romania when our perspective predicts little feminization of poverty, Magyari et al. challenge one of the central hypotheses of this proposal. They also point to ways in which our conceptualization of poverty must be reexamined through empirical research. We suggested that the feminization of poverty occurs only if women are overrepresented among the poor. At the household level of analysis, therefore, poverty can be feminized only if female-headed households are overrepresented among the poor. Magyari et al. challenge this premise because they argue that poverty may be feminized within households if there are systematic asymmetries in access to scarce resources within the family or household unit. For example, females may be under-nourished within patriarchal families or may be poor in nonpoor households.

Finally, following in this spirit of inquiry into the possibilities of underclass formation, we put Michael Stewart's Chapter 7, which questions the very use of the term "underclass" as the conclusion. In so doing, we hope that his chapter, far from providing the final, concluding word, serves instead to renew the debate about our hypotheses and our terminology. Stewart suggests that although there is little doubt that poverty has increased dramatically in Southern and Central Europe, we should think twice before applying the term "underclass." He notes that the supposed social exclusion that sometimes seems to accompany poverty is perceived as such only by the nonpoor. The poor themselves are, all the while, engaged in a variety of social activities and strategies, without which they would certainly not be able to survive. Stewart reminds us of the important point running throughout this volume that acts of social classification have a directionality inherent in them. A negative group label is often used to maintain privilege and hierarchy, not to describe social groups neutrally. Acts of social science classification are not necessarily exceptional in this respect.

CONCLUSIONS

We use our theoretical perspective and the available evidence from Central Europe and Southern Europe to make these hypotheses:

1. If the neo-classical position is correct, the relationship between economic growth and poverty will follow an inverted U-curve. As marketization proceeds, poverty will increase for a while, but eventually the benefits of economic growth generated by the market economy will trickle down to the poor, decreasing absolute poverty.
2. By incorporating the perspectives of Mitev, Tomova, and Konstantinova (Chapter 2) and Radicová and Vašecka (Chapter 6) into the neo-classical framework, it is possible to argue that a gradualist strategy of market transition may initially delay the growth of poverty, but when poverty begins to increase, it may actually reach higher levels than under conditions of "shock therapy." Thus, we can imagine two inverted U-curves with slightly different shapes and heights, depending on whether the transition was gradual or sudden. In the case of shock therapy, we expect rapid growth of poverty early in transition. The height of the U curve, however, may be relatively low, and the curve may decline rapidly after peaking. Such a curve may describe well the dynamics of poverty in Poland and Hungary: it increased rapidly right after 1989 but peaked as early as 1993 and declined gradually in the past five years. In countries that followed gradualist policies (Romania and Bulgaria), the growth of poverty may have been smaller and slower during the early years of the transition (in Romania poverty probably declined right after 1989), but poverty continued to increase after it began to decline in Poland and Hungary. Furthermore, in Romania and Bulgaria absolute poverty may have been higher than where shock therapy was implemented.
3. We also hypothesize that the presence of an ethnic minority affects the shape of the U-curve. Ethnicity may be used to launch successful struggles to racialize poverty and, therefore, to create an underclass. We argue that the racialization of poverty is likely to occur as the U-curve begins to decline. Without racialization, poverty may decline monotonically. With racialization, this decline may stop if an underclass emerges that reproduces itself and consequently perpetuates absolute poverty. While we do not expect that feminization will have strong effects at this stage of marketization, it is possible that feminization and racialization may have analogous effects on the shape of the U curve describing the relationship between marketization and poverty.

We can summarize the different ways that poverty is constructed under the conditions of the market transition in Central Europe. How do racialization and feminization alter the theoretical controversy between traditional institutionalist and neo-classical economists? If there is an ethnic minority in a society that has an elective affinity with poverty, there will be a tendency toward the formation of an underclass, depending on the outcome of the classificatory struggle. Where such an underclass develops, it is less likely that absolute poverty will be reduced as market institutions develop and as economic growth occurs. When poverty is feminized, an underclass may also develop that inhibits the elimination of absolute poverty. Racialization and feminization of poverty, however, are strongly affected by access to labor markets. In the transition from socialist redistribution to capitalist markets, the historical legacy of socialism may provide some advantages for women in the labor market at the same time that it disadvantages the Roma. These historically specific attributes of markets are missed by both the institutionalist and the neo-classical economists. The evidence presented in this introduction begins to address these issues, as do the other chapters in this volume.

ACKNOWLEDGMENTS

We would like to thank Rachel Cohen and János Ladányi for their assistance with this chapter.

REFERENCES

Aponte, Robert. 1990. "Definitions of the Underclass: A Critical Analysis." Pp. 117–137 in *Sociology in America*, edited by H. Gans. Newbury Park, CA: Sage.

Ayres, Ron, and David A. Clark. 1998. "Capitalism, Industrialization and Development in Latin America: The Dependency Paradigm Revisited." *Capital and Class* 64:89–118.

Barany, Zolton D. 1994. "Living on the Edge: The East European Roma in Postcommunist Politics and Societies." *Slavic Review* 53:321–344.

Barth, Fredrik. 1969. "Introduction." Pp. 9–38 in *Ethnic Groups and Boundaries: The Social Organization of Cultural Difference*, edited by F. Barth. Boston: Little, Brown.

Beck, Sam. 1989. "The Origins of Gypsy Slavery in Romania." *Dialectical Anthropology* 14:53–61.

Becker, Gary S. 1991. *A Treatise on the Family*. Cambridge: Harvard University Press.

Beskid, L. 1997. "Ubostvo w Polsce" (Poverty in Poland). Raport Rády Strategii Spoleczno-Gospodarczej przy Radzie Ministrow RP.

Blank, Rebecca M. 1997a. *It Takes a Nation: A New Agenda for Fighting Poverty*. Princeton, NJ: Princeton University Press.

Blank, Rebecca M. 1997b. "Why Has Economic Growth Been Such an Ineffective Tool Against Poverty in Recent Years?" Pp. 27–42 in *Poverty and Inequality: The Political Economy of Redistribution*, edited by J. Neill. New York: W. E. Upjohn Institute for Employment Research.

Bokor, Ágnes. 1987. *Szegénység a mai Magyarországon* (Poverty in Hungary Today). Budapest: Magvető Kiado.

Bourdieu, Pierre. 1991. *Language and Symbolic Power*. Cambridge: Harvard University Press.

Caplan, Lionel. 1996. "Dimensions of Urban Poverty: Anglo-Indian Poor and Their Guardians in Madras." *Urban Anthropology* 25:311–349.

Casper, Lynne M., Sara S. McLanahan, and Irwin Garfinkel. 1994. "The Gender-Poverty Gap: What We Can Learn from Other Countries." *American Sociological Review* 59:594–605.

Central and Eastern Europe Business Information Center. 1998/1999. "Country Commercial Guides 1998/1999." American Embassy Staff, (http://www.mac.doc.gov/eebic/ceebic.html).

Central Statistical Office. 1991. *Statistical Yearbook of Hungary, 1990.* Budapest: Central Statistical Office.

Cornia, Giovanni Andrea. 1994. "Income Distribution, Poverty, and Welfare in Transitional Economies—A Comparison between Eastern Europe and China." *Journal of International Development* 6:569–607.

Cornia, Giovanni Andrea, and Sheldon Danziger. 1997. *Child Poverty and Deprivation in the Industrialized Countries, 1945–1995.* Oxford: Clarendon Press.

Crowe, David. 1991. "Conclusion." Pp. 151–157 in *The Gypsies,* edited by D. Crowe and J. Kolsti. London: M. E. Sharpe.

Davidova, Eva. 1995. *Romano drom—Cesty romu: 1945–1990.* Olomouc: Univerzita Palackeho v Olomouci.

Erdei, Ferenc. [1943] 1983. "A magyar társadalom a két világháboru között" (Hungarian society during the interwar years). Pp. 291–346 in *A magyar társadalomról* (On Hungarian Society), edited by F. Erdei. Budapest: Akadémiai Kiadó.

Esping-Andersen, Gosta. 1996. "After the Golden Age? Welfare State Dilemmas in a Global Economy." Pp. 1–31 in *Welfare States in Transition: National Adaptations in Global Economies,* edited by G. Esping-Andersen. London, England: Sage.

Ferge, Zsuzsa. 1969. *Társadalmunk rétegzödése* (Social Stratification in Hungary). Budapest: Közgazdasági és Jogi Könyvkiadó.

Fodor, Eva. 1997. "Power, Patriarchy, and Paternalism: An Examination of the Gendered Nature of State Socialist Authority." Ph.D. thesis, Department of Sociology, University of California, Los Angeles.

Frackiewicz, L. 1983. *Sfery niedostatku* (Spheres of Deficiency). Warsaw: IWZZ.

Fraser, Angus M. 1992. *The Gypsies.* Oxford: Blackwell.

Friedman, Milton, and Rose Friedman. 1980. *Free to Choose.* New York: Avon Books.

Gheorghe, Nicolae. 1991. "Roma-Gyspy Ethnicity in Eastern Europe." *Social Research* 58:829–844.

Hayek, Friedrich August von. 1944. *The Road to Serfdom.* Chicago: University of Chicago Press.

Hayek, Friedrich August von. 1960. *The Constitution of Liberty.* London: Routledge and Kegan Paul.

Headey, Bruce, Robert E. Goodin, Ruud Muffels, and Henk-Jan Dirven. 1997. "Welfare over Time: Three Worlds of Welfare Capitalism in Panel Perspective." *Journal of Public Policy* 17:329–359.

Hungarian Central Statistical Office. 1993. *Labor Force Survey.* Budapest: Hungarian Central Statistical Office.

Illyés, Gyula. [1936] 1955. *A puszták népe* ("The People of the Pusta"). Budapest: Szepirodalmi Konyvkiado.

Jarosz, Maria. 1984. *Nierownosci spoleczne* (Social Inequalities). Warsaw: KiW.

Jenkins, Richard. 1994. "Rethinking Ethnicity: Identity, Categorization, and Power." *Ethnic and Racial Studies* 17:198–227.

Kemény, István. 1972. "Az alacsony jövedelmü családok életkörülményei Magyarországon" (Living Conditions of Low Income Families in Hungary). Manuscript, Budapest.

Kemény, István. 1976. *Beszámoló a magyarországi cigányok helyzetével foglalkozó 1971-ben végzett kutatásról* (Report on the 1971 Survey of Hungarian Gypsies). Budapest: MTA Szociológiai Intezete.

Kemény, István, Gábor Havas, and Gábor Kertesi. 1995. "Beszámoló a magyarországi roma (cigány) népesség helyzetével foglalkozó 1993 oktobere és 1994 februárja között végzett kutatásról" (A Report on the Survey of the Hungarian Roma Population, 1993–94). Manuscript.

Kenworthy, Lane. 1999. "Do Social-Welfare Policies Reduce Poverty? A Cross-National Assessment." *Social Forces* 77:1119–1139.

Kornai, János. 1980. *The Economics of Shortage*. Amsterdam: North Holland.

Kornai, János. 1996. "Reform of the Welfare Sector of Post-Socialist Countries—a Normative Approach." Paper presented at the National Research Council Meetings, November 1996, Washington, DC.

Korpi, Walter, and Joakim Palme. 1998. "The Paradox of Redistribution and Strategies of Equality: Welfare State Institutions, Inequality, and Poverty in the Western Countries." *American Sociological Review* 63:661–687.

Kuznets, Simon. 1955. "Economic Growth and Income Inequality." *The American Economic Review* 45:1–28.

Lal, Deepak, and H. Myint. 1996. *The Political Economy of Poverty, Equity, and Growth: A Comparative Study*. Oxford: Clarendon Press.

Levy, Frank. 1977. "How Big Is the Underclass?" Urban Institute, Washington, DC.

Lewis, Oscar. 1966. "The Culture of Poverty." *Scientific American* 215:19–25.

Li, Hong Yi, Lyn Squire, and Heng-fu Zou. 1998. "Explaining International and Intertemporal Variations in Income Inequality." *The Economic Journal* 108:26–43.

Lucassen, Leo. 1991. "The Power of Definition, Stigmatisation, Minoritisation, and Ethnicity Illustrated by the History of the Gypsies in the Netherlands." *The Netherlands Journal of Social Science* 27:80–91.

Massey, Douglas S., and Nancy C. Denton. 1993. *American Apartheid*. Cambridge: Harvard University Press.

McAll, Christopher. 1990. *Class, Ethnicity and Social Inequality*. London: McGill-Queen's.

Milanovic, Branko. 1994. "A Cost of Transition—50 Million New Poor and Growing Inequality." *Transition* 5:1–4.

Miles, Robert. 1982. *Racism and Migrant Labour*. London: Routledge and Kegan Paul.

Myrdal, Gunnar. 1963. *Challenge to Affluence*. New York: Pantheon Books.

Myrdal, Gunnar. 1964. "The War on Poverty." *The New Republic* 150:14–16.

Okely, Judith. 1983. *The Traveller-Gypsies*. Cambridge: Cambridge University Press.

Pinchuk, Ben-Cion. 1990. *Shtetl Jews under Soviet Rule*. Oxford: Basil Blackwell.

Polanyi, Karl. 1944. *The Great Transformation*. Boston: Beacon Press.

Pronai, Csaba. 1995. *Cigánykutatás és kulturális antropologia* (Gypsy Research and Cultural Anthropology). Budapest-Kaposvár: N.p.

Ricketts, Erol R., and Isabel Sawhill. 1988. "Defining and Measuring the Underclass." *Journal of Policy Analysis and Managment* 7:316–325.

Rodgers, Harrell R., Jr. 1996. *Poor Women, Poor Children: American Poverty in the 1990s*. Armonk, NY: M. E. Sharpe.

Rogger, Hans. 1986. *Jewish Policies and Right-Wing Politics in Imperial Russia*. London: Macmillan Press.

Russell, George. 1977. "The American Underclass." *Time*, August 28, pp. 14–27.

Smedley, Audrey. 1993. *Race in North America: Origin and Evolution of a World View*. Boulder, CO: Westview.

Smith, Joan. 1984. "The Paradox of Women's Poverty: Wage-Earning Women and Economic Transformation." *Signs: Journal of Women in Culture and Society* 10:291–310.

Stack, Carol B. 1974. *All Our Kin: Strategies for Survival in a Black Community*. New York: Harper and Row.

Standing, Guy. 1996. "Social Protection in Central and Eastern Europe: A Tale of Slipping Anchors and Torn Safety Nets." Pp. 225–255 in *Welfare States in Transition: National Adaptations in Global Economies*, edited by G. Esping-Andersen. London, England: Sage.

Stephens, John D. 1996. "The Scandinavian Welfare States: Achievements, Crisis, and Prospects." Pp. 32–65 in *Welfare States in Transition: National Adaptations in Global Economies*, edited by G. Esping-Andersen. London, England: Sage.

Stewart, Michael. 1997. *The Time of the Gypsies*. Boulder, CO: Westview.

Stigler, George. 1970. "Director's Law of Public Income Distribution." *Journal of Law and Economics* 13:1–10.

Szelényi, Iván, and Donald Treiman. 1992. "Social Stratification in Eastern Europe after 1989." NSF Grant Proposal.

Szonda Ipsos. 1997. "Survey 'TF3' Machine Readable Data Set." Szonda Ipsos, Budapest.

Tienda, Marta. 1989. "Puerto Ricans and the Underclass Debate." *The Annals of the American Academy of Political and Social Sciences* 501:105–119.

Tomova, Ilona. 1995. *The Gypsies in the Transitional Period*. Sofia: International Center for Minority Studies and Intercultural Relations.

Townsend, Peter. 1970. *The Concept of Poverty*. London: Heinemann.

Tulli, R. 1978. *Jednoosobowe gospodarstwa domowe* (Single Households). Warsaw: IFiS PAN.

Tymowski, A. 1973. *Minimum socjalne. Metodyka I proba okreslenia.* (Social Minimum. Method and Measurement). Warsaw: PWN.

Ward, David. 1989. *Poverty, Ethnicity and the American City: 1840–1925*. Cambridge: Cambridge University Press.

Warzywoda-Kruszynska, Wielislawa, and J. Grotowka-Leder. 1996. *Wielkomejska bieda w okresie transformacji* (Poverty of a Great City in the Period of Transition). Lodz: Instytut Socjologi Uniwersytetu Lodzkiego.

Weber, Max. 1978. "The Belief in Common Ethnicity." Pp. 387–393 in *Economy and Society*, vol. 1, edited by G. Roth and C. Wittich. Berkeley and Los Angeles: University of California Press.

Williams, Brackette. 1989. "A Class Act: Anthropology and the Race to Nation across Ethnic Terrain." *Annual Review of Anthropology* 18:401–444.

Wilson, William Julius. 1978. *The Declining Significance of Race: Blacks and Changing American Institutions*. Chicago: University of Chicago Press.

Wilson, William Julius. 1987. *The Truly Disadvantaged*. Chicago: University of Chicago Press.

Zamfir, E. and C. Zamfir. 1995. *Dimensiunile Saraciei* (Dimensions of Poverty). Bucharest: Editura Expert.

2

The Price of Procrastination? The Social Costs of Delayed Market Transition in Bulgaria

Petar-Emil Mitev, Ilona Tomova, and Liubena Konstantinova

INTRODUCTION

Poverty is the greatest social problem in Bulgaria.[1] The form and scope that it takes are not so much the result of the economic reform itself as of its delay. The dilemma whether privatization or restitution should have priority was the focus of a direct political clash back in 1991,[2] but it took until 1998 to resolve it through a practically complete restitution.

The ex-communist Bulgarian Socialist Party (BSP) and the anticommunist Union of Democratic Forces (UDF) differed primarily in the form of capitalism they proposed (i.e., pass property on to the nomenclature or restore precommunist property relations) rather than in their attempts to prevent "rampant capitalism."[3] The protomarket economy of the Bulgarian transition is a strange combination of *market, nonmarket, pseudomarket and antimarket* phenomena. Outside of the market still remain not only the natural economy but also land—the main property of almost half the Bulgarian population. The so-called financial pyramids can be viewed as a pseudomarket mechanism. The "entry-exit" economy has a typical antimarket character.[4]

The main advantage of the market over other forms of economic integration is that it stimulates competition. The paternalism of "*Nashism*" or "our people" proved to be the most powerful antimarket factor in Bulgaria.[5] In Bulgaria—unlike in Bosnia—the borderline between "our people" and "others" has been drawn on ideological and political grounds, rather than on religious or ethnic ones. Yet, when the "cold civil war" ended in February 1997, ethnicity began to play a more important role again. It became clear that the Roma does not have much chance to become "one of us" thus to be accepted as a member in the network of party clients. The ideology of "our people" furthermore prevented the feminization of poverty, since the exclusion was not drawn by gender (except in the case of Roma women, who tend, indeed, to be the poorest).

POVERTY IN BULGARIA

Poverty as a Problem

Poverty Measures

Poverty has become the most serious social problem in Bulgaria. Yet there are no commonly accepted definition of poverty and no agreement about what the appropriate policies should be to deal with poverty.[6]

In 1991 the National Commission on Interests Coordination defined the *social minimum* as a measure of poverty. However, given the fast decline of living standards, this soon had to be revised. In 1992 a "consumer basket" was established to measure *subsistence minimum*. This indicator was used only in research and never gained policy implementation. Instead, a more a conventional definition of *minimum basic income* was used in policy making. This is really not a "poverty line"—it only indicates at what level of income the government has the financial capacity to offer welfare payments.

Poverty: Income or Property

One unique feature of poverty in Bulgaria is a glaring imbalance between income rates and property—the income poor can be quite well-off in terms of property. This importance of the "shadow" and natural economy is, at least in part, responsible for this.

An Information Problem

There has not been enough research on poverty in this country. The most important investigations of the World Bank have been kept secret for quite a long period of time. The mass media remain generally aloof from issues of poverty. The wish of each government to see its citizens as less poor than they are in reality and the desire of opposition parties to convert poverty into a political argument render evasion of the problem into a sign of loyalty and conformism.

It appears that Bulgarian society has been ill prepared for the encounter with poverty—economically, psychologically, and academically.

The Concept of Poverty

Poverty has various meanings in various national contexts; it means one thing in Asia, and another in Europe, one thing in Bulgaria, and another in Italy.

The scholarly literature often defines two types of poverty used in academic writing. One of them is *economic*. The other type of definition is *sociological*. "Poverty affects all aspects of daily life and is manifest in the absence of capabilities to satisfy the basic needs of life. In this sense, it is a way of life and any attempt to confine it to the inability to possess one thing or another, irrespective of the rest, is piecemeal and doomed to failure" (Zhelyazkova, 1997:34).

There is no contradiction between the two definitions; rather, they complement each other. Indeed, sociologists tend to state alternately that the phenomenon of "poverty" means "deprivation of the requisites essential for a sound existence and an acceptable quality of life" (Fotev 1997:7) and "the lack of material values required to establish and maintain basic living conditions" (Yosifov and Naumov 1998:191). Nonetheless, the sociological understanding tends to be more complex.

Economic definitions emphasize the *objective* aspects of poverty. Sociologists are also concerned with the perception of poverty, with *subjective* poverty.

Measuring Poverty

In Bulgaria the traditional "consumer basket of goods," as calculated by experts, continues to be used for measurement of poverty.[7] The *social minimum* was first calculated in 1991 and then recalculated in 1995, on the basis of the consumer basket principle. It is based on 297 goods and services (including 80 food items). The *subsistence minimum* was calculated in 1992 on the basis of the consumer basket principle, which was reduced in 1995 to 184 goods and services (including 70 food items). The *survival minimum* was calculated on the basis of physical needs and based on a basket of 27 goods and services used by the poorest 20% of the country.

The social, subsistence, and survival minima are used for statistical surveys and academic research. They are not used as a tool of official policy. Trade unions give higher estimates of the social and subsistence minima based on their own techniques and their own data about price fluctuations—both of which digress from those of the National Statistics Institute.

The *base minimum income* was renamed in November 1998 as the *guaranteed minimum income* (GMD). This is the politically recognized minimum fixed by a decision of the Council of Ministers on the basis of a consumer basket of 22 food goods and energy consumption only. As a rule, the base minimum income is low and does not reflect needs, but rather the financial capabilities of the state. In 1998 it was Bulgarian leva (BGL) 29,500 (=US$18.6—a loaf of bread costs roughly BGL550 =US$0.34).

The Scope of Poverty

Table 2.1 shows monthly incomes in Bulgaria for June 1997.[8]

Table 2.1
Average Monthly Incomes (June 1997)

	BGL[9]	Equivalent in US$
Minimum salary	41,290	26.0
Average salary	152,230	96.2
Minimum pension	24,300	15.3
Average pension	44,500	28.1
Maximum pension	56,900	35.9

Source: Ministry of Labour and Social Policy (MLSP)

At the same time[10] the minimum poverty criteria are shown in Table 2.2.

Table 2.2
Minimum Poverty Criteria (June 1997)

	BGL	Equivalent in US $
Subsistence minimum	111,752	70.6
Survival minimum	69,494	43.9
Base minimum	23,460	14.8
Social minimum (average)	161,866	102.3
Social minimum (per pensioner)	117,373	74.1
Social minimum (per child)	136,461	86.2
Social minimum (per employed person)	117,373	74.1

Sources: MLSP; UNDP (1997), 25–27.

Thus, the average salary is below the social minimum, whereas even the maximum pension is below the survival minimum. Various estimates of the percentage of the population in poverty are: 80% (Noncheva 1997), 86-87% (Center for the Study of Ideologies [CSI] 1998), 88% (CSI 1998), 95% on the base of social minimum in 1989 (Zhelyazkova 1998; CSI 1998); the *Statistical Barometer* of the National Statistics Institute (NSI) has shown (1996) 92.5% (NSI 1997c: 48).

A good indicator of poverty is *the relative share of general consumer expenses made up by food*. Those who spend 40–45% of their income on food are usually regarded to be poor. In 1989 food expenses in Bulgaria were around 38% of total consumption expenses. During the period of transition they constantly rose. In March 1997, as a result of the hyperinflation shock, food expenses skyrocketed to 60% of total consumer expenditures; they subsequently declined but remained above 50%. After the stabilization, food expenses declined to 47.9% in 1998. For the very poor they are above 60–70%.[11]

At the same time, the number of people on welfare support dwindled: in 1993 these were 510,705; in 1995, 236,897; in 1996, 218,945; and in 1997, 155,364.

In a joint United Nations Development Programme/International Labour Office (UNDP/ILO) project, the base minimum income is accepted as the lower limit of poverty and the sum of BGL95,500 is estimated to be the upper limit of poverty. Percentages of poor households according to these poverty thresholds are shown in Table 2.3.

Table 2.3
Poor Households, Share According to the Poverty Thresholds (%)

Poverty thresholds	Poor	Non-poor	Total
BGL29 500 (US$17.1)	3.9	96.1	100.0
BGL95 500 (US$55.5)	65.5	34.5	100.0

Sources: NSI, 1997a; ILO/UNDP 1998a: 33.

The Shadow Economy

The National Statistics Institute collects no data on the informal ("shadow") economy,[12] but according to a survey by the World Bank, the informal economy's share of GDP is about 40% (ILO/UNDP 1998a: 5). This "shadow" economy is in the "shadow" mainly for the purposes of taxation. A vicious circle is thus created. Poor people contribute to the poverty of the state by hiding their taxes; the poor state is thus incapable of supporting poor people.

Given the high levels of poverty subsistence, production is of great importance. Between 1990 and 1996 the portion of subsistence production increased from 11% to 23% (Noncheva 1997:61). Since land was restituted, 42.5% of Bulgarians own land (usually just small plots).[13] According to data from one opinion poll, a considerable proportion of the population consumes homemade foodstuffs (milk and cheese—28% in total [% who produce all of their milk and cheese at home], 16% in part [% who produce part of their milk and cheese at home]; meat—24% in total; 30% in part; fresh vegetables and fruit—37% in total, 32% in part; canned food—51% in total, 22% in part; alcoholic beverages—25% in total, 23% in part) (Kolev 1997).

Social Inequality

The extremely high proportion of persons in poverty may create the impression that everyone is equally poor in Bulgaria. This is not true. Income inequality of the population is increasing (ILO/UNDP 1998a: 7).[14] In 1995 the ratio between the income of the most affluent 20% and the poorest 20% of households in Bulgaria stood at 6.5%. In 1996 the poorest 10% of the Bulgarian population received 2.3% of total income—half their share in 1989. Over this period, the richest 10% of the population increased their share of total income from 19% to 28%.

The ratio between average income earners and those in poverty (the *poverty gap*)—according to data of the World Bank study—has increased from 4.6% in 1991 to 9.9% in 1995 (Noncheva 1997:64).

Public perception of social stratification is changing. The study "Social Stratification and Inequality" (1998) "explicitly determined the shift of the dominant [criterion]—the criterion of social stratification in the mass consciousness" (Tilkidjiev 1998b:125). Until recently the public perceived the dominant form of stratification to be tied to a person's social and professional status; now two-thirds of the people interviewed divide the population according to the criteria of affluence/poverty.

Bulgarians are egalitarian. People feel that a dual social injustice is being done: while some get poorer, undeservedly, others get richer. The wealthy have a *negative image*.[15]

Limitation of Consumption

Impoverishment means that people consume less. In the typical words of a respondent: "I consider all people poor who cannot afford to buy meat, milk or cheese and have instead to eat only vegetarian potato soups and bread" (BBSS 1998). According to data gathered by Mediana Agency (August 1997), 15% of those polled had stopped eating meat, and another 54% had reduced meat consumption; 5% had stopped eating cheese, and 49% had reduced consumption; 3% had stopped using milk and yoghurt, and 45% had reduced consumption; 6% had stopped eating fresh fruit and vegetables, and 38% had reduced consumption (Kolev 1997; NSI 1997b).

Unemployment

The unemployment rate is one of the highest in Eastern Europe.[16] The proportion of long-term unemployed is high, and there is much unemployment among the young. In 1996 the long-term unemployed accounted for almost one-third of all unemployed. In June 1999 there were 487,503 unemployed; of these 30.5% were 29 years of age or less, and 32.8% had been registered as unemployed for over a year (National Service with Employment 1999). Ethnic minorities and women tend to be overrepresented among the unemployed.

There are regional variations in unemployment. In June 1999 the level of registered unemployment in Sofia was 3.38; in Plovdiv district—10.45; in Rousse—15.14; in Smolyan—19.57; in Targovishte—24.51.

Sociodemographic Profiles of Poverty

The expansion of poverty is different in different social groups. Poverty is particularly widespread among the pensioners (2,400,000); the handicapped (240,000); and the Roma (600,000).

Children

Data from the National Statistics Institute show that in extreme poverty (poverty line: BGL29,500) the number of households with one child and the number of households with two children are approximately the same. However, when the poverty line is defined as BGL95,500 families with two children are at a disadvantage. Families with three or more children are always worse off than families without children (Table 2.4).

Table 2.4
Share of Households below the Poverty Line by Number of Children under 18 Years of Age (%)

Poverty lines	Total	1 child	2 children	3 or more children	Adults only
BGL29,500 (US$17.1)	100.0	100.0	100.0	100.0	100.0
Poor	3.9	6.1	7.1	35.6	1.8
Nonpoor	96.1	93.9	92.9	64.4	98.2
BGL95,500 (US$55.5)	100.0	100.0	100.0	100.0	100.0
Poor	65.5	65.6	73.1	97.8	62.7
Non-poor	34.5	34.4	26.9	2.2	37.3

Sources: NSI 1997a; ILO/UNDP 1998a: 30.

Education

The less educated tend to be poorer, but the *majority* of households headed by a person with higher education are also poor (Table 2.5).

Table 2.5
Share of Households below the Poverty Line by Level of Education (%)

Poverty lines	Total	Un-educated	Primary education	Secondary education	Higher education
BGL29,500 (US$17.1)	100.0	100.0	100.0	100.0	100.0
Poor	3.9	8.6	3.8	3.8	1.6
Nonpoor	96.1	91.4	96.2	96.2	98.4
BGL95,500 (US$55.5)	100.0	100.0	100.0	100.0	100.0
Poor	65.5	76.6	68.1	65.4	53.0
Nonpoor	34.5	23.4	31.9	34.6	47.0

Sources: NSI 1997a; ILO/UNDP 1998a:33.

Regional Aspects

Absolute poverty is lowest in the capital, whereas relative poverty is lower in the villages. Country towns are in the most disadvantageous position, especially those with a population of over 5,000, as they are deprived of the opportunities for income found in the capital as well as the substantial support provided by the natural economy of the village (Table 2.6).

Table 2.6
Households below the Poverty Lines by Size of Residence Location (%)

Poverty lines	Total	Capital city	Cities over 5,000	Cities up to 5,000	Villages over 2,000	Villages 1,000-2,000	Villages up to 1,000
BGL 29,500 (US $17.1)	3.9	1.9	3.8	5.2	5.9	3.1	3.3
BGL 95,500 (US $55.5)	65.5	64.6	70.1	68.3	66.7	55.0	57.8
BGL 29,500	100.0	6.8	28.8	30.4	15.3	8.5	10.2
BGL 95,500	100.0	14.0	32.1	24.0	10.4	8.9	10.6

Sources: NSI 1997a; ILO/UNDP 1998a:32.

The Stratification of Poverty

According to a survey conducted by the National Statistics Institute (headed by Dr. I. Nourkova) in January 1997, the respondents classify the population the following way:[17]

Rich	0.6%
Neither poor nor rich	35.2%
Somewhat poor	43.3%
Very poor	20.8%

The New Poverty

In 1989 Zbigniew Brzezinski believed that Bulgaria was the most politically stable East European country (Brzezinski 1989). This stability was, in great measure, the result of government policies: minimum salaries were close to average, and they guaranteed sustenance needs. There were no unemployment and no "homelessness." The state provided free health care, education, maternity leave, and childcare. During socialist times "the poor" were those who could afford only a panel flat and could not afford a car. Today, the poor are those who cannot afford to heat their flat during the winter or who must sell the flat itself. Some of the differences in the characteristics of poverty under communism and postcommunism are shown in Table 2.7.

Table 2.7
Characteristics of Poverty under Communism and under Postcommunism

Indicator	Under communism	Under postcommunism
Everyday life problems	Lack of commodities	Lack of money
Social life problems	Lack of information for everyone	Lack of food/energy for some
Social limits	Administrative	Economic
Dominant trends	Egalitarian	Social differentiation
Poverty of the lowest paid	Relative	Absolute
Extent of poverty	Limited	Massive

We are witnessing the emergence of a new poverty. The poverty of the past was exclusively social poverty; the new poverty is becoming a biological issue. According to one World Bank survey, the majority of respondents were poor before the beginning of the transition but believe that their former poverty was not as distressing as their current poverty.

In 1989 households were differentiated by per capita income (Table 2.8).

Table 2.8
Per Capita Income of Households (1989)

Up to BGL1,200	4.3%
1,200 – 1,430	5.0%
1,431 – 1,670	8.4%
1,671 – 2,150	20.2%
2,151 – 2,630	18.8%
2,631 and above	43.3%

Source: NSI 1990.

The per capita monthly social minimum in 1989 averaged BGL185 (US$200).[18] At this time the average monthly salary was BGL274 (US$295), and the minimum salary was BGL140 (US$150); the ratio of the minimum to the average monthly salary was 51.1%; 9.3% of all those employed received a monthly remuneration of less than, or equal to, BGL160 (US$172); 6.8% received between BGL160 (US$172) and BGL180 (US$194). The leveling of incomes between different social strata was typical. High academic qualifications were not a material advantage. Incomes above BGL350 (US$378) were paid to 24.4% of workers, but only 16.2% of university graduates.

In 1989, 40.9% of the population had incomes below the social minimum (NSI 1990). Within seven years that percentage had doubled. To this was added a qualitative difference, namely, the emergence of a part of the population with extremely low incomes.

Macrolevels and Microlevels

The case of Bulgaria elicits an unambiguous answer to the question of whether poverty is produced by economic change. The most significant research project yet completed concluded that "Bulgaria's shift to a market oriented economy has led to significant impoverishment of the population" (ILO/UNDP 1998a:5). However, the answer, while clear, is not straightforward.

It was not so much the transition as the way in which it was implemented that generated impoverishment on a scale that constituted a social disaster. When Bulgaria entered the transition process, it had little international debt, it had a well-functioning, energy-producing industry, and its machine-building and food-processing, electronic, oil-processing, and chemical industries were quite highly developed. Mechanization in agriculture achieved high levels. The young generations were well educated. The savings of the population in 1989 were substantial: BGL20.6 billion (NSI 1990).

During the period of transition were three parallel, interrelated processes: GDP declined, capital stock shrank, and people became poorer. State industry was drained out, instead of being modernized. Agriculture became fragmented.

A so-called entry–exit economy emerged. Private companies, which were generally managed by relatives, friends, or partners of the director of the state enterprise (and sometimes the director himself), controlled the "entry" of raw materials into the public firms, and they also controlled "exit"; thus, they distributed the products of the firms for sale. As a result profits from the state enterprise were transferred to these private companies. State firms became loss-making, which brought their value down so they could be privatized at a low price.

In this way, instead of being channelled into the fueling up of the transition, the state industry, the credit system, and the savings of the population have been transformed into channels that drain the economy and rob the people. In addition, there were negative consequences of the property restoration strategy. Land restitution has left most Gypsies without land. The restitution of land in its "real limits" has brought agriculture back to the inefficient and extremely fragmented state typical of former times.

The question whether economic growth will contribute to a reduction in poverty can be answered only conditionally. In 1995 the socialist government increased production but at the cost of postponing restructuring and "pouring" financial resources into unprofitable, state-owned enterprises. The economic standards of the population were temporarily maintained, but their maintenance induced an economic slump at the end of 1996. In other words, economic growth can provide an alternative to impoverishment only when it is combined with structural change.[19]

The social and cognitive challenges of poverty have found expression in the issue of the formation of a social bottom.

The Social Bottom

Expert opinion (CSI 1998) spans a wide spectrum: from the point of view that there are "big masses of poor and at risk" constituting the "social bottom" (E. Tzekova), to a rejection of the very category of social bottom either methodologically, as being not economic (V. Dimitrov), or empirically, as an inadequate description (S. Kostadinova).

Poverty in contemporary Bulgaria is *diffuse*. It penetrates everywhere. This is evident in the merging social demographic profiles of the poor. Diffusion turns poverty from an individual or social group trait into a national trait, a backdrop to all personal and public life. But it does not follow from this that there are no qualitative differences between groups of people with respect to poverty. There is a simultaneous *concentration* of poverty. More chronic forms of poverty become the fate of particular social and ethnic groups. Some of these groups form the social bottom. However, its characteristics are not only economic.

Extreme and long-term poverty brings about lifestyle changes; people increasingly lose their ability to make social contacts and reintegrate into society. Characteristically, possibilities for participation in the "shadow economy" decrease; in particular, use of the produce from the family farm is very restricted as this requires an initial investment of resources that are not at the disposal of the poor. The standard of living of the extremely poor is one of *deprivation*—not only deprivation of income and of economic assets but also the absence of any social possibilities for self-development. Poverty makes it impossible to defend *social rights*.[20] There is a trend for chronic poverty to become *hereditary*. Parents cannot provide for their children or secure for them the conditions for a good start in life, and thus poverty is inherited. The school dropout rate is very high, reaching 50,000 in 1995, partly due to forced child labor.

The most significant fact in the formation of a social bottom is the dangerous "sinking" of a large ethnic group—the Bulgarian Roma.

ETHNIC DIMENSIONS OF POVERTY

Statistical and sociological data show that there is a strong relationship between poverty and ethnicity in postcommunist Bulgaria. Data from the World Bank survey of poverty in Bulgaria in 1996 (Table 2.9) show the pattern of poverty among different ethnic groups.

Table 2.9
Poverty Rates by Ethnic Group (%)

Group	Adults without children	Adults with children	Old-age pensioners	Total
Bulgarian	10.4	14.7	18.9	15.0
Turkish	24.5	41.6	30.1	34.8
Roma	65.1	76.5	63.3	71.4

The ratio between Bulgarian Christians (the majority of the country's population) and the Roma minority is greater than nine-to-one and reveals a trend toward ghettoization of the Roma. Increasing differentiation in living standards and the labor market makes ethnicity appear more salient in postcommunism.

Poverty among Gypsies

The Number of Gypsies in Bulgaria

According to 1992 population census data for Bulgaria, 313,326 people (3.7% of the population) identified themselves as Gypsies. Because of the low social status of the group, a significant number of its members prefer to identify themselves as Bulgarians, Bulgarian Turks, or Wallachs. Thus, the number of people self-identifying as Gypsy is hardly greater than half the number that the surrounding population identifies as Gypsies.

In January 1989 the number of Gypsies was approximated to be 577,000 (or 6.45% of the Bulgarian population). This figure was based on "objective criteria" and the estimation of the officers of the Ministry of Internal Affairs and city mayors. Elena Marushiakova and Vesselin Popov, two Bulgarian Gypsiologists, hypothesize that in many places the number of Roma may be even higher (Marushiakova and Popov 1993:95). Jean-Pierre Liegeois and Nicolae Gheorghe, basing their estimation on the above hypothesis, estimate the number of Gypsies in Bulgaria to be approximately 700,000–800,000 (Liegeois and Gheorghe 1995:34).

Intergroup Structure of the Gypsy Community

The Roma are the most heterogeneous minority in the country. In fact, the Roma are perceived as a coherent minority group only by other parts of the population, since differences within the group are more significant than differences between the group and the rest of the population. Subgroups differ in terms of religion (which includes Muslim, Orthodox, Reformed Christian, and other denominations, even Jewish), mother tongue (the Roma speak in various Roma dialects as well as Turkish, Bulgarian, and Vlach dialects), traditional work patterns and crafts, time of settlement, and lifestyle.

Gypsies rarely have a common "Roma" consciousness. Gypsies identify themselves with subgroups: the Kardarash, the Thracian tinsmiths, the Burgudias, the "Turkish Gypsies," the Lingurars, and so on. Only a few Roma intellectuals and leaders of the numerous Roma organizations have an awareness of a more united community or ethnic group. This awareness of a shared ethnicity is sometimes expressed among wider circles of the Gypsy population as a reaction to press racism or discriminatory social or economic policies; that is, Roma ethnicity is construed from the "outside."

Different processes of ethnic identification are taking place among the numerous groups of Roma in Bulgaria. The quantitative data about the proportion of Gypsies who prefer to identify themselves as something else have to be interpreted with caution. The way of presenting the self to "others" depends on various situational factors. At the time of the census at least half of the people who were identified by the surrounding population as Gypsies identified themselves as Bulgarians, Turks, or Wallachs. Yet, in 1994, two-thirds of the representatives of the 1,844 Roma households that were interviewed declared an affiliation to the Roma community (Tomova 1995). A preferred Turkish identity was selected by 22%, mostly from regions with mixed

(Roma and non-Roma) populations. A further 10% of respondents identified themselves as ethnically Bulgarian and 5% as Wallach (Tomova 1995:19).

In the preceding study 47% of the people who self-identified as Gypsies indicated that they belonged to the subgroup of "Bulgarian Gypsies" (they also infrequently call themselves "Dasikane Roma" or, more rarely, "Gadjikane Roma"). Three-quarters of this group did not indicate any other name for their group in any other way. The remainder most frequently identified themselves with reference either to the traditional (or modern) craft practiced by their group or to the specific name by which other groups know them. Twenty-one subgroups of "Bulgarian Gypsies" emerge out of these various forms of self-identification. Many of the crafts that have given names to subgroups long ago ceased to be practiced by members of the subgroups. In addition, some of those self-identifying as "Bulgarian Gypsies" say that their grandparents were Muslims but that they are now Christians (i.e., that they have transferred from the group "Turkish Gypsies" to the group "Bulgarian Gypsies"). Traces of the old religion are preserved in some groups. For instance, boys are still circumcised, and funerals are performed by an imam. Forty-six percent of respondents with a Roma self-identification additionally identify as "Turkish Gypsies." Of these, over two-thirds do not indicate any other subgroup. The rest are dispersed into 18 subgroups.

"Wallach Gypsies" accounted for only 5% of self-identified Roma. They self-identify themselves more specifically as Wallachs, Wallachors (or Lachors), Whittlers, Ursars, and Spindle-makers. The smallest group in the population of self-identified Roma (1.6%) were the Kardarash and Lovara (1.6 (Tomova 1995).

In contrast to the West European understanding of Gypsies as nomads, most Gypsies in Bulgaria have been settled since the time of the Ottoman empire (Crowe 1995; Fraser 1992).

The long-settled Gypsies selectively include, and incorporate into their culture, large chunks of the traditional culture of the surrounding population. In this way their group culture loses its unique features (e.g., their own institutions and, in some cases, language and traditional crafts). In the nomadic subgroups and in those that were seminomadic until the middle of the twentieth century, especially in the Kardarash and Lovara groups (which are still mobile), there has been the greatest preservation of traditional Gypsy culture. Only they retain their unique institution—the meshere (Gypsy court). Eighty-five percent of the population of these subgroups actively use their language (Tomova 1995).

Socioeconomic Status

Although to a lesser extent than in Western and Central Europe, Gypsies on the Balkans have been constantly subjected to discrimination and rejection by surrounding populations.

Due to the modernization of Bulgarian society and the sharp decline in the demand for services provided by Gypsies, the negative attitude toward them has increased. They began to be considered people incapable of coping with the problems of a changing reality, useless to society, and parasitically reliant on personal charity and social services. Gypsies are gradually becoming isolated, "dropping" out of "our" world. This, in turn, leads to the objective deterioration of the position of Gypsies in all social spheres: in education, culture, socioeconomic life, and political participation.

In the past 10 years of deep economic and social crisis the social distance between Gypsies and representatives of other ethnic groups has consistently increased. Constant negative stereotypes and prejudices toward members of the Gypsy community produce discriminatory attitudes and behavior against them. As all of this occurs against a background of the settling down and normalization of relationships between Bulgarians and Turks and between Christians and Muslims found in many studies conducted since 1990, it is especially painful to Gypsies (Georgiev et al. 1992; Zhelyazkova 1994; Mitev et al. 1997; Tomova 1997; Mitev 1998b).

Gypsies are overrepresented among the unemployed, and the rate of unemployment is increasing faster among Roma than among other Bulgarians (Table 2.10).

Table 2.10
Proportion of Unemployed, by Ethnic Group

Month/Year	Bulgarians	Ethnic Turks	Roma
June 1993	8.9	19.8	50.0
June 1994	10.1	31.5	54.8
June 1995	11.3	31.0	69.6
June 1996	12.5	32.4	73.6

Source: BBSS Gallup International 1998.

One of the reasons for high Roma unemployment is land restitution. Most Gypsies did not own land before the establishment of cooperatives, and so they did not receive anything from restitution. At the moment unemployment among Gypsies in rural regions is above 85%. Gypsies also tend to be more rural than ethnic Bulgarians: 48% of all Gypsies in Bulgaria live in the villages (NSI 1994a).

Urban Gypsies are also overrepresented among the unemployed. They are typically unqualified and used to work in heavy and construction industries. These branches of the economy were the hardest hit with the increase of unemployment.

Very few Gypsies have preserved or managed to adapt their traditional craft to the changed conditions (as few as 10%). The craftsmen that still earn their living by their crafts are blacksmiths (especially in the villages), bell-makers, solid-fuel-stove makers, tool and instrument makers, tinsmiths and whitesmiths, and those making copper vessels. Some from the groups traditionally engaged in carpentry requalified as furniture producers and repairers, while others still manage to sell the pressboard items they produce (baskets, linen baskets, tables, chairs, etc.). Some items, like wooden spoons and other wooden vessels and cutlery that come in various forms and sizes for home cooking, are still purchased directly from Gypsies. A good income can also be secured by making wooden coal, by collecting herbs and mushrooms, or by logging. In addition, a number of Roma families earn their living by entertaining the surrounding population. The most sought-out entertainers are musicians and dancers. Travelling animal trainers and their bears and monkeys are also still seen touring the Black Sea coast and the large cities during the summer season, and fortune-tellers and "healers" offer various herbs or spells to their clients as a way of overcoming problems.

Very few Gypsy households own arable land (as few as 8.5%), and what land they do own is usually small, limited to the land in their backyard. According to Tomova (1995), 14% of Gypsy households breed poultry; 9%, sheep and goats; and 2%, cows. According to Georgiev et al. (1992), these figures were twice as high two years earlier. At the same time comparative analysis shows a strong negative tendency in midterm perspective (Tomova 1995; Georgiev et al. 1992).

There are various indicators of Gypsy poverty. The data from National Statistical Institute (1992 census) show Gypsies to have the shortest life expectancy, the highest birthrates and death rates, and the highest mortality rate among females during childhood and the period of active fertility. These figures place them at roughly the level that the rest of the Bulgarian population was at in 1926. The age structure of the Gypsy community differs considerably from that of the rest of the Bulgarian population. While 66% of Gypsies are children or young adults (from 0 to 29 years of age), children and young adults constitute hardly 37% among ethnic Bulgarians. While 22% of ethnic Bulgarians are over 60, this age group makes up barely 5% among Gypsies (NSI 1994a).

There is a chronically sick member in 44% of Roma families, and in every fifth of them there are two or more sick or disabled members of the family (Tomova 1995). According to official statistics, the percentage of people with disabilities is lower among the Roma than the national average and almost twice as low as it is among Bulgarian Armenians and Jews (NSI 1994b). However, Tomova reports that people over 16 with disabilities occur in the Roma ethnic group at a rate of 81 per 1,000 of the population (i.e., more than twice as frequently as the national average). It is also worth bearing in mind the early age for acquiring disability among this group; children with disabilities are not included in the figure of 81 per 1,000, yet they account for 38% of the disabled people registered during the research (Tomova 1995).

The level of education and qualification among the Roma community continues to lag a long way behind that of the rest of the population in Bulgaria. In 1992 the educational structure of the economically active population in the larger ethnic groups in the country appeared as shown in Table 2.11.

Table 2.11

The Structure of the Ethnic Groups According to Education (18+ Years of Age)

Education	Bulgarian Christians (%)	Ethnic Turks (%)	Roma (%)
University/Institute graduates	20.2	2.0	0.9
High (11th–12th grade)	54.0	24.6	7.8
Basic (to 8th grade)	22.6	55.0	46.2
Primary (to 4th grade)	3.0	16.0	36.7
Illiterate	0.2	2.3	8.5

Source: NSI 1994a.

In the transition period a lot of Roma children dropped out of the educational system or never attended classes. The experts estimate that 52% of Roma children of the age for compulsory education (7–16 years) do not go to school (NSI 1993).

The low levels of education and qualifications of representatives of the Roma community turned out to be a great handicap for their competitiveness in the labor market. Only about one-tenth of the Roma population over 18 years of age are highly qualified.

A considerable part of the Roma population lives in separate neighborhoods, which tend to have the appearance of ghettos. These places are normally overcrowded, and most Roma houses do not meet acceptable living standards. A Roma house is, on average, inhabited by 6.9 people, whereas 2.6 people usually live in a Bulgarian house (according to the last census data). One Gypsy has an average use of 7.1 sq. m., while the figure for the average Bulgarian citizen (including the Roma) is 16.9 sq. m. In 17% of Roma houses there is no furniture, not even beds on which to sleep, and the 1992 census shows that in only 37% of Roma houses is a water system available (NSI 1995b; Tomova 1995).

The proportion of better-off Roma is small. About 10% live in decent and hygienic houses and flats of about 20 sq. m. floor area per person. About 6% run their own businesses, and 8% declare savings and have the capacity to put aside a portion of their current income. About 20% to 30% of Roma individuals lead a way of life that is typical of the average Bulgarian: quite modest, often accompanied by many kinds of privation, but still bearable. Into this category falls part of the (not numerous) Roma intelligentsia; qualified workers who have managed to retain their jobs; some of the Roma who live in the villages, possess some land, and breed domestic animals or are engaged in village cooperatives; and some craftsmen.

The rest of the Roma (60–70%) are poor. Poverty is a traditional characteristic of the Gypsy community, and it deepened considerably at the end of the nineteenth century and the beginning of the twentieth century with the decline of handicrafts in Bulgaria. In the 1950s modernization and urbanization delivered a new blow to the traditional way of life of whole communities of

Roma, who had previously made their living through the provision of various cheap services to the village population. Then, during communist rule, considerable effort was made to raise the educational level of the Roma population and to integrate them in the economic life of the country (mainly as unqualified workers), thus ensuring them an income that approximated the national average.

Bulgarian ethnologists Marushiakova and Popov estimate that until 1990 the strongly marginalized group constituted up to 1.5–3% of the Roma (Georgiev et al. 1992). In this period Roma would isolate anomic Gypsies, ending all contact with members of their families. Thus, this group was doubly marginalized—once from society at large and second from within the Roma community. However, this was an effective way to localize and isolate destructive phenomena in large Roma neighborhoods.

The main reasons for the dramatic impoverishment of the Roma minority over the last several years are the discriminative legal and social policy against them, the massive and lasting unemployment, and the rapid decrease in wages for unqualified labor. Recently (during the deep economic crisis), the existing negative stereotypes against Gypsies were strengthened. These constantly reproduce discriminative attitudes and behaviors toward Roma individuals in all fields of social life. Many studies of the ethnoreligious situation in Bulgaria demonstrate an increasing distance between Roma and *all* other communities (Georgiev et al. 1992; Zhelyazkova 1994; Mitev et al. 1997; Mitev 1998b).

Poverty among Bulgarian Turks and Bulgarian Muslims (Pomaks)

The other two, big minority groups in Bulgaria that are characterized with higher than the average poverty ratio are Bulgarian Turks and Bulgarian Muslims (Pomaks).

Number and Locality

According to NSI data from the 1992 census, 800,052 individuals, or 9.4% of Bulgarian citizens, identify themselves as ethnic Turks. If we take into consideration the fact that their neighbors identify not less than 100,000 of these people as Muslim Gypsies as well as the fact that about 60,000 Bulgarian Muslims identify themselves as Turks, the number of people in what has traditionally been accepted to be the biggest minority group in Bulgaria turns out to be approximately the same as the number of Gypsies in Bulgaria.

Bulgarian Turks are concentrated in two regions: northeast Bulgaria (the Deliorman) and southeast Bulgaria (the Rhodope Mountains). At the moment poverty among people living in the mountain region is much greater than among people living in northeast Bulgaria. The majority of Bulgarian Muslims (the Pomaks, of whom there are estimated to be about 200,000) also live in the Rhodopes. This is the group who, after the Roma, suffered the worst from changes during the period of transition.

Socioeconomic Situation

The mountainous and the semimountainous regions, inhabited by Bulgarian Turks and Bulgarian Muslims, are among the most economically backward areas in the country. This backwardness was the basis for a sharper manifestation of the economic crisis in these areas.

Bulgarian Turks and Bulgarian Muslims predominantly live in villages. The ratio of village living to town living among the Turk population is approximately 68:32 (NSI 1994a). The ratio for Bulgarian Muslims is roughly the same. This population distribution exerts a considerable influence on the preservation of a traditional way of life and on ethnic and religious differentiation. It is of crucial importance in the struggle to find jobs under conditions of increasing unemployment, in accessing relatively good educational and cultural institutions, in getting quick and effective medical aid, and in making use of social services and public utilities. In this respect the village population in Bulgaria is extremely deprived. However, under conditions of economic crisis people in villages turn out to be in a privileged position with regard to the provision of food (and food is the main expense for Bulgarian households at the moment).

Mass emigrations of Bulgarian Turks in the summer of 1989 in connection with the forcible assimilation policy of the Communist Party resulted in the shutdown of many unprofitable enterprises in Turkish villages. But after almost one-third of those who emigrated returned to Bulgaria, more than half remained unemployed. Most of the unemployed, even in the beginning of 1990, were Bulgarian Turks.

According to the NSI 1992 census data, the level of unemployment among the economically active population varied considerably across different ethnic groups. Of Bulgarians, 14.4% were unemployed, as opposed to 25.5% of Turks. Since the 1992 census, no data about unemployment in different ethnic groups have been gathered. However, analysis of data about unemployment in different municipalities shows unambiguously that since 1993 unemployment among Bulgarian Turks and Pomaks has been two to three times more prevalent than among Bulgarians. The fact that unemployment is a typical phenomenon for Turks, Pomaks, and Gypsies is, inevitably, interpreted by them as discrimination on an ethnic and religious basis and could be transformed from a social to an ethnic or a religious conflict.

The tendency for a high level of unemployment to persist among Turk and Pomak communities will continue over the medium term. The reasons lie with the peculiarities of the local economy and the future closure of mines in the Middle Rhodope Mountains, as well as in the fact that Bulgarian Turks' and Pomaks' qualifications and education are poorer than Bulgarian Christians'.

There are considerable differences in the levels of education of people who identify themselves as Bulgarians, Turks, Pomaks, and Roma (differences that have attracted the attention of researchers, politicians, and society at large). According to census data, only 2% of adult Turks have university or college education (as against 20.2% of adult Bulgarians), 24.6% of Turks (and 54% of Bulgarians) have secondary school education, 55% of Turks (and 22.6% of

Bulgarians) have primary education, and 16% of Turks (3% Bulgarians) have completed only elementary school (NSI 1994a).

In many homogeneous Turkish villages in the northeast of Bulgaria and in the Rhodope Mountains families speak no Bulgarian, and children start school without understanding the official language. This is an important obstacle for successful mastery of school subjects, and many children leave school after the eighth grade. Poverty in Turkish and Pomak families is another reason for their children to stop attending school after the eighth grade, as this is the time when many of them have to begin commuting to another town in order to continue their education.

The high level and continuous nature of unemployment, as well as the loss of personal savings following inflation and bank bankruptcies, have caused the abrupt impoverishment of a large number of Bulgarian Turks and Pomaks. Turks suffered many losses in connection with the emigration campaign of 1989. They sold property and animals dirt-cheap. These problems are some of the reasons that the economic situation of many Turkish families has changed for the worse.

The Subjective Effect

The subjective effect of the disastrous situation "now" can be seen in groups' estimation of the socialist "yesterday"; present impoverishment sheds a rosy glow on ethnic groups' evaluation of state socialism, as is seen in Table 2.12.

Table 2.12
How Do You Estimate the Period September 9, 1944–November 10, 1989?

	Positive answers	Neutral answers	Negative answers	Don't know
Bulgarian Christians	32	26	33	9
Bulgarian Muslims	44	24	19	14
Ethnic Turks	34	24	20	21
Roma	45	17	13	25

Bulgarian Christians are most critical of the socialist period, while the "dark" ethnic groups are the most "red." Only one-fifth of ethnic Turks negatively evaluate the state socialist period. These evaluations of ethnic minorities are more a reflection of problems in their economic situation today than of strong ethnic identification with conditions in the past.

WOMEN'S POVERTY

Is There a "Feminization of Poverty" in Bulgaria?

Data on the gender profile of poverty are rather contradictory. Different interpretations of World Bank data are also at variance. The ILO/UNDP report[21] suggests that there has not been feminization of poverty. Table 2.13 shows little difference in poverty rates between men and women.

Table 2.13
Poverty Rates by Gender—1995 (%)

	Adults without children	Adults with children	Old-age pensioners	Total
Male	12.5	21.2	18.8	17.6
Female	12.4	20.4	20.9	18.6
Total	12.4	20.8	20.1	18.1

However, there are other evaluations: "One of the reasons for the considerable impoverishment of the Bulgarian family is women's unemployment. That is why we are not entirely unjustified in talking about the feminization of impoverishment" (Stoyanova et al. 1997). This point was also made at a conference to discuss poverty, where Dimova explicitly stated that "in Bulgaria there is a feminization of poverty" (Dimova 1998). More extreme opinions also exist.

In pursuing research for this book we have, over the period May–June 1998, sought expert opinions from members of Parliament (mostly members of the Social Care Committee), as well as from syndicate activists and sociologists (CSI 1998). The aim of this has been to solve the contradiction in impressions about the feminization of poverty or, if the contradiction remains, to express it more clearly. According to some, there is no reason to talk about a feminization of poverty in Bulgaria (S. Dyankova, K. Gramatikova). But others hold the opposite opinion: the feminization of poverty remains the most severe problem in the development of poverty (M. Hristov, L. Mestan). A ream of more cautious answers lies between these two poles of opinion; their general sense is, "The feminization of poverty in Bulgaria can be viewed only in the narrow sense of the word" (Tzekova 1997).

Women live longer (their life expectancy is 74.6 years) than men (67.1 years); but their "extra" years of life turn into a punishment for them. Women have lower incomes, but this does not necessarily mean that they claim a smaller part of the budget that is determined for the whole household.

The problem of the feminization (or not) of poverty becomes circular if it is studied from a purely economic perspective. Its solution is not to be found in unemployment percentages and income indices alone. Instead, if poverty is understood as the narrowing of the possibilities for human self-affirmation and development, then we must conclude that women are suffering the most from the transition. The boom in the "informal economy" as a means of survival placed a new and heavier load on women. The reduction of the family budget also unevenly affects women, and the sharp reduction in publicly sponsored child support and problems with the education system impose additional burdens on them. In this context the role of "the single mother" (and the hardship associated with this role) becomes a part of everyday life. At the same time, the number of illegitimate children has increased constantly (in 1992 illegitimate births were 28.1% of all live births). Impoverishment leads to a reluctance to enter into marriage; that is, there is a flight from the responsibility of supporting a child, and the illegitimate child becomes "an important factor for poverty among women" (ILO/UNDP 1998b:6). In this way general and, in particular, masculine impoverishment is transformed into female poverty. It is not therefore surprising that Bulgaria has one of the highest rates of abortions in the world (in 1995 the ratio of abortions to live births was 1.34:1), a fact that carries with it significant consequences for women's health (especially the health of the impoverished Gypsy minority). In addition, general instability in the country and increased crime rates unevenly affect women, who become easy prey. Lastly, understanding poverty as a general, not a purely economic, phenomenon is important in looking at the rise of prostitution among young girls and women. This offers them a road away from economic poverty toward a world of luxury, but at the expense of moral and spiritual degradation.

An idea of differences in the situation of men and women is given by using the Human Development Index (HDI), which evaluates quality of life using three basic criteria (1) a longer life in good health; (2) the possibility of acquiring knowledge; and (3) access to the necessary resources for a higher standard of living, and the Gender Development Index (GDI), which reflects differences between men and women (Table 2.14).

Table 2.14
Indexes of Human Development in Bulgaria (1990s)

Human Development Index (HDI)	0.774
Gender Development Index (GDI)	0.757

Source: UNDP 1998.

The lower value of the GDI than the HDI is mainly due to differences in the income of men and women and also to a fall in girls' attendance at educational institutions during levels one, two, and three (this trend is largely shaped by girls from the ethnic minorities, who are usually the first to stop attending classes). These differences are somewhat compensated for by women's longer life expectancy (the qualitative aspect of this "advantage" is not under consideration for these indices). As a result the HDI and the GDI do not very differ significantly, showing a certain, but not dramatic, asymmetry between the situation of the sexes. Nevertheless, in order to analyze what is "hidden" by the index, it is necessary to study the ethnic side of women's poverty.

Women's unemployment is higher than men's. In 1996, 55% of all registered unemployed were women; in June 1999 they made up 53.4% (National Service with Employment [NSE] 1999). At the same time, the proportion of women in the employed population is always below 50% (in 1996 it was 41.5%). The structure of unemployment is not favorable to women either: they stay unemployed for longer periods of time and, given an equal educational status, are less preferred and lower paid. Fifty percent of unemployed married women and more than 60% of unemployed divorced and widowed women are permanently unemployed. In most cases the unemployment of women over 35–40 is transformed into long-term unemployment since younger women are preferred for the few vacant jobs available. Continuous unemployment disqualifies the female workforce, decreasing its competitiveness in the labor market.

Discrimination against women in the labor market is not inherited from the communist era. On the contrary, the labor protection for women that existed then is now falling apart. Prior to 1989 women's pay relative to men's pay was higher in Bulgaria than in Western Europe. Now it is lower. In 1970–1985 women's pay in Bulgaria was 81% of men's pay, whereas this proportion was 69% in England, 74% in Finland, and 78% in France. In 1992 Bulgarian women received only 72% of what men received, while English women received 73%, Finnish 74%, and French 77% (Stoyanova et al. 1997: 126). In the Bulgarian transition "market conditions in general cannot be considered favorable for the female labor force" (ILO/UNDP 1998b:8).

The concept of "female household" refers to households headed by women—21.4% of all Bulgarian households. There are different reasons for women to head a household: most are widows (54.3%), divorced (25.5%) or single (3.2%) (i.e., "incomplete" families). However, 13.8% are married women who, in spite of tradition, head their households. Data indicate that households with a female head are much poorer than those with male heads (ILO/UNDP 1998b:11). According to the same study almost two-thirds of female households (64.9%) are poor, using the criteria for *absolute poverty*.

Divorce is a factor in poverty among women (ILO/UNDP 1998b:17–18). Whereas in earlier times the moral and psychological issues of separation were key, now the economic ones distinguish it. Divorced women find jobs very quickly after joining the labor market because they cannot afford the "luxury" of choosing. One-fifth of interviewed women who had secondary education (and specific qualifications) were forced to work as cleaning women. The fact that divorced women spend more than 70% of their incomes on food highlights their low standard of living. The child allowances they receive from the state and their children's fathers are far from sufficient. Their subjective poverty—pessimism and feelings of desperation—adds an additional burden to their economic poverty (ILO/UNDP 1998b:18). All this leads to the paradox of accumulating tension and worsening relationships in most male households but a decline in divorce rates. One of the reasons for this is probably a growth in women's amenability. In spite of family burdens the single life of women has become far more difficult, and divorce turns into a luxury.

While illegitimate births rose in the 1980s, the situation of single mothers (women with illegitimate children who are without judicially identified fathers) underwent a significant change after the beginning of the reform. Under state socialism these women received social protection, and their only problem was the negative attitudes of a conservative social environment. Today these prejudices have been outlived, but single mothers fall into an economic abyss. It is not surprising that in questionnaire responses we find explicit statements by single mothers that their condition was much better before 1990. Only in 10% of households is the per capita income more than DM50 per month. Food consumption has been reduced to a minimum.

The central reasons for the greater poverty of Gypsy women are the cultural peculiarities of Gypsies and the social consequences of the marginalization and impoverishment of the majority of the group.

One of the most serious consequences of the crisis in the Gypsy community is the *destabilization of the Gypsy family*. More and more young and not so young men leave their wives and children or go to prison, placing severe pressure on their families. Over the past years in the Gypsy community there has been a sharp rise in the proportion of single mothers and divorced women who take care of their numerous children on their own.

Until 1989 the traditional way of life for most Gypsy women followed the following pattern: early marriage with short-term employment (often as cleaning women in state enterprises), pregnancy, and the birth of a child every two to three years. According to pretransition laws, this counted as a long term of service and made possible early retirement and maternity and child allowances at a level that could be lived on. While raising a child of under three years, a mother would receive special remuneration at a rate close to her salary, and this period of time would be counted as part of her service. Women who gave birth to, and raised, three or more children gained an especially privileged status with the right to an early retirement and various social privileges. Now this pattern of "spending" one's life is disastrous for women, but their attitudes have not changed fast enough.

With an increasing number of broken marriages and unbearably high rates of unemployment among Gypsies, the situation of Gypsy women has become tragic. The tradition in many Gypsy subgroups is that the physical survival of the family is the responsibility of women. Husbands, even when they remain in the family, continue to expect and require their wives to meet this responsibility and punish their wives severely if they cannot handle what is often an unbearable task. Chronic hunger, living in misery, and constant violence (rooted in both chance cultural proclivities and in the spread of alcoholism among men) all lead to extremely high death rates among fertile Gypsy women, their quick physical exhaustion, a large number of premature births (frequently of children with serious diseases), and a high incidence of disability (often occurring as early as childhood).

The subcultural peculiarities of the Gypsy community place women in a very vulnerable situation. Most of them have low levels of education and are without qualifications. This is due to parents' inability to educate their children, itself a result of families' past impoverishment and the Gypsy community's rejection of education as a value. Usually the beginning of menstruation is a sign to parents for their daughters to stop attending classes. These girls enter a new stage of life: as they will soon be married, it is unacceptable for them to visit places where there are many boys and no parental control. Even if parents have previously allowed girls to attend classes, marriage (usually below the legal age of consent—often as young as 14) leads automatically to the termination of girls' educational activities. Poor education and the bearing of children at an early age place additional difficulties on young Gypsy women as they search for work.

The condition of Bulgarian Muslim and Turkish women has been peculiarly affected by the sharp increase in female unemployment. The closure of village workshops, most of which offered women work, has led to the unemployment rates among these groups rising to over 70%. While Turkish women in northeastern Bulgaria can, in the short term, cope with this change in their situation if they own some land that they can cultivate with their children, the low quantity and quality of land in the Rhodopes do not allow households to lead a normal life on the miserable income possible from agricultural activities.

In order to survive, families largely depend on products from their private plots of land, which are again managed by women. However, low levels of monetary income and a harvest limited to the fruits and vegetables that grow in the mountain region lead to inadequate and monotonous forms of nourishment. Only the existence of a cow or a goat can save a household from starvation.

Additional impoverishment can be expected in these communities over the next few years as the demand for tobacco on international markets decreases and as there is an increase in competition on the potato market (the other product grown by Bulgarian Turks and Muslims).

Poverty among Bulgarian Turkish and Muslim women in the Rhodope region is deepening as a result of their limited access to social services and benefits. As most of these women were engaged in tobacco growing, since the closure of the Agricultural Co-operative Enterprises they do not have any social insurance. For most young women their work in tobacco growing is an obstacle to obtaining a document for a seven-day period of employment women with illegitimate children who are without judicially identified fathers and so automatically makes them ineligible for receipt of maternity allowances.

Women, more than men, believe that they live in misery and privation (Table 2.15). Probably some of their responses are tempered by the specific sociopsychological characteristics of men and women, features such as men's self-confidence and vanity or the psychological vulnerability of women: men are more reluctant to admit that they cannot cope with particular economic situations for which they feel responsible as heads of their households, while women are more sensitive about a lack of possibilities and means. However, these psychological layers are also deposited on objective differences. Women experience the cataclysms of the transition more sharply. The project *Catastrophic Consciousness in Modern Bulgaria* proved that Bulgarian women are significantly more psychologically insecure than men (Mitev 1998).

Table 2.15
Self-Evaluation of the Quality of Life of Men and Women

	Men (%)	Women (%)
Living in abundance	1.3	0.6
Living without privation	12.1	9.2
Living with some privation	55.3	50.4
Living with much privation	23.7	28.3
Living in misery	7.5	11.5

Source: National Centre for Public Opinion Research (NCPOR) 1998.

Conclusion

The influence of gender on impoverishment is linked to, and interdependent with, other factors—place of work, occupation, family status, place of residence, and ethnicity. Poverty integrates, subjects, and modifies women in similar and in different ways than it does men. There are also some important ways in which it strengthens women. The ILO/UNDP study summarized: "Women are not inherently poorer than men, but the uneven distribution of the burden of the crisis has formed groups of women, which undoubtedly comprise the poorest population strata" (ILO/UNDP 1998b).

The feminization of poverty occurs where gender combines with another critical variable (age, marital status, or ethnicity). It is worth noting that inequality is broader than can be gauged by a strictly economic measurement. It is only in some groups that the narrowing of opportunities under the pressure of circumstances is striking and takes an economic shape.

In the conditions of the Bulgarian transition we have reason to talk about a *tendency toward a feminization of poverty,* which may increase over the next few years. The prospect is not predetermined and will depend on the presence (or not) of an effective national policy in relation to women in poverty. So far such a policy has not been invented, but the prerequisites exist.

Poverty is the new—and let us hope the last—stage in the *incomplete emancipation* of Bulgarian women.

CONCLUSION

The specificity of Bulgarian poverty is determined by the following:

- A critical decline in incomes and dramatic increase in a majority of people with incomes under the social, and in many cases even the survival, minimum; food expenses are the majority of all outgoing income;
- Massive unemployment;
- Depletion of savings due to inflation, bank insolvency, and financial "pyramids," as well as the need to maintain the household budget;
- Development of a "shadow economy" that operates as a compensation mechanism but at the same time becomes a poverty reproduction factor;
- Residual resources (property acquired under administrative socialism—primarily housing);

- Acquired resources (property acquired during the transition period—primarily restituted land).

In Bulgaria over 90% of the people own their homes.[22] At the same time about 90% of the people have incomes below the social minimum.[23] The Bulgarian paradox is that the Bulgarians are property owners and are poor. People do have property, but it is of low liquidity, so it cannot be capitalized. All attempts to grasp this paradox place us face-to-face with another one: on its way to the *market* economy Bulgarian society has developed a large-scale *natural* economy. These two paradoxes are genetically interrelated. They both stem from the delay of the transition as a result of striving to subjugate it and derive dubious profits from it by social groups that are already powerful or just gathering strength.

In a protomarket space the average Bulgarian citizen works in a state enterprise prepared for privatization. He has a low salary, which is often paid only irregularly. She has land that she does not cultivate and could not sell. He used to have savings but they are now appropriated by the financial pharaoh or gone with the bankrupt bank. She feels not only poor but robbed as well—both in the literal sense and metaphorically.

In a protomarket time it is as if this same citizen is alternately subjected to hot and cold showers being poured over him indiscriminately. The dynamism is described by a steep curve running from relative stability to constant decline, going through an inflationary slump to stabilization holding as yet unknown prospects.

Today the Human Development Index (HDI), a general benchmark for development, stands at 0.774 in Bulgaria,[24] whereas in the industrialized countries it is 0.916, and in the developing world, 0.570. In the course of the transition the country's place in world civilization changed. In the 1980s Bulgaria was ranked 27th in the world according to the Human Development Index (NSI 1990), in 1991, 33rd, in 1994, 48th (UNDP 1995:13). In 1995 Bulgaria ranked 69th (Tzekova 1997).

The basic traits of Bulgarian poverty serve as criteria that provide an opportunity to address the issue of the feminization of poverty. Only along two of the indicators (namely, the decrease in personal income and unemployment) are there obvious variances. In both cases women are placed in a less favorable position, but in neither of them are the differences significant enough to point to a general process of feminization of poverty. The syndromes of poverty affect women's subgroups (such as divorced women, single mothers, and widows in cities).

However, this is not the case with ethnic minorities, particularly not with Bulgarian Roma. Their situation is more or less affected by all indicators: a radical dip in incomes, ubiquitous unemployment, large concentration of the shadow economy in the most shadowy, that is, criminal, sectors, and far fewer residual resources. The Roma constitute the only group where restitution does not manifest itself as a new resource but as a new loss of resources.

The average statistical picture will be misleading if we do not take differentiation into account. Between the bottom and the top layer of those 90%

in Bulgaria with incomes below the social minimum there are differences that can be measured by the ontological category *survival chances*.

A social bottom is being formed in Bulgaria by people who have lost hope as well as the chance of finding a way out of poverty, people thrown into social isolation, anomie, and degradation. A large portion of the Bulgarian Roma are threatened by this social disaster.

Due to the modernization of Bulgarian society and the sudden limitation of the services offered by Gypsies, the negative attitude toward them has increased. They are considered incapable of coping with the problems of a changing reality, useless to society, and parasitically reliant on personal charity and social services. Gypsies are gradually becoming isolated, "falling" out of "our" world. This, in turn, leads to the objective deterioration of the position of Gypsies across all of society: in education, culture, socioeconomic status, and political participation.

In past years the social distance between Gypsies and representatives of other ethnic groups has consistently increased. Constant negative stereotypes and prejudice toward members of the Gypsy community produce discriminatory attitudes and behavior. As all of this occurs against a background of the settling down and normalization of relationships between Bulgarians and Turks and between Christians and Muslims (found in all studies conducted since 1990), it is especially painful to Gypsies.

NOTES

1. Prime Minister I. Kostov: "The main foes of the Government are misery and crime." S. Kostadinova, sociologist: "Poverty and crime are the two key-words which constantly rival the first place amongst the dominants in mass conscience during the years of transition. The rivalry is serious, indeed, but the common element between them is their anti-social essence. Poverty and crime burn to ashes our human nature as such and delineate the parameters for the degradation of the nation" (Kostadinova 1997:17). According to a public opinion survey, two-thirds of the Bulgarians feel a strong alarm and constant fear about the downfall in the standard of living and impoverishment (Mitev 1998a).

2. In their preelection platforms (1991) the Union of Democratic Forces proclaimed restitution "before and parallel to the privatisation," while the Bulgarian Socialist Party rejected all restitution and proposed compensation through privatization bonuses (BSP 1991; UDF 1991).

3. Transformation in Central Europe and on Balkans contained alternatives (Zoon 1994; Mitev 1994; Offe 1996).

4. The concept of "entry–exit economy" is given an interpretation further on in the text.

5. *Nashi hora* ("our people") is a widespread expression in Bulgarian political journalism and everyday communications. It is employed to designate a high degree of closeness and trust that has a personal nuance and exceeds or runs counter to relations regulated by ethic norms and the law. Bulgarian political slang accepted some terms for "our people" borrowed from informal and family relations and applied them to political colors: "friendly circle" for the red and "cousins" for the blue. *Nashism* or the syndrome of "our people" is a new coinage in political jargon. It denotes surrounding oneself by one's own "reliable" people, which has recently grown to be a principle and an ersatz

ideology. The concept first appeared in postcommunist Russia. It is synonymous with the phenomenon of party clients and dubious business relations. As a result of *nashism,* "Private property of ones own is more important than private property of others" (K. Stoichev, sociologist, director of Balkan British Social Survey (BBSS) Gallup International; Monitor newspaper, March 9,1999).

6. "The issue of poverty was formally recognized for the first time in Bulgaria in March 1991 when the 'second safety net' was established. Since then, however, Bulgaria has lacked a definition of the 'poverty line' which is required in order to determine who—and how many—are the poor in Bulgaria" (ILO/UNDP 1998a:10). The cited monograph, *Poverty in Transition: Strengthening the National Policies and Strategies for Poverty Reduction in Bulgaria,* is the main academic publication dealing with poverty in Bulgaria. It contains the results of an UNDP/ILO project and includes critical analysis of the completeness and reliability of available data and of alternative approaches to measuring poverty; household equivalence scales and how they are implemented; assessment of the current extent and profile of poverty; and recommendations for the administrative and financial management of social benefits in the future.

7. "The consumer basket method is the one applied most often in Bulgaria, and has the longest tradition in social assistance practice" (ILO/UNDP 1998a:11). Alternative methods are the method of M. Orshansky and the food share method by Engel. About the definitions of the social subsistence, survival, and base minima, see UNDP 1997:26–27.

8. In 1999 monthly incomes in Bulgaria were as follows:

	BGL	Equivalent in US$
Minimum salary	64.00	35.5
Average salary	182.0	101
Minimum social pension	35.83	20
Minimum pension	41.20	23
Average pension	66.50	37

9. The national currency of the country—the Bulgarian leva (BGL)—suffered dramatically through the years of transition. Relatively stable during the starting years and periodically devaluated, later on it reached a hyperinflation shock in the beginning of 1997. In the middle of that same year (on July 1, 1997) the Currency Board at the International Monetary Fund was established, and BGL was correlated to the deutsche mark (DM) in the ratio BGL1000 = DM1. As of July 5 BGL was denominated, and now BGL1 = DM1.

10. Expected guaranteed minimum income in 1999 was BGL37.30. It is equal to 0.58 of the minimum salary and 1.04 of the minimum pension.

11. The source for the structure of general expenditure of households is the National Statistics Institute. The ratio of food expenses of the very poor is an expert evaluation (CSI 1998).

12. The National Statistics Institute is developing a methodology for a pilot project under Eurostat.

13. Source: Committee for Agriculture, Forests and Agrarian Reform at the Parliament 1999.

14. The Gini coefficient has changed as follows: 1989—21.7%; 1990—22.8%; 1991—23.5%; 1992—33.7%; 1994—36.6%; 1995—37.8%.

15. "The image of the rich man is too distorted to serve as a behavioural model and it cannot inspire a living 'Bulgarian dream' (ILO/UNDP 1998a:53; Bulg. ed.).

16. Registered unemployment in some countries of Central and Eastern Europe:

Unemployment	1995	1996	1997*	1998**
Czech Republic	2.9	3.5	5.0	6.0
Hungary	10.4	10.5	10.0	9.0
Russia	8.8	9.3	9.1	9.0
Bulgaria	11.0	12.5	16.5	19.0
Poland	14.9	13.6	11.9	11.5
Romania	8.9	6.1	9.2	9.0

* Preliminary data.

**Forecast.

Source: Business Central Europe 1997.

17. The following data show the relationship between monetary incomes and self-assessment of social category (%):

Category	Monthly monetary income per had of a family in thousand BGL			
	Up to 30 (US$18)	30–60 (US$18–36)	60–120 (US$36–72)	Over 120 (US$72)
No privation	8	26	41	25
Some privation	13	44	38	5
Big privation	30	60	10	-
Live in misery	45	55	-	-

18. The National Statistics Institute (1990) provided the figures in BGL. The official exchange rate has been used for calculating the equivalent in US$. At that time the Bulgarian lev had a low exchange rate abroad but provided a high level of domestic buying power. For example, one loaf of bread = BGL0.26; one liter of milk = BGL0.30; One kilogram of cheese = BGL1.80; one kilogram of pork meal = BGL3.50. The monthly rent of a one-room, state-owned apartment was BGL10. The city bus and tram tickets were BGL0.05, and the airplane ticket along the longest route (Sofia to Varna) was BGL24.

19. After the completion of land property restitution the agricultural land was divided into 25 million plots, or an average of 2–3 decares each. The number of tractors was reduced from 53,653 in 1989 (NSI 1990) to 24,967 in 1996 (NSI 1997b); the number of harvesters for the same period was reduced by more than half, from 14,215 to 7,035. Farming also suffered extreme losses.

20. The following are some examples: "I sang with a Roma choir. I was a soloist. When the choir was disbanded, I was not given a document. I have 40 years of service but only 20 of them are recognized." "I was told that I cannot buy a voucher book to participate in the mass privatization because I did not take part in the municipal elections." "I haven't had a passport for 5 years now. I have to go to the town of Vidin to get one. I have no money for bread, let alone for travelling to Vidin!" (Zhelyazkova

1997:35).

21. The monograph *Women in Poverty* (ILO/UNDP 1998b) contains results from the most significant study on the subject. It was presented to an international conference in Sofia in June 1998. The publication is a new starting point for scientific work and can become the basis for government decisions. The data have been interpreted in reports presented during the same conference. See Bobeva (1998) for the main results of the study; also Dimova (1998) and Tomova (1998).

22. According to the census data in 1992, 94.2% of people own their homes (NSI 1995c). According to the sociological study of the National Statistics Institute (1994c), one-third of the households also own a second living place, villa, or country house (Vladimirova 1997).

23. Official information about social minimum has not been published. The figure recorded here is a result of expert evaluation (CSI 1998). According to sociological studies, "generally speaking 10% of people in the country over 18 years of old determine themselves as living without privation" (NCPOR 1999:36).

24. The Human Development Index in 1991 was 0.899, in 1993, 0.820, in 1995, 0.805 (UNDP 1995; 1998). "The shortfall is mainly due to the serious fall of education coefficient (from 0.925 in 1993 to 0.888 in 1996) as well as to the adjusted per capita real GDP [Gross Domestic Product] index from 0.770 to 0.676 within the same period" (UNDP 1998:11–12).

BIBLIOGRAPHY

Andrews, Emily S. 1996. *Income Maintenance Programs and Poverty in Bulgaria*. A background paper prepared for the Bulgaria Poverty Assessment Study of the World Bank, July 29.

Balcerowicz, Leszek. 1995. *Socialism, Capitalism, Transformation*. Budapest, London, and New York: Central European University Press.

BBSS Gallup International. 1998. *Poverty Assessment in Bulgaria 1997*. Report. Sofia.

Bobeva, Daniela. 1998. *Zheni v bednost* (Women in Poverty). Paper presented at the international conference "Poverty in Transition: Women in Poverty," Sofia.

Bogdanov, Boris. 1994. *Bednost i linii na bednost* (Poverty and Poverty Lines). In *Statistika Journal,* no. 6, pp. 57–70.

Bogdanov, Boris. 1996. *Izsledvane na bednostta chres pokazateli za sustoyanie na lishenie* (Research on Poverty on the Basis of Indicators of Privation). In *Statistika Journal,* no. 1, pp. 10–24.

Brzezinski, Zbigniew. 1989. *The Grand Failure*. New York: Scribner.

Bulgarian Socialist Party. 1991. *Pre-Election Platform*. Sofia: BSP.

Business Central Europe. 1997. *The Annual 1997/98*.

Central Statistical Department. 1986. *Statisticheski godishnik na Narodna Republika Bulgaria* (Annual Statistics of the Peoples Republic of Bulgaria). Sofia: CSD.

Centre for the Study of Ideologies. 1998. *Bulgarskata bednost. Expertni otzenki* (Bulgarian Poverty. Expert Evaluations). Sofia.

CONSENSUS Programme/PHARE. January 1998a. *Minimum Income for Survival*. First Report. Sofia: PARTEX.

CONSENSUS Programme/PHARE. June 1998b. *Minimum Income for Survival*. Final Report. Sofia: PARTEX.

Crowe, David M. 1995. *A History of the Gypsies of Easter Europe and Russia*. New York: St. Martin's Press.

Demery, Lionel, and Kalpana Mehra (assisted by Galina Sotirova and Gnanaraj Chelleraj). 1996. *The Incidence of Social Spending in Bulgaria*. A background paper prepared for the Bulgaria Poverty Assessment Study of the World Bank.

Dimova, Lilia. 1998. *Women in Poverty—Strategies for a Way Out of Poverty.* Paper presented at the international conference "Poverty in Transition: Women in Poverty," Sofia.

Dinkova, Maria. 1997. *Brakat kato predstava, tzennost i realnost* (The Marriage as a Concept, Value and Reality). Report from an empirical sociological study. Sofia: ASSA-M.

Fotev, Georgi. 1997. *Sotzialna reintegratzia na bednite i sotzialno izclyuchenite* (Social Re-integration of the Poor and the Socially Excluded). In Nepravitelstveni organizatzii i darzhavni institutzii sreshtu bednostta (NGOs and State Institutions against Poverty). Sofia: Perspektiva.

Fraser, Angus M. 1992. *The Gypsies.* Cambridge, MA: Blackwell.

Genov, Nikolai, and Anna Krasteva (eds.). 1999. *Bulgaria 1960–1995.* Sofia: National and Global Development.

Georgiev, Zhivko, et al. 1992. *Etnokulturnata situatzia v Bulgaria '92* (Ethnocultural Situation in Bulgaria '92). Manuscript. Sofia.

Gocheva, R., and K. Stoyanova (eds.) 1994. Sotzialna zashtita na bednite, bezrabotnite i potrebitelite pri prehoda kam pazarna ikonomika (Social Protection of the Poor, Unemployed and the Consumers in the Transition to a Market Economy). Sofia: Bulgarian Academy of Sciences.

ILO/UNDP. 1995. *Bulgaria 1995. Situation of Women.* Geneva: ILO.

ILO/UNDP. 1998a. *Poverty in Transition: Strengthening the National Policies and Strategies for Poverty Reduction in Bulgaria.* Geneva: ILO.

ILO/UNDP. 1998b. *Women in Poverty: An Assessment of the Bulgarian Anti-poverty Policies and Strategies.* Geneva: ILO.

Kabakchieva, Petya. 1997. *Problemite na bednostta i problemite na sotzialnata politika* (The Problem of Poverty and the Problems Facing Social Policy). In Nepravitelstveni organizatzii I darzhavni institutzii sreshtu bednostta (NGOs and State Institutions against Poverty). Sofia: Perspektiva.

Kolev, Kolyo. 1997. *Nepazarnata lichnost* (Non-market Person). In: *24 Chassa* newspaper, August 27. Sofia.

Kostadinova, Snezhana. 1997. *Prestupnostta—izhod za bednite?* (Crime—Break a Deadlock for the Poor?). *Socialdemocratzia* magazine, 13, pp. 17. Sofia.

Kostov, Georgi, S. Todorova, Z. Toneva, and T. Rakadjiiska. 1993. *Sotziologicheski problemi na bednostta* (Sociological Problems of Poverty). *Sotziologicheski Pregled* (Sociological Review) 17, no. 2. Sofia.

Liegeois, Jean-Pierre and Nicolae Gheorghe. 1995. *Roma/Gypsies: A European Minority.* London: Minority Rights Group.

Marushiakova, Elena, and Vesselin Popov. 1993. *Tziganite v Bulgaria* (Gypsies in Bulgaria). Sofia.

Marushiakova, Elena et al. 1993. *Etnicheskata kartina v Bulgaria* (Ethnic Picture in Bulgaria). Sofia: Klub '90.

Miller, Jeffrey B. 1998. *Social Dimensions of Economic Change: Is the Private Market a Solution to Bulgaria's Economic Problem?* In J. Bell (ed.), Bulgaria in Transition. Boulder, CO: Westview Press.

Minev, Duchomir. 1998. *Political Democracy. Transition and Poverty. The Weakness of Paradigms.* In P.-E. Mitev (ed.), The Bulgarian Transition: Challenges and Cognition. Sofia: LIK.

Mirchev, Mikhail. 1998. *Dynamics of the Social Structure in the 1990's in the Light of Impoverishment and Poverty in Bulgaria.* In P.-E. Mitev (ed.), The Bulgarian Transition: Challenges and Cognition. Sofia: LIK.

Mitev, Petar-Emil. 1994. *Post-Totalitarian Development: Proto-Democracy or Proto-Authoritarian Regimes*. In N. Genov (ed.), Sociology in a Society in Transition. Sofia: BSA.

Mitev, Petar-Emil. 1998a. *Catastrophic Consciousness in Modern Bulgaria*. Manuscript. Michigan State University.

Mitev, Petar-Emil. 1998b. *Discriminatory Attitudes*. In Bozidar Jaksic (ed.), Racism and Xenophobia. Beograd: Rebublika.

Mitev, Petar-Emil. 1999. *From Neighbourhood to Citizenship*. In Bozidar Jaksic (ed.), Tolerancija/Tolerance. Beograd: Republika.

Mitev, Petar-Emil, et al. 1997. *Vrazki na savmestimost i nesavmestimost mezhdy christiani i myusyulmani v Bulgaria '97* (Relations of Compatibility and Incompatibility between Christians and Muslims in Bulgaria '97). Manuscript. Sofia: IMIR.

National Centre for Public Opinion Research. 1998. Bulletin, March. Sofia: NCPOR.

National Centre for Public Opinion Research. 1999. Bulletin, July. Sofia: NCPOR.

National Service with Employment. Informatzionen buletin za yuni 1999 (News bulletin, July 1999). Sofia.

National Statistics Institute. 1990. *Statisticheski godishnik na Republika Bulgaria, 1989.* (Annual Statistics of the Republic of Bulgaria, 1989). Sofia: NSI.

National Statistics Institute. 1993. *Osnovni rezultati ot prebroiavane na naselenieto kam 2 dekemvri 1992* (Major Results of the Census, 2 December 1992). Sofia: NSI.

National Statistics Institute. 1994a. *Demografska i sotzialna charakteristika na naselenieto*, tom 1 (Demographic and Social Characteristics of Population, vol. 1). Sofia: NSI.

National Statistics Institute. 1994b. *Demografska i sotzialna charakteristika na naselenieto*, tom 2 (Demographic and Social Characteristics of Population, vol. 2). Sofia: NSI.

National Statistics Institute. 1994c. *Ikonomicheskata sigurnost v zhivota na domakinstvata* (Economic Security in the Life of Households). Sofia: NSI.

National Statistics Institute. 1995a. *Granitzi na bednost* (Poverty Boundaries). Sofia: NSI.

National Statistics Institute. 1995b. *Rezultati ot prebroiavaneto na zhilishtniya fond, tom 1* (Results of the Census of Housing, vol. 1). Sofia: NSI.

National Statistics Institute. 1995c. *Rezultati ot prebroiavaneto na zhilishtniya fond, tom 2* (Results of the Census of Housing, vol. 2). Sofia: NSI.

National Statistics Institute. 1995d. *Zhenata i semeistvoto v Bulgaria* (The Woman and the Family in Bulgaria). Sofia: NSI.

National Statistics Institute. 1996. *Byudjetat na domakinstvoto v Republika Bulgaria* (The Household Budgets in the Republic of Bulgaria). Sofia: NSI.

National Statistics Institute. 1997a. *Bednite domakinstva v Bulgaria (*Poor Households in Bulgaria. Sofia: NSI.

National Statistics Institute. 1997b. *Dohodi, razhodi I potreblenie na domakinstvata. Tretoto trimesechie na 1996 I 1997* (Incomes, Expenditures and Consumption of Households. The Third Quarters of 1996 and 1997). Sofia: NSI.

National Statistics Institute. 1997c. *Statisticheski barometar, 25.09.1997* (Statistical Barometer, 25.09.1997). Sofia: NSI.

National Statistics Institute. 1998a. *Statisticheski godishnik na Republika Bulgaria, 1997.* (Annual Statistics of the Republic of Bulgaria, 1997). Sofia: NSI.

National Statistics Institute. 1998b. Statisticheski spravochnik 1998 (Statistical Manual 1998). Sofia: NSI.

Ninno, Carlo Del. 1996. *Poverty Profile*. A background paper prepared for the Bulgaria Poverty Assessment Study of the World Bank.

Noncheva, Tatyana. 1997. *Kriterii za identifikatzia na bednite i riskovite grupi* (Criteria for Identification of Poor and Risk Groups. In Nepravitelstveni organizatzii I darzhavni institutzii sreshtu bednostta (NGOs and State Institutions against Poverty). Sofia: Perspektiva.

Offe, Claus. 1996. *Varieties of Transition: The East European and East German Experience*. Cambridge: Polity Press.

Petrov, Georgi. 1990. *Krahat na totalitarnata ikonomika* (The Failure of Totalitarian Economy). Sofia: Nauka i Izkustvo.

Przeworski, Adam. 1991. *Democracy and the Market Political and Economic Reforms in Eastern Europe and Latin America*. New York: Cambridge University Press.

Rakadjiiska, Temenuga. 1994. *Social and Economic Identity of the Bulgarian Households according to the Status "Rich–Poor."* In N. Genov (ed.), Sociology in a Society in Transition. Sofia: BSA.

Russanov, Valerii. 1994. *Aspekti na etnokulturnata situatzia v Bulgaria* (Aspects of Ethno-Cultural Situation in Bulgaria. Sofia: AKSES.

Rutkowski, Jan J. 1996. *Labor Markets and Poverty in Bulgaria*. A background paper prepared for the Bulgaria Poverty Assessment Study of the World Bank, July 29.

Skoufias, Emmanuel. 1996a. *An Analysis of Social Transfers and the Safety Net System in Bulgaria*. A background paper prepared for the Bulgaria Poverty Assessment Study of the World Bank, October 29.

Skoufias, Emmanuel. 1996b. *Seasonality in Household Consumption in Bulgaria*. A background paper prepared for the Bulgaria Poverty Assessment Study of the World Bank, October 29.

Stoyanova, K. et al. 1997. *Semeina sotzialna politika. Problemi, prioriteti, provezhdane* (Family Social Policy. Problems, Priorities, Realization). Sofia: Goreks Press.

Tilkidjiev, Nikolai (ed.). 1998a. *The Middle Class as a Precondition of a Sustainable Society*. Sofia: AMCD.

Tilkidjiev, Nikolai (ed.). 1998b. *Sotzialna stratifikatzia i neravenstvo* (Social Stratification and Inequality). Sofia: M-8-M.

Tomova, Ilona. 1995. *The Gypsies in the Transition Period*. Sofia: IMIR.

Tomova, Ilona. 1997. *Religioznite naglasi na bulgarskite romi* (Religious Attitudes of Bulgarian Roma). Manuscript. Sofia: IMIR.

Tomova, Ilona. 1998. *Poverty among Women from the Minority Groups*. Paper presented at the international conference "Poverty in Transition: Women in Poverty," June 9–10, Sofia.

Topalova, Velina. 1996. *Sotzialna identifikatzia 'bedni—bogati' v parvite godini na prehoda* (Social Identification "Poor–Rich" during the First Years of Transition). In Bednost i fragmentatzia na bulgarskoto obshtestvo (Poverty and Fragmentation of Bulgarian Society). Sofia: Perspektiva.

Tzekova, Evgenia. 1997. *Semeistvoto na granitzata na bednostta* (Family at the Boundary of Poverty). Manuscript. Sofia: Institute of Demography, Bulgarian Academy of Sciences.

Union of Democratic Forces. 1991. *Pre-Election Platform*. Sofia: UDF.

UNDP. 1995. *Bulgaria 1995. The Human Development*. Sofia: UNDP.

UNDP. 1997. *Early Warning Report*. Sofia: UNDP/Open Society Foundation, September-October.

UNDP. 1998. *National Human Development Report*. Sofia: UNDP.

Vladimirova, Katia. 1997. *Promenite v dohodite, potreblenieto i sotzialnata diferentziatzia na naselenieto prez godinite na prehod kam pazarna ikonomika* (The Changes in Incomes, Consumption and Social Differentiation of Population during the Transition to Market Economy). In *Problemi na truda Journal*, pp. 3–4.

Voynova, Emilia. 1998. *Poverty in Bulgaria*. In P.-E. Mitev (ed.), The Bulgarian Transition: Challenges and Cognition. Sofia: LIK.

Yitzhaki, Shalomo. 1996. *The Effect of Changes in Policy on Inequity and Poverty in Bulgaria*. A background paper prepared for the Bulgaria Poverty Assessment Study of the World Bank, September 25.

Yossifov, Assen, and Iliya Naumov. 1998. *Poverty—Cultural Models and Mass Attitudes*. In P.-E. Mitev. (ed.), The Bulgarian Transition: Challenges and Cognition. Sofia: LIK.

Zhelyazkova, Antonina. 1998. *Bulgaria's Muslim Minorities*. In J. Bell. (ed.), Bulgaria in Transition. Boulder, CO: Westview Press.

Zhelyazkova, Antonina (ed.). 1994. *Relations of Compatibility and Incompatibility in Everyday Life between Christians and Muslims in Bulgaria*. Sofia: IMIR.

Zhelyazkova, Maria. 1997. *Bednost, sotzialna zashtita i NPO* (Poverty, Social Defence and NGOs). In Nepravitelstveni organizatzii I darzhavni institutzii sreshtu bednostta (NGOs and State Institutions against Poverty). Sofia: Perspektiva.

Zhelyazkova, Maria. 1998. *Poverty and Integration. The Diverging Roads of a Society in Transition. The Case of Bulgaria*. In P.-E. Mitev (ed.), The Bulgarian Transition: Challenges and Cognition. Sofia: LIK.

Zoon, Hans van. 1994. *Alternative Scenarios for Central Europe*. Avebury: Ashgate.

3

The Hungarian Neoliberal State, Ethnic Classification, and the Creation of a Roma Underclass

János Ladányi

INTRODUCTION

Eastern European communist elites legitimated their power by rapidly decreasing social inequalities and by the abolition of poverty. They understood state-socialist society as highly egalitarian, containing only minor inequalities that had been inherited from the previous capitalist regime and that would disappear in the near future. Thus, poverty and ethnicity became off-limits as topics for social research.

In Hungary during the end of the 1960s and the early 1970s it was, for the first time, possible to conduct research on poverty and ethnicity. These studies tended not to be theoretically oriented (a point to which I will return). Their aim was, above all, to prove that absolute and relative poverty were both present and continuously reproduced in a "classless society." The existence and continuous reproduction of ethnic disadvantages meant that extreme social disadvantages existed in Hungary, as did ethnic discrimination against the Gypsy population. The most important message of these studies was that these inequalities were not "left over" from the previous capitalist regime but were produced by the state-socialist redistributive system.

By the beginning of the 1980s, traditional poverty was confined to marginal groups. However, social inequality increased significantly, and the exclusion of Gypsies became more explicit. Most state-socialist measures to aid the poor, such as free and compulsory elementary education, free or practically free health insurance, and heavily subsidized state housing, proved very expensive and often counterproductive. Their expense meant that, after the collapse of the centralized redistributive system, these mechanisms could not be maintained. The measures were counterproductive because, instead of favoring the poor, the income redistribution worked as a camouflaged form of discrimination that made the poor (Gypsies in particular) even poorer. For example, the theoretically equal elementary education system included special classes for poor, especially Roma pupils; and while special programs for those living in traditional Gypsy settlements improved their housing conditions, these policies reproduced the extreme residential segregation of the rural Roma and provided Gypsy families with only very little, low-quality housing that was without land for self-maintenance farming. These countereffective programs "helped" the poor without asking them how they wanted to be "helped" or treating them like partners and often were contrary to their preferences, thus not making it possible for them to help themselves after a certain period of time.

This is why the most important achievements of state-socialist social policy collapsed almost within a fortnight of the end of the communist regime. Many of these achievements became a "dead end" for those who previously had been "favored" by the system. Furthermore, the postcommunist economic crisis resulted not only in the temporary decline of the standard of living for the poor and the reappearance of traditional poverty within large social groups but also in poverty of a new character. A new Eastern European underclass is emerging. There is a social group divided from the rest of society by strict borders. Poverty is becoming highly ethnicized. Thus, poverty and ethnicity are coming to mean significantly different things than they did during state-socialism. I believe that this is the most unfavorable social consequence of the postcommunist transition.

POVERTY

In Hungary there are no official definitions of poverty and no poverty lines that are accepted by experts. This results in much confusion in the discourse about poverty. In this section I review the various definitions of poverty used in Hungary.

In the "Hungarian Household Panel" (HHP), a survey carried out annually between 1992 and 1997, the following definitions of poverty were used:

1.   The lowest 20% based on household income per capita.
2.   Those with less than 50% of the national average income per consumer unit.
3.   Those with less than 60% of the national average income per consumer unit.
4.   In 1996 and 1997 Andorka and Spéder used an additional definition based on a subjective concept of poverty. They assumed that people have an image of how much income they need for a minimum standard of living. They also asked, "How much money does your family household need per month as a minimum?" Then, based on answers to this question and other data, they defined a subjective poverty line (Andorka and Spéder 1997).

The World Bank in its report "Hungary: Poverty and Social Transfers" (April 1996) used the following definitions from the Hungarian Central Statistical Office (CSO):

1.   The CSO calculates regularly a subsistence minimum for different types of households. The subsistence minimum is the cost of buying a given subsistence food basket. It includes an allowance for housing costs and other nonfood expenses. Subsistence food expenditures are based on a seasonal weekly menu that meets the different dietary intake requirements of active adults, children, and pensioners, as prescribed by the National Research Institute of Dietetics. Nonfood expenditures are

based on actual observations of households whose food expenditure is plus or minus 20% of the subsistence food expenditure level. The resultant subsistence minima (there are several) are therefore household-specific, embodying both scale economies and the different consumption needs of active adults, children, and pensioners. The usefulness of the subsistence minimum for poverty analysis has decreased over time, and recently the CSO has suspended its calculation. This is because the method of calculating this minimum predates the economic transition, and at that time the relative prices of different goods were different than they are today. In 1993 the real value of the subsistence minimum increased to a point where it was barely less than the average household expenditure (the equivalent of U.S.$166 per month), thereby classifying more than 50% of the population as "poor." Clearly, this makes the level difficult to interpret as a genuine "subsistence minimum," meaning that those below it live in absolute poverty.

2.   Among the benchmarks used in the social transfer system, only the minimum pension has a poverty connotation, as it implies the minimum sum of money needed for a single retired adult to live on. It is also used as the basis for various social assistance programs. In 1993 the minimum pension was, on average, 6,400 Hungarian forint (HUF) per month (U.S.$70). The minimum pension in 1993 was worth only 73% of its real 1989 value. This poverty line can be used to identify the very poorest individuals in Hungary in 1993.

3.   There is a strong tradition in Hungary of using relative poverty lines—lines derived from the data themselves. Relative poverty analysis often uses a set fraction (one-third, one-half, two-thirds) of mean income/expenditure as a poverty benchmark. This analysis uses both one-half and two-thirds of the mean as poverty lines. Since both these lines fall between the minimum pension and the subsistence minimum, they serve as a useful device for showing the sensitivity of poverty estimates to the poverty line selected.

According to Andorka and Spéder, "The poverty line based on the relative definition of poverty is about the same as the poverty limit based on minimum income used by the CSO between 1982 and 1994" (Andorka and Spéder 1997:32).

Different poverty lines result, of course, in different numbers and percentages of poor. The estimates in Table 3.1 are from the "Hungarian Household Panel" (Andorka and Spéder 1997:41) and the household survey of the CSO (Szívós 1994).

Comparing the pre- and postcommunist periods on the basis of all of these definitions of poverty, we can conclude that the number of poor significantly increased during the postcommunist period and that the most radical changes took place between 1989 and 1993.

Because of the previously mentioned methodological problems, changes in the number of people below the "subsistence poverty line" are of least use. Based on CSO data, the percentage of people in this category increased from 13.9%, to 45.2% between 1989 and 1993 (based on 1989 prices). In the same period, those living on less than 50% of the average household income increased from 4.3%, to 34.6%. Those with less income than the minimum pension increased from 1.6% in 1989, to 8.6% by 1993.

Table 3.1
The Percentage of Poor According to Different Poverty Lines, 1993 and 1994

Poverty line used	Persons	Households
Hungarian Household Panel estimates, 1994		
Lowest 20% of family income per capita	20.1	14.0
Less than 50% of national average income	14.0	11.6
Less than 60% of national average income	22.7	20.5
Subjective poverty limit	35.7	41.2
CSO estimates, 1993		
Minimum Pension	4.5	-
50% of average income	9.3	-
Below the subsistence poverty line	58.3	-

Andorka and Spéder came to very similar results: the percentage of those receiving less than 50% of national average income per capita increase by 35.9% between 1993 and 1996 (Andorka and Spéder 1994:41).

During the first four or five years of the postcommunist transition, Hungary suffered its deepest economic crisis. During this period, not only did the number of poor increase and poverty become more intense, but the nature of poverty also went through significant changes:

1. Income inequalities increased significantly. This had begun in the early 1980s, but the process accelerated after the collapse of the communist regime. The income share of the highest decile compared to the lowest decile was 3/1 in 1989. The same share was 5.3/1 in 1993.
2. A substantial part of the middle classes slipped down into poverty. Those placed within the middle-income deciles (4th, 5th, and 6th) have a smaller share of income than before the changes. The middle classes experienced a high degree of polarization. "Socialist entrepreneurs" who had made high profits in the "second economy" during the 1970s and 1980s faced declining incomes and standards of living during the postcommunist transition. This was especially true for farmers who could not sell their products at good prices (if they could sell them at all) because Hungarian agriculture lost most of its traditional markets in Eastern Europe. Thus, the "socialist entrepreneurs" are among the losers in the postcommunist transition. A substantial part of the middle class is in danger, or feels itself to be in danger, of becoming poor. Initially, this appears to be explained by the increase in unemployment and the deterioration of wages and pensions, but the idea of the entire middle class becoming impoverished is far from reality. Many of the beneficiaries of the postcommunist transition period were members of the late-Kádár middle class and foremost among them were those with better education and skills.

3. The most significant change in the nature of poverty during the transition period was the birth of a new underclass. This means that poverty is no longer something that can be described merely in terms of social inequalities. The new kind of poverty must be described in terms of social integration because it no longer means just less income, worse housing, and a lower standard of living; it now also means that a new social group, the underclass, is emerging, which is segregated from the rest of society and discriminated against. Those in the underclass have almost no chance of finding roles in the new division of labor or of having "normal" jobs, income, housing, social security, or access to better education for their children.

It is now evident that this is a problem that will not be solved automatically by economic growth. For three years, between 1989 and 1992, Hungary lost more than one-third of its jobs. The decline of the economy ended in 1994 as more and more indicators pointed toward economic prosperity. However, the number of jobs did not increase during this period. Instead, the number of jobs declined.

It is important to mention that the problem of the underclass did not disappear in those regions of Hungary where economic prosperity started earlier or where the increase was stronger (in particular, the western and northwestern regions). There is also, already, a labor shortage in certain qualification-based and well-respected types of work. However this has not affected the mostly-Gypsy-origin underclass. Instead, it has highlighted that they are a social group that has become useless (from the perspective of the emerging economic system). This explains the increase in ethnic conflicts that have taken place during the last couple of years (particularly in western and economically successful regions of Hungary and in west Hungarian, economically prosperous cities, e.g., in Székesfehérvár).

In 1969 István Kemény conducted the first survey designed to study poverty. Because the expression "poverty" could not be officially used at that time and for quite some time thereafter, the research was officially aimed at studying the "life circumstances of the low income population." The survey was coordinated by the CSO, and the sample population was taken from the lowest decile of households, in terms of income per head, from the 1967 national income survey. Kemény has often noted that, due to the compromises he had to make for political reasons, his sample did not cover the entire poor population of Hungary:

The 600 forints per head monthly income limit was arbitrary and does not reflect how many people live in poverty nation-wide. The CSO Department of Economics came to the conclusion that, on the basis of 1968 prices, the minimal income per head for a single household was 1,100 forints per month. For a dual household it was 970 forints per month. For a 3-person household it was 880 forints per month. For a 4-person household it was 830 forints, and for a 5-person household it was 780 forints per month. If we accept these limits as social subsistence minimums, we ought to come to the conclusion that in 1967, 32% of the population lived under the poverty limit. It is, however, misleading to draw a strict limit based on a certain income. It is better to speak about an income range between the poor and the rest of the population. For example, some commuter workers might have quite reasonable incomes per capita, but their families could still be poor because of high transportation costs, the cost of expenditure on two households, and the high costs of renting an apartment, room, or a bed in the city. Other families with reasonable incomes might, anyway, be poor because of the costs of building a house for themselves. In addition, other families, who do not have the previous costs, live in very poor housing conditions and this prevents them from living under "normal" conditions. This is why it is better to speak about the poor rather than people with low incomes, as well as to take more dimensions into account, making the definition of poverty include all those poor who are not able to live as others do. (Kemény 1972)

Kemény returned several times to the problem of poverty. Notable are his research on the Hungarian working class and his national census of Gypsies, done in 1971 and 1993 (Kemény 1970a, 1970b, 1972, 1976). The most important result of Kemény's research can be summarized as the finding that there were many people living in poverty; that is, there were social groups that were not able to take part in the social changes that were leading to substantial increases in standards of living in "socialist Hungary," a country where political leaders legitimated themselves through their ability to achieve full employment, get rid of poverty, and create a society constantly moving toward equality.

Kemény's research on poverty and Gypsies established a new school of young social researchers. Worth mentioning is the work of Ottilia Solt, Gábor Havas, Zsolt Csalog, and Kálmán Rupp (Kemény et al. 1976) on the culture of poverty and the excellent work of Péter Ambrus (1988) on a segregated urban ghetto.

Differing somewhat from Kemény's statistically oriented studies is the work of Zsuzsa Ferge (1969) on poverty. Also important is her work on poverty and education (Ferge 1976) and poverty and social policy (Ferge 1980; 1986).

Tamás Kolosi's research at the Research Institute of the Hungarian Socialist Worker's Party was also statistically oriented but already, by the middle of the 1980s, included multivariable analysis. In addition, Ágnes Bokor's (1987) book on poverty has to be mentioned.

During the last 30 years, sociological research on poverty has been heavily politicized due to the fact that the word "poverty" could not be officially used. The euphemistic expressions that were used instead include "multifactoral, unfavorable situation," "absolute and relative deprivation," "those in peripheral situations," and "those left out of the mainstream." Some of these categories are, of course, used in the international literature on poverty, but they have been misused, or used with many different meanings, in Hungary. Under these political conditions it was not possible to have open theoretical discussion about issues of poverty and inequality or even about structural versus cultural approaches to poverty analysis.

In 1963, for the first time since the communist takeover, the CSO coordinated a study on social stratification in which national data were collected and which enabled us to analyze poverty. Since 1963, the CSO has carried out a national income survey every five years. Thus, we have comparable data from 1967 to study poverty at national and regional levels by social strata, by sex, and by other demographic criteria. Since the early 1960's, there are also annual household surveys, coordinated by the CSO, that allow us not only to analyze income by household types but also to do detailed analysis on the structure of expenditures.

From the end of the 1960s many surveys have been done on nationally representative samples, providing us with data on salaries, incomes, household expenditures, housing conditions, and the supply of durable consumer goods in the postcommunist transition period. Notable is the "Hungarian Household Panel" survey, which since 1992, has returned annually to question the same families. This survey is extremely important because it supplies information about changes in poverty in the postcommunist transition period.

The nature of poverty has changed quite a lot since the end of the 1970s because of the rapidly increasing rate of inflation, growing importance of the "second economy," and (after the collapse of state subsidies) changes in the structure of expenditures. All this has resulted in increasing methodological problems in measuring poverty. There are, of course, no "real methods" to eradicate these problems. Some improvement has come as, alongside the measurement of incomes, expenditures have also started to be analyzed.

Because, by the end of state socialism, traditional poverty was linked to small and completely marginalized groups, relative definitions of poverty were often used. Kemény explained the essence of these definitions 10 to 15 years ago: "Poverty is when somebody cannot live like others do."

CLEAVAGE BETWEEN POOR AND NOT-SO-POOR

As I have already mentioned, the appearance of an underclass has been the most important change in the nature of poverty during the postcommunist period. The emergence of the underclass was the result, more or less, of the same tendencies in Eastern Europe as in advanced capitalist countries of the West. The key transformative tendency was a major technological change, often called the "third industrial revolution," that began in the late 1960s, becoming more intense in the 1970s and early 1980s, and that resulted in a completely changed world economy. State socialism could not stop this major economic change but was able to delay it for quite a long period of time. This policy, of "stopping unfavorable changes at the borderline of communism," is, in large part, responsible for increasing Hungary's national debt, creating enormous shortages, and decreasing the standard of living in other state-socialist countries. The policy is also responsible for the fact that these changes (when they did occur) resulted in the decline of entire economic regions and industrial branches and occurred much more dramatically in Eastern Europe than in the capitalist world. In ex-Soviet bloc countries, economic restructuring occurred simultaneously with the collapse of the state-socialist economy. The shock was intense because neither social institutions nor families were ready to handle the new problems (including massive unemployment, impoverishment, and homelessness).

Long explanations are not required to understand that in a country that had full employment, where social welfare was a citizen's right, and where "basic consumption" was centrally subsidized, the result is extreme inequalities and rigid, castelike segregation when massive unemployment and a collapse of the welfare system (or, generally speaking, the collapse of the redistributive system) happen. The formation of the underclass had the most effect on unskilled workers in highly subsidized state industries, many of Roma origins. Young people from such families and workers over 50 years of age had no chance of finding a new job. Those able to cushion their unemployment in the "first" (state-organized) economy with increasing possibilities in the "second" economy were able to create a better situation for themselves (some middle-class Roma are included among this group). However, those who were not able to do so because they were too old, did not have enough cultural capital, and/or lived in deprived economic regions faced a rather hopeless situation. These are the people who now live at the level of the Third World poor, in castelike segregation from a society that, over the next few decades, has a good chance of coming closer and closer to living conditions approximating those in the countries of the European Union.

The concepts of "underclass" or "undercaste" were almost never used in Hungarian research until now. This may be partly explained by the fact that some Hungarian researchers are used to thinking in old ways about old schemes and still hope that after the end of the postcommunist economic crisis, the Hungarian welfare state can be reconstructed (although they tend to hope that this reconstruction can follow the model of Western European welfare states). Other Hungarian researchers are not very interested in the problem of the underclass because they believe that economic prosperity will soon arrive and will result in a rise of the standard of living for the whole of the society.

Highlighting problems like the development of the underclass is important research on the labor market (Kertesi 1994; Nagy and Sik 1996) and the problem of the underclass in the school system (Kertesi 1995).

According to János Ladányi and Iván Szelényi (1997), reintegration of the underclass, besides ensuring the circumstances for sustainable economic growth, is one of the most important tasks of the facilitator state.

More or less, the same statistical surveys and sociological research could be used for research into the underclass as have already been mentioned in the section about poverty. The survey data of Iván Szelényi and Donald J. Treiman's (1993–1994) research, "Social Stratification in Eastern Europe after 1989," could also be of help. Using these data, Ladányi has provided an analysis of the demographic, social, and economic characteristics of the poor, as well as the Gypsy population, in five ex-Soviet bloc countries (Ladányi 1996).

The data of the Szelényi–Treiman research do not prove the conclusions in the Polish Country Report (Chapter 4 this volume) about the existence of a strong Polish underclass. I agree with our Polish colleagues that a substantial part of the postcommunist Polish society lives amid poverty and that this poverty is broader and more intense than that in Hungary. I disagree that the social and spatial segregation of poverty is as strong or that the borderline of the poor and the not-so-poor is as rigid in Poland as it can be empirically proven to be in Hungary. I hypothesize that this sharp borderline is a product of the ethnicization of poverty, namely that "poverty" and "Gypsy-ness" (in intermarriage and as social and political terms) are analogous. As there have been hardly any Roma in Poland since the Holocaust, such an ethnicization of poverty is not possible, and, I hypothesize, this is the primary reason that, despite stronger and longer poverty, the borderline between poor and not-so-poor is less rigid than it is in Hungary and that there is no Polish underclass.

I disagree with the Slovak Country Report (Chapter 2 this volume) for exactly the opposite reasons. According to this report, no underclass emerged in Slovakia during the postcommunist transition because of an encompassing set of state social policies. However, the data from the Szelényi–Treiman research show that the number of Gypsies in Slovakia is roughly the same as it is in Hungary and that the intensity of social and spatial discrimination is also very similar. Additionally, reports about attacks on Gypsies and the ways in which these attacks are handled by the state prove the existence of state-sponsored discrimination against Roma, rather than the opposite.

To study "the poorest of the poor" or even to give a strict definition of this group on the basis of relative income raises rather serious methodological problems. This is because the incomes of this group are unstable, and ways of earning an income are different than they are in the rest of society. This results in serious barriers concerning the validity of data. The results of minimum standard-of-living calculations could be of use, however:

1. As already been mentioned, research in the Central Statistical Office that defines the minimum standard of living is already some decades old.
2. Research since 1949 on "minimal and optimal" standards of nutrition has been done at the National Institute of Health (Országos Táplálkozástudományi Intézet). This shows that the minimal nutrition level isn't determinable with exact scientific methods. Nutritional norms vary a great deal even over a short period of time and can sometimes be explained by political decisions (Ladányi 1976).
3. Since 1990 (earlier within the framework of Ujpesti Családsegitö Központ and later within the framework of Léthatáron Alapitvány under the supervision of György Mezei) there has been very detailed research carried out on minimum standards of living (Mezei and Sarlós 1995). The results could be used in the search for a definition of the Hungarian underclass.

In analysis of the recent Hungarian underclass, studies with an ethnographic orientation that were carried out during the interwar period should not be forgotten. These focused on the "underclass" of that time, the landless agrarian proletariat. The work of Ferenc Erdei is probably the most important from these studies. Studying Hungary's "dual social structure," Erdei describes the "class under the society" as a product of incomplete capitalist growth (Erdei 1944; 1976).

ETHNICITY

As a result of the peace agreements after World War I, Hungary lost two-thirds of its territory and half of its population. Thus, Hungary became almost ethnically homogeneous. Only 8% to 10% of the population consider that they belong to another ethnicity than Hungarian, and half of this group are considered to be Roma. This is why the ethnic issue in Hungary becomes "a Roma issue." The Roma issue is a special one because poverty and ethnicity are linked together only in the case of this particular ethnic minority.

The intensity of the link between ethnicity and poverty is highly dependent on whom we define as a Gypsy. This is why we first discuss the definitional issue.

In Hungary, as everywhere in the world where Gypsies live, there are very different estimates about the number (or population share) of the Roma. Earlier, I was of the opinion that "a real number" could be found with scientific methods of measurement and that divergence from this "real" number could be explained as the result of using incorrect or less correct methods of estimation. I also believed that the causes of variation in estimates of the number of Roma were, on the one hand, that ethnic minorities in general (and in particular a disadvantaged ethnic minority like the Roma in Hungary) have very good reasons not to declare their ethnic identity and, on the other hand, that nationalist leaders (belonging to either the majority or minority) often inflate the number of Roma. Indeed, the lowest estimates of the Gypsy population in most Central and Eastern European countries come from national censuses: in Hungary the 1990 census found that 0.7% of the population were "Romani-speaking" and 1.4% of "Gypsy nationality" (KSH 1994). In contrast, the highest estimates usually come from anti-Gypsy or Gypsy nationalist sources (Ladányi 1996). However, while estimates based on "scientific methods" are usually between these low- and high-point estimates, they can be very different from other estimates, also based on "scientific methods." These differences are often twofold or greater.

Table 3.2 shows some research that estimates the population share that is Roma.

Table 3.2
Estimates of the Roma Population in Hungary (%)

Ethnicity	Survey on which estimation is based				
	Kemény*	HHP	Szonda–Ipsos**	Szelényi–Treiman**	CSO
Roma	4.7%	3.1%	6.6%	3.9%	3.9%
Don't Know	-	9.1	2.2	1.2	0.8
Non-Roma	95.3	87.8	91.2	94.9	95.3

* Percent Roma in total Hungarian population.
**Percent Roma in total Hungarian population over the age of 18.

The variations in the data in Table 3.2 cannot be explained by methodological mistakes in the research. Only one of the set of percentages, from the Kemény survey, refers to the share of the Roma population in the entire Hungarian population. The Szonda–Ipsos and Szelényi–Treiman data refer to the population older than 18. As the average number of children per household is much higher among the Gypsy population than in the average Hungarian household, the real percentage of Roma in the entire Hungarian population is, according to the Szonda–Ipsos survey, greater than 10% and, according to the

Szelényi–Treiman survey, somewhat less than 7%. Both figures are much higher than the 4.7% from the Kemény survey.

There are other important methodological differences. For example, in the Hungarian Household Panel Survey (HHP) all people over 16 were interviewed, whereas in the other surveys only one person per household was interviewed. This made it hard for interviewers, visiting families that were evidently ethnically mixed, to decide whether the interviewed person was Gypsy or not.

In the Szelényi–Treiman research, besides relying on interviewer classification, the interviewed persons were also asked if they considered themselves Roma and if there had been any Roma in their parents' families. Percentages of self-identified Roma are much lower: 2.1% of the sample of 18-year-olds and over considered themselves Roma, and 2.6% considered their parents and/or themselves to be Roma, while interviewers classified 3.9% as Gypsy and 5.1% as either definitely or perhaps Gypsy (Ladányi 1996:32). The percentages of interviewer-classified Roma are fairly high despite the fact that there is reason to believe that interviewers were less likely to classify those respondents as Gypsy who had earlier identified both themselves and their parent's families as non-Gypsy. This is why the Szonda–Ipsos survey, relying solely on interviewer classification, gives a much higher percentage for the Gypsy population than does the Szelényi–Treiman survey.

Not only is there a significant difference between the Kemény research and research from the Central Statistical Office (CSO) with regard to the number and the proportion of Roma in the population, but there is also a big difference between Kemény's research and the surveys done by the CSO and Szonda–Ipsos (which both used fairly large samples) in terms of the social and demographic composition of the "Gypsy" populations. This is due to the different mode of classification used in the Kemény research. "The classification of the social environment" in the Kemény research, in effect, meant that experts in the local council, social, and educational institutions classified families in the randomly chosen neighborhoods as "Gypsy and non-Gypsy." Because of their jobs and everyday experiences, it is understandable that these experts would be more likely to classify "problematic families" as Gypsy and that those Roma "who are clean and decent as if they were not Gypsies" will be underrepresented. Thus, the Kemény research provides a good estimate of Gypsies who are recipients of social welfare, and we agree with Kemény that the situation of this group is the most serious social problem currently in Hungary. This does not, however, mean that this is the only possible or the only scientific definition of the Roma population. It is very important to mention that as far as we know, no one has examined the classification of the "non-Roma social environment" until now. This would be an interesting issue to pursue.

Another important methodological note is that Kemény's research used only the Gypsy/non-Gypsy dichotomy, whereas in the other, previously mentioned research there were three possibilities. It is not difficult to see that ethnically mixed families, who are usually more assimilated than ethnically homogeneous ones, will be more likely to be categorized as non-Gypsy families when only two possibilities are given than when there is a third choice (Table 3.3).

Table 3.3
Some Social Demographic and Economic Characteristics of Different Roma Groups in Hungary

	Persons per house-hold	% with primary educ. or less	% employed	% un- and semi-skilled workers	Standardized monthly per capita household income (USD)	% of group in Hungarian population
Roma 1	5.0	42.4	29.2	48.0	76.6	3.3
Roma 2	4.9	37.0	32.1	45.7	82.7	4.0
Roma 3	4.6	31.4	40.0	42.9	84.6	5.6
Roma 4	4.3	28.2	43.3	44.9	91.6	6.9
Non-Roma	3.2	17.7	50.0	22.4	145.6	-

Roma 1 = Those who considered themselves Roma.
Roma 2 = Roma 1 + those who considered their father or mother as Roma.
Roma 3 = Roma 2 + those who were considered by the interviewer as Roma.
Roma 4 = Roma 3 + those who were considered by the interviewer to be perhaps Roma.

Source: (Ladányi 1996:32.)

It is evident from Table 3.3 that different definitions of the Roma, more or less, describe groups experiencing different levels of integration. It can be seen that the sociodemographic characteristics of the more integrated and more ethnically mixed groups differ less from those of the non-Roma than do the sociodemographic characteristics of less integrated groups. However, even the most integrated Roma group is in a much worse position than the non-Roma population.

Because of the rather low number of cases in the Roma subsample of the Szelényi–Treiman research, these data should be interpreted cautiously. However, it is important to note that in all three of the surveys where, besides the "Roma category," a "don't know" was possible, the results have been, as in the Szelényi–Treiman survey, that the latter group appears to be much more socially integrated than the clearly Roma one (and the Szonda–Ipsos and CSO surveys include a rather high number of cases).

The significantly different estimates from these surveys could be explained by the fact that the Gypsy and the non-Gypsy populations of Hungary are not two clearly separated groups. It is true that ethnic classification, in the case of such a poor and discriminated against social group as the Roma, functions as a self-fulfilling prophecy. Those who are considered Gypsy by the social environment will be treated as Gypsies by this environment, and, alternately, those who are not considered to be Gypsy will not be treated as such. But survey data and everyday experience prove that this classification process is highly dependent on the particularities of a social situation. Moreover, identification and self-identification change over time with changes in the economic and political situation. There are historic periods, such as the 1970s and 1980s in Hungary, that are periods of assimilation. On the other hand, there are periods, like the 1990s, when assimilation strategies that had seemed fairly successful collapse.

Gypsy studies have a long history in Hungary. There have been Gypsy censuses since 1724, when "traveling Gypsies" were counted in order to find out the number of Roma living in the country. In the second half of the eighteenth century, during the reign of Maria Theresa and Joseph II, a Gypsy census was carried out.

The Hungarian national census since 1941 provides information about the language spoken (respondent's mother tongue) and languages other than the mother tongue that are spoken. A question on nationality is also included. However, calculating the size of the Hungarian Gypsy population on the basis of either nationality or language spoken is rather misleading. Most Gypsies in Hungary do not speak another language than Hungarian, and, as mentioned before, many Gypsies do not declare their "nationality" when census takers ask this question.

Another methodological problem of the census method is that it collects responses from the individual only and does not refer to the origins, behavior, or way of life of the family or household. Other statistical surveys often use additional indicators that measure "way of life" or include interviewers' classifications.

The Hungarian Statistical Office made the first effort to find out the total number of Hungarian Gypsies in 1893. Before that, censuses focused exclusively on either "traveler" or "settled" Gypsies. There has not been a Gypsy census (i.e., a survey of the total Gypsy population) in the country since then. The CSO report of 1955 (based on responses to the nationality and spoken language questions from the 1941 and 1949 national census data), which dealt with the victims of the Gypsy Holocaust in the Second World War as well as some demographic and migration data, estimated that there were 50,000 Gypsies in Hungary. Another report, done in 1961, estimated the number of Gypsies in Hungary to have reached 200,000. Kemény's research at the Institute of Sociology Hungarian Academy of Sciences in 1971, based on a 2% national representative sample, estimated the number of Gypsies to be 320,000. Data from local councils, collected in 1977 and 1978, showed there to be 325,000 Gypsies living in Hungary. The national census gives figures for people who speak Romany as their mother tongue (Table 3.4).

For the same years, Table 3.5 shows the populations that declared themselves (also) to belong to the Gypsy (Roma) nationality in Hungary.

Some of these huge changes in the size of the Roma population cannot be explained by physical demographic trends but rather are related to changes in the politics (and policies) toward minorities and the reaction of the Roma to these.

Table 3.4
Number of National Census Respondents Who Speak Romany as Their Mother Tongue

Year	Romany speakers
1960	40,000
1980	46,000
1990	71,000

Table 3.5
Number of National Census Respondents Claiming Roma Nationality

Year	People claiming Roma nationality
1960	56,000
1980	6,400
1990	143,000

As already mentioned, the Hungarian Statistical Office, in its Gypsy census of 1893, considered the community living together as the unit of analysis (OMKSH 1985). Recent surveys also follow this definition. During the surveys of the Institute of Sociology of 1971 and 1993, households were defined as Gypsy when they were considered by the "non-Gypsy environment" to be as such (Kemény 1976; Havas and Kemény 1995).

During the CSO Gypsy survey, connected to the national labor survey of 1993, 27,000 "Gypsy" households were surveyed. Interviewers with "extensive local knowledge" classified households according to their "way of life" (KSH 1994). The classification possibilities were as follows: "households with a Gypsy way of life" and "transitional, (uncertain) way of life" and "non-Gypsy way of life" households.

Recently, a discussion has started in Hungary about the issue of defining the Hungarian Roma population. I do not think that there is a single "correct" definition. Various definitions, whether by the local environment or by interviewers' classifications, are socially meaningful. It is important to find methods that would enable us to capture the continuum of the Roma population—from the non-Hungarian-speaking, most traditional Gypsies living in Gypsy settlements, to the "almost completely successfully assimilated" groups of Roma. In sampling (for a survey) the Hungarian Gypsy population or any other group, the best method seems to be to take a random sample of the entire population. A random sample, big enough to significantly represent even the largest ethnic group, would be very costly. Thus the groups most important for the research must be overrepresented. The problems of overrepresentation could be solved by making the sample approximately five times larger and:

- asking interviewees whom they consider Gypsy in their neighborhood
- asking to interview experts of local authorities such as local councils, teacher, social workers, and so on (this method is the most similar to the methodology that Kemény

followed in his surveys) and to compare these lists with the list gained from neighbors' classifications

• combining the preceding lists with the results of interviewers' classifications

• combining all the preceding classifications with lists of respondents' self-classification and with their classification of their families' and ancestors' ethnicity

One of the most important issues to examine is how much the previous and other "mental maps" match each other, how much they differ from each other, and what the demographic and social characteristics are of the groups formed by these different "mental maps."

As the Hungarian Roma are highly spatially concentrated, we have to take a spatially concentrated sample that overrepresents poor and Gypsy settlements, "new projects" and ethnic slums in the cities, and rural Gypsy ghettos.

REFERENCES

Ambrus, Péter. 1988. *Dzsumbuj*. Budapest: Magvetô.

Andorka, Rudolf, and Zsolt Spéder. 1994. Szegénység az 1990-es évek elején. In Rudolf Andorka and Kolosi és Vukovich (eds.), *Társadalmi riport 1994*. Budapest: TÁRKI.

Andorka, Rudolf, and Zsolt Spéder. 1997. Szegénység. In Sík Endre and Tóth István György (eds.), Az ajtók záródnak Jelentés a Magyar Háztartás Panel 5. hullámának eredményeirôl. Budapest: BKE-TÁRKI.

Bokor, Ágnes. 1987. *Szegénység a mai Magyarországon*. Budapest: Magvetô.

Erdei, Ferenc. 1944, 1976. A magyar társadalom a két világháború között I. - II. Valóság. 4-5 szám.

Ferge, Zsuzsa. 1969. *Társadalmunk rétegzôdése*. Budapest: Közgazdasági és Jogi Könyvkiadó.

Ferge, Zsuzsa. 1976. *Az iskolarendszer és az iskolai tudás társadalm meghatározottsága*. Budapest: Akadémia Kiadó.

Ferge, Zsuzsa. 1980. *Társadalompolitikai tanulmányok*. Budapest: Gondolat.

Ferge, Zsuzsa. 1986. *Fejezetek a magyar szegénységpolitika történetébôl*. Budapest: Magvetô.

Ferge, Zsuzsa. 1995. *Societies in Transition. International Report.of the SOCO Project*. Vienna: Institute for Human Studies.

Gábor, László, and Péter Gyôri. 1990. Adósságok kicsiben. Valóság, 2. szám.

Gyôri, Péter. 1995. Eladósodott társadalom. Esély. 3-4 szám.

Havas, Gábor. 1994. A megélhetési módok és a többségi társadalomhoz fûzôdô viszony változásai a magyarországi cigányok különbözô csoportjaiban. Kandidátusi értekezés, sokszorosítva, Budapest.

Havas, Gábor, and István Kemény. 1995. A magyarországi romákról. Szociológia 3. szám.

Iványi, Gábor. 1997. Hajléktalanok. Budapest: Sík Kiadó.

Kemény, István. 1970a. *A Csepel Vas- és Fémmûvek munkásai*. Budapest: Társadalomtudományi Intézet.

Kemény, István. 1970b. *Pest megye munkásai*. Budapest: Társadalomtudományi Intézet.

Kemény, István. 1970, 1992. A szegénységrôl. In *Szociológiai írások*. Budapest: Replika Könyvek.

Kemény, István. 1972. Az alacsony jövedelmû népesség életkörülményei Magyarországon. Budapest. (kézirat).

Kemény, István. 1976. *Beszámoló a magyarországi cigányok helyzetével foglalkozó, 1971-ben végzett kutatásról.* Budapest: MTA Szociológia Kutató Intézet.

Kertesi, Gábor. 1994. Cigányok a munkaerõpiacon. Közgazdasági Szk. 11.szám.

Kertesi, Gábor. 1995. Cigány gyerekek az iskolában, cigány felnõttek a munkaerõpiacon. Közg. Szkk. 1. szám.

KSH. 1994. A cigányság helyzete, életkörülményei 1993. Budapest: KSH.

Ladányi, János. 1976. A táplálkozási szokások változtatásának lehetõségei és korlátai. Egészségnevelés. 1. szám.

Ladányi, János. 1993. Patterns of residential segregation and the Gypsy minority in Budapest. *IJURR.* 17, No. 1.

Ladányi, János. 1995. Economic restructuring and social inequalities in Eastern Europe—the case of Hungary. In Gerlich and Glass (eds.), DEr schwierige Selbstfindungsprozess. Österreichische Gesellschaft für Mitteleuropaische Studien. Wien (pp. 237–250).

Ladányi, János. 1996. Romák Közép-Kelet-Európában. *Társadalmi Szemle* 51, No. 4.

Ladányi, János, and Iván Szelényi. 1997. The new social democrats? *Social Research* 64, No. 4.

Ladányi, János, and Iván Szelényi. 1998a. "Adalékok a csenyétei cigányság történetéhez" (A Sketch of the History of the Roma in Csneyete). In Zsuzsa Kereszty and Zoltan Polya (eds.), Csenyete Antologia. Csenyete-Budapest-Szombathely: Bar Konyvek (pp. 9–31).

Ladányi, János, and Iván Szelényi. 1998b. Class, Ethnicity and Social-Ecological Change in Postcommunist Hungary and Budapest. In Enyedi György (ed.), Social Changes and Economic Restructuring in Central Europe. Budapest: Akadémiai Kiadó.

Matesz, Éva. 1990. Önkényes lakásfoglalók, kilakoltatottak.

Mezei, György, and Katalin Szarlós. 1995. *Nyomorskála.* Budapest: Léthatáron Alapítvány.

Nagy, Gyula, and Endre Sik. 1996. Munkanélküliség. In Társadalmi páternoszter. Budapest: TÁRKI.

OMKSH. 1985. A Magyarországban 1893. január 42-én végrehajtott czigányösszeírás eredményei. Országos Magyar Királyi Statisztikai Hivatal. Budapest.

Szelényi, Iván, and Donald Treiman. 1992. "Social Stratification in Eastern Europe after 1989." NSF Grant Proposal.

Szívós, Péter. 1994. A szegénység kialakulása Magyarországon, 1987–1992. Budapest: KSH.

Tóth, Pál, and Istvánné Páczelt. 1991. A falusi cigányság. MTA RKK Észak-Magyarországi Osztály, Miskolc.

World Bank. 1996. "Hungary: Poverty and Social Transfers. A World Bank Study." Country Studies Series.

4

An Underclass without Ethnicity: The Poverty of Polish Women and Agricultural Laborers

Elzbieta Tarkowska

INTRODUCTION

Poverty, like any complex and multidimensional social phenomenon, is a product of both the present and the past. It is true about the so-called new poverty in Poland, associated with transition to the market economy but at the same time deeply rooted in the past. The specific features of contemporary poverty in Poland, especially the phenomenon of an emerging underclass, are strongly shaped by the social processes that took place in the past. The period of the state socialism, when poverty officially didn't exist, has formed a fertile ground for processes of today's economic deprivation and marginalization of certain categories of Poles. This is the main idea of this chapter.

Poverty, like many other concepts and categories used in the social sciences, is ambiguous, defined and measured in many ways. Increasingly, researchers of poverty indicate that it is more than just an economic phenomenon: "Poverty today is a matter not just of financial deprivation, but also, increasingly a deprivation of rights and marginalisation from power" (Curtin, Haase, and Tovey 1996:8–9). Particular negative social and cultural characteristics are found alongside low or very low incomes. Some authors (e.g., Curtin et al. in *Poverty in Rural Ireland: A Political Economy Perspective*) differentiate between two different meanings of the term "poverty": poverty in the narrow sense, limited to the economic dimension, and poverty in a broader sense, containing both an economic dimension and the social, political, and ideological exclusion of individuals from participation in society (Curtin et al. 1996). Terms such as "exclusion" or "marginalization" are increasingly seen in poverty studies and discussions and express the multidimensionality of poverty, taking into account its extraeconomic aspects (or even concentrating on them). Nolan and Whelan (1996:225) make this distinction: "Poverty is unidimensional, 'just about money,' whereas social exclusion relates to multidimensional disadvantage."

What is more, the terms "exclusion" or "marginalization" suggest the dynamic or temporal aspects of poverty. Tied to the issue of contemporary poverty are questions of its continuation and durability: the so-called reproduction of poverty or the vicious cycle of poverty, the creation and re-creation of mechanisms that exclude large numbers of people from society and push them onto the margins of social life, thus forming a so-called underclass.

In this chapter I give a quantitative presentation of poverty in Poland, as this is necessary for international comparison; however, I would like to underline that behind the numbers is hidden a complicated, qualitative picture. I focus on material poverty, but the social, cultural, psychological, and other aspects of poverty should not be forgotten.

The many concepts of poverty, as well as the many ways of measuring it and its range and depth, make comparison over time, either internationally or within one country, a difficult, limited, and approximate project. In Poland multiple poverty measures (or "poverty lines") have been used.[1] In this chapter I focus on three of them, which have been applied by the Central Statistical Office and the Institute of Labor and Social Studies (the bulk of my presentation is based on the research and estimates that have come from these institutes). The three poverty lines are (1) social minimum, (2) subsistence minimum and (3) relative poverty line.

1. The *social minimum* identifies the sphere of privation. It takes into account "the basket of goods and services recognized as indispensable for the normal functioning of man in society"; during the last few years the level of the social minimum was very close to the average expenditure level in households.

2. The *subsistence minimum* is the absolute poverty line and is more than twice as low as the social minimum. It takes into account exclusively those needs that must be met without delay—any lower level of consumption leads directly to biological destruction.

3. The *relative poverty line* is set at 50% of the average household expenditure per capita (equivalent unit), estimated for the total number of households in the country (*Poverty Indicators* 1997:51–52).

There are other measures used and quoted here. An important example is the *official poverty line*, which is equal to the minimum retirement pension (presently 39% of the average wage). This is the socially relevant poverty line, because income at or below this level enables people to receive social benefits. Researchers on poverty differ in their evaluation of the various indicators. The social minimum seems especially questionable, and some researchers maintain that it indicates a threat of poverty rather than poverty itself; they see the social minimum as a kind of "warning measure" (Ochocki 1997:127; Golinowska 1996a:9). However, others regard the social minimum as an important measure of poverty and consider the subsistence minimum to be a measure of destitution (Beskid 1999a:41). Kazimierz W. Frieske, a sociologist who highlights the extraeconomic dimensions of poverty, makes a statement in line with this latter position: "Poverty is not only the lack of money; it is a set of specific circumstances which disallow people from participating in collective life and which diminish in essential ways their ability to participate in basic social institutions, from the family to the system of justice" (Frieske 1996:236).

The last few years have witnessed an increasing amount of research around the world dealing with poverty and the related phenomena of exclusion, marginalization, and the emergence of an underclass. This trend is also seen in Poland, where poverty is a frequent research subject within the social sciences. In these studies different methodologies—both quantitative surveys made on representative samples, as well as qualitative research such as case studies, in-depth interviews, and life-history methods—are used.

The sociological study of poverty in Poland is almost as old as institutionalized sociology in this country. The first Polish sociological research institutions, such as the Institute of Social Economy (Instytut Gospodarstwa Spolecznego) in the Warsaw School of Economics, studied poverty, unemployment, and the economic migrations of the 1920s and 1930s. Besides information recorded by official census and family budget inquiries, the poverty of this period was documented by independent sociological investigations and—unique to Polish research—autobiographical materials (diaries collected during special competitions) (Tarkowska and Sikorska 1998). The famous work of Thomas and Znaniecki, *The Polish Peasant in Europe and America* ([1918] 1958), is the best example of this tradition. Therefore, the poverty, unemployment, and homelessness of the Great Depression era in Poland are relatively well documented.

This rich prewar research tradition was interrupted during the period of the communist regime as poverty became a political issue—a social, political, and ideological taboo. Poverty at this time was dismissed as a remnant of the former regime or the result of transitional difficulties, and poverty and the poor were euphemistically described by terms like "sphere of deficiency" or "low-income groups."[2] As Wielislawa Warzywoda–Kruszynska comments, the term "poverty" was never used in book or report titles in Poland before 1989 (Warzywoda–Kruszynska and Grotowska–Leder 1996:68). The absence of policies to counteract poverty (apparent in the lack of related legislation) is also indicative of the neglect of poverty as an issue during this period (Tarkowska and Sikorska 1998).

Empirical documentation of postwar poverty and scientific investigations in this field were limited. The most important studies took place in the periods of political freedom (e.g., after October 1956, the early Gierek period—the early 1970s, the "Solidarity" period of 1980–1981). Highlights from this body of research are the first estimations of the social minimum and the proportion of the population living below it (Deniszczuk 1972; Tymowski 1973); the Central Statistical Office's calculations of the number of people living in the "sphere of low incomes"; the remarkable study of Renata Tulli on single households of old retired people (1978); and new studies of "spheres of deficiency" and "spheres of unsatisfied social needs" (Frackiewicz 1983) or of social inequalities (Jarosz 1984). Thus, in spite of ideological and political prohibitions, important and interesting research initiatives were taking place. However, some results of these studies did not become public. Their publication was severely restricted,[3] and several were published only after 1989.[4] This contributed to the "poor visibility" of poverty in the postwar period and to its almost complete absence in the social memory of Poles today.

In addition, state labor market policy (the phenomenon of hidden unemployment), income-equalizing policies, and the subsidization of food, energy, housing, and so on allowed people to make ends meet and survive and so helped to relieve the problem of poverty and make it less visible.

These obstacles to the analytic reconstruction of poverty in the communist period combine with the fact that today past poverty is rarely made a subject of research. Instead, researchers are primarily interested in the so-called *new poverty* that has emerged from the transformation to capitalism. This topic is approached within the context of unemployment, gender, family life, old people, the young generation, and so on.

However, the limitations placed on poverty research during state socialism have also led to an absence of theoretical or methodological discussions about poverty in Polish sociology. The concept of poverty (its content and ways of measuring it), the ideas of the culture of poverty, social exclusion, marginalization, and the underclass issue, all frequently debated in American and West European social sciences, were not discussed (or not discussed openly[5]) until the beginning of the 1990s. This long-overdue discussion is only now taking place, centering on the concept of poverty (Toczyski 1991; Kraczla 1993; Warzywoda–Kruszynska and Grotowska–Leder 1996; Zalewska 1997), the underclass and marginalization (Wodz 1994; Frieske and Sikorska 1994; Warzywoda–Kruszynska and Grotowska–Leder 1996; Polawski 1997a), and the effects of welfare (Hirszowicz and Neyman 1997).

PAST POVERTY IN POLAND

Due to the rural character of the country, poverty in Poland was of a peasant nature. The poor and overpopulated countryside was the base of economic migrations, famously documented by Thomas and Znaniecki ([1918–1920] 1958). Agrarian reform, which helped peasants as a class, and the general impoverishment of the whole of society after World War II changed this situation dramatically.

Estimates of the extent of poverty in the period of state socialism vary, according to the poverty line used. For example, the following are estimates of those living below the social minimum level:

1. at the end of the 1960s—20% of the population (Tymowski 1973);
2. in 1975, 28% of the population, mostly employees—a secret estimate made by the Institute of Labor and Social Studies (Rajkiewicz 1993:52);
3. at the end of the 1980s, about 30% of the population—estimates made by Lucyna Frackiewicz (1993:43);
4. according to World Bank estimates, the percentage of the population living below the social minimum level was 14.2% in 1981, 27.2% in 1983, 25.3% in 1987, and 16.3% in 1989 (Golinowska 1996c:231).

According to Lucyna Frackiewicz (1993:42) in the period 1978–1987 the number of the poor rose from 3.3 million to 8.6 million. The 1980s are thus seen as a period of "the expansion of the poverty sphere" (*Poverty Indicators* 1997:52). Stanislawa Golinowska expresses a similar statement: "Poland began its transformation period with ca 20% of its population threatened with poverty, though this does not mean absolute poverty," although she adds: "No estimation of poverty can be calculated based on the research conducted at that time" (Golinowska 1996b:69).

Using measures stronger than the social minimum, estimates of the extent of poverty in Poland at the end of 1980s are 5–7% (Warzywoda–Kruszynska and Grotowska–Leder 1996:69); 6% (Milanovic 1996:60), or 5–10% (World Bank experts; see Ochocki 1997:128).

The different estimates and different measures used show that in the time of the communist regime in Poland poverty constituted a serious problem; yet its extent, scale, and social consequences are overshadowed by the *new poverty*, because of the dramatic growth of the latter during the transformation period.

The most characteristic feature of poverty in the socialist period was its *dispersion*, both in geographical and in social space (Glinski 1983). Poverty appeared in the countryside and in rural families with many children (rural workers' incomes were consistently lower than urban workers'), as well as in towns, in the households of unskilled workers, old-age pensioners, the single and disabled, single-parent families, and "pathological" families (families tied to alcoholism and crime), and in the households of young intelligentsia couples, just starting an independent life. Poverty in this period was generally connected with family dysfunctions (serious sickness, the loneliness of elderly people, abuse, alcoholism) and with dramatic incidents that disorganized life and decreased incomes. It was a cross-strata phenomenon.

The bundle of ills that befell people at this time, the "accumulation of insufficiency," characteristically included very low incomes, substandard housing, a lack of resourcefulness in searching for help from institutions (the extensive possibilities of different institutions were at that time not used), and low level of education and pathological phenomena, such as alcoholism or crime in family (Jarosz 1984:198; Frackiewicz 1983). Although researchers connected poverty with forms of social pathology, they did not understand there to be a culturally distinct concentration of urban people—lumpen proletariat—with a distinct life-style or subculture (or culture of poverty; Glinski 1983).[6]

The social location of this *old* poverty was as follows. First of all, poverty was most common among pensioners and people living on disability payments (e.g., in 1979, according to the Central Statistical Office estimates, 40–50% of pensioners and disabled families lived at a level below the social minimum [Glinski 1983]). Second, poverty affected workers belonging to the lowest income categories (agricultural workers, unskilled workers, laborers). For example, in 1974 almost half of all workers (48%) belonged to "low income groups" and in 1979, according to the Central Statistical Office report, 10% of people in workers' families lived below the social minimum level (Glinski 1983). However, according to some researchers, "poverty did not appear among the employed and their families, since full employment guaranteed subsistence, however modest and uniform" (Golinowska 1996d:350–351). Third, poverty affected families with several children (e.g., in 1974, 60% of children lived in families below the social minimum level) and young families just starting an independent life (Glinski 1983). Poverty affected also single-parent families and families with disability, serious illness, alcoholism, and other problems (Frackiewicz 1983; Glinski 1983; Jarosz 1984).

Thus, poverty at this time was also *transitory*; it frequently occurred in the form of temporary stages in one's life cycle: at the beginning of family life and at its end.[7]

At the same time, poverty was *differentiated*: sometimes it was very deep, close to the subsistence minimum (as was the case for the single, old, and disabled pensioners, described by Renata Tulli [1978]), but sometimes poverty was partial, existing in only one part of peoples' lives (e.g., a lack of adequate accommodation could alone change the financial situation of Polish families).

Taking on additional jobs (formal and informal, legal and illegal) was the most common way of coping with economic difficulties. In the state socialist period there were many ways to "capitalize one's time" (e.g., selling *queuing time*—which involved waiting in a queue in the place of somebody else). The practice of capitalizing time meant that poverty was often accompanied by serious shortages of time. With an increasing *jar economy* (the home production of food and clothing, reparations, painting of apartments, etc. for economic gain), this time pressure affected the whole of family life. Lack of leisure time was one of the most widespread impoverishments suffered by Poles (Frackiewicz 1983; Wnuk–Lipinski 1981).

Another characteristic of poverty under state socialism was the minimal involvement of social assistance institutions in ameliorating people's lives. This was caused both by the lack of pro-active interest taken by these institutions and by poor people's lack of awareness of their rights. According to Piotr Gliski (1983), social assistance fulfilled only 14% of poor people's needs. Therefore this old poverty was not only *dispersed and temporary* but was also *private, invisible, unofficial, and ininstitutionalized*.

The 1980s—the period of economic depression and of the so-called *economy of shortages* witnessed a change in this picture: "Poverty was no longer a phenomenon strictly found among those at the 'margins of society' and the socially ill-adapted, but it also touched those willing and able to work" (Golinowska 1996b:69).

The ideological and political rationale for the marginalization of poverty under state socialism meant that it became seen as marginal, caused by unusual life events and pathology, rather than being a usual, "normal" part of life. However, a precise identification of this old poverty is extremely important when addressing the question of the persistence of poverty, its repetition, reproduction, and transmission from one generation to another (i.e., underclass formation). These processes can be seen clearly in the research "Old and New Forms of Poverty," made in 1998, within the international research project *Social history of poverty in Central Europe* (Szalai 1995) which reconstructs poor families' lifestyles. I refer to it in the last section of this chapter.

I would like to stress the fact that Poland (like Hungary) belongs to a group of countries from the former socialist bloc, where studies on poverty have a long and rich tradition within the social sciences. Under state socialism these studies were limited in many ways; nevertheless, we possess today statistical and sociological materials informing us about past poverty, its scope and forms.

Poverty in the period of state socialism was different in each socialist country, but there were certain common features. Such phenomena as the social dispersion of poverty, its transitory character, connected with individuals' and families' life cycles, and the political and ideological taboo of this issue can also be found in the socialist pasts of the Czechs (Mares and Mozny 1995), Hungarians (Ladanyi 1998) and Slovaks (Radicova and Vasecka 1988). The *new poverty* in these countries also presents certain similarities.

THE *NEW* POVERTY

The so-called new poverty in Poland differs in many respects from past poverty: the extent of poverty, its social location, and the lifestyle of poor people as well as the ways of coping with poverty are all different. In addition we can now study it in an open way, with the help of the State Committee for Scientific Research.

Quantitative Description of the New Poverty

Estimates of the new poverty differ according to the measures used. These differences apply to the beginning of transformation (the fall of communism in 1989), as well as to its course and dynamics during the transformation period.

Nonetheless, all estimations confirm a doubling in the rate of poverty in the period just after the fall of communism (in the years 1989–1990) and during the introduction of reforms leading to the market economy. The direct causes of this big increase in poverty were serious contraction of the Gross Domestic Product (GDP) (due to the opening of markets to international competition and the collapse of COMECON), a rapid growth of unemployment, a considerable decrease in real incomes and in consumption, the cutting of state subsidies for basic consumer goods, the limitation or reduction of social benefits provided by the workplace, high inflation, and depreciation of savings.

Interpretations of poverty dynamics, its extent and depth, in the years 1990–1996 differ. For example, Lidia Beskid, a Polish sociologist who has studied Polish families' lifestyles and patterns of consumption for many years, divides this period into two parts. She argues that the years 1990–1994 saw a growth of poverty (especially 1990), while in the second period, the years 1995–1996, this trend stopped, and poverty gradually started to decrease. Now she speaks about the stabilization of the extent of poverty in Poland (Beskid 1999a:39). Stanisawa Golinowska, author of many studies on poverty within the Institute of Labor and Social Studies and the editor of the most complete book about poverty in contemporary Poland (Golinowska, ed. 1996), claims that earlier, in the period 1993–1995, certain stabilizing tendencies started as a result of increasing wages and real incomes in 1994 (the first growth in wages in the 1990s) (Golinowska 1996d: 355).

Therefore, although there remain disputes about the timing, there is a broad consensus that the sharp rise of poverty at the beginning of the 1990s was followed a few years later by processes that stabilized and decreased it.

Therefore, when presenting the quantitative characteristics of this new poverty, it is important to isolate two periods: the first period—years 1989–1993 (or 1994 or 1995)—and the second period—years 1994 (or 1995)–1996 (the last year of available data).

According to Lidia Beskid, the main characteristics of poverty in the first period are:

1. The emergence of a new group of poor people—the unemployed;
2. A rapid increase in the extent of poverty among people in those socioeconomic categories where the ratios of the poor were lowest before the transformation. For example, 11.8% of employees in 1989 and 41.2% in 1994 were below the social minimum; 10.7% of employees—farmers in 1989 and 51.0% in 1994 were below the social minimum; 19.8% of farmers in 1989 and 59.5% in 1994 were below the social minimum (Beskid 1999a: 40).
3. A relatively low growth in the poverty rates of retired people and pensioners, because the percentage of poor in this category was relatively high at the starting point — 22.4% in 1989 and 38.6% in 1994 were below social minimum (Beskid 1999a: 40).

In the first period the percentage of the people living at a level below the social minimum was gradually increasing (Table 4.1).

Table 4.1
Percentage of People Living Below the Social Minimum (1989–1994)

	World Bank[a]	Inst. of Labor and Soc.Studies[b]
1989	16.3	14.8
1990	33.4	31.2
1992	44.1	32.4
1993	52.0	34.8
1994	54.0	54.0

[a](Golinowska 1996c: 231).

[b](Golinowska 1996d: 353–356).

Stanislawa Golinowska (1996d:356–357) argues that increasing income differentiation, which led to the growing wealth of the rich and the increasing impoverishment of the poor in Poland, was one of the reasons for the rise of poverty in 1991–1993.

The second period (i.e., the years 1994–1996) witnessed a gradual decrease in poverty: the percentage of people living below the subsistence level was 6.4% in 1994 and 4.3% in 1996; below the social minimum level—58.2% in 1995 and 46.7% in 1996. This tendency is seen by estimates of Szulc's *corrected social minimum*:

1995   34.6%   (of households)
1995   28.7%   (of households)
1996   30.8%   (of households)

1996 25.3% (of households) (Beskid 1999a:41)

The last available publication of the Central Statistical Office general figures[8] describes poverty in Poland in 1996 in the following way: 46.7% of the population lives below the social minimum; 4.3% of the population is below the subsistence minimum; and 14.0% of the population (i.e., 5.4 million) lives below the relative poverty line, equal to 50% of the average expenditure of households (*Poverty Indicators* 1997:53).

More Comprehensive Description of the New Poverty

Characteristic of today's poverty in Poland is the determinate role played by the following factors: (1) youth, (2) unemployment (especially long-term unemployment), (3) a large number of children per family, (4) a low level of education of the household head, (5) residence in the countryside or in a small town, especially in the areas affected by structural unemployment, and (6) a connection with agriculture (as farmer or farm-employee) (*Poverty Indicators* 1997:54; Ochocki 1997:129). In the face of mass unemployment such correlates of poverty as serious illness, old age, alcoholism, or drugs are less important than they were before the transformation.

One of the most characteristic traits of this new poverty is child poverty. Whereas poverty in the 1970s affected mostly old people (the retired and pensioners), today *child poverty* is most striking. People 65 years old and older constitute 5% of the poor population, and children under 14, 30% of this population (Topinska 1996:83). The probability of being poor increases with an increase in the number of children in the family. Researchers estimate that poverty affects from 800,000 to 3 million children, depending on the method of estimation. If the minimum subsistence level is the criterion, nearly half of the poor population is under 19 years old; and one-third of this population is children under 14 (*Poverty Indicators* 1997:54). These numbers are dramatic. Child poverty threatens the biological, physical, and intellectual and cultural development of a whole generation. While parents try to protect their children, the danger of the transmission of poverty to the next generation is palpable. Yet, interestingly, public opinion seems to underestimate child poverty. The stereotype of the poor retired and elderly pensioner remains popular (Falkowska 1997; Wciorka 1999).

In Polish conditions, poverty always affects *families with many children*. In 1994 more than 30% of the members of such families lived below the subsistence minimum, and almost 86%, below the social minimum level (Golinowska 1996d:360). It is interesting to note that large families tend to be considerably more vulnerable to poverty than single-parent families. In 1996, 80.0% of people from families with four or more children were below the social minimum level, and 16.0% were below the subsistence minimum, whereas the respective percentages for single-mother families were 45.3% and 4.0% (see Appendix).

New poverty is closely related to *unemployment*. In 1995, 15.2% of the population was unemployed. In 1996, 77.8% of people in households "living on unearned resources" (usually social security benefits) lived at a level below the social minimum, and 21.0% lived below the subsistence level (see Appendix). Thus, poverty is today also related to the receipt of social assistance. The central role of this institution in dealing with poverty is a new phenomenon in Poland. Now over 1.5 million Poles receive social benefits. Alongside persistent unemployment, the *welfare trap* (long-term dependence on social assistance), a phenomenon very well known from Western and American countries, forms the basis for the recurrence of poverty and underclass formation.

Educational level is another important factor related to poverty. The self-employed, the retired, and pensioners, as well as educated people, are the least vulnerable to poverty. People with a university education are virtually immune to poverty at the subsistence level. However, in 1995, 17% of people with higher education lived below the social minimum level, and in 1996, 14%. This group largely works for, and is paid by, the state; thus, their persistent, albeit low, level of poverty suggests that wages in this sector are not high. In the first period of transformation highly educated workers were particularly affected by growing poverty.

The temporal dimension of the new poverty in Poland has been noted by both scholars (Tarkowska 1996) and politicians (Kuron and Zakowski 1997). In the 1970s and 1980s families coped with poverty by accumulating additional jobs. As a result, their lives were plagued by time shortages. Now, in different circumstances (e.g., a changing labor market situation, changing availability of social assistance benefits), there are many poor families with no members working and no official income (although they may participate in the *shadow economy*). They are dependent on social benefits. As a result, the new poor suffer from an abundance of time, rather than its shortage. Although some researchers have classed poor people as the "idle milieu" (Kraczla 1993:43), I think that this classification is erroneous. Excess time is an extremely difficult and destructive experience (see Tarkowska 1996); and when combined with a lack of opportunities, it can be the breeding ground for pathological behavior (alcoholism, violence, crime), especially among the young. It is worth noting that an excess of time does not affect all members of the family to the same degree. In particular, women, trying to cope with a difficult family situation, tend to remain busy satisfying everyday family needs (I return to this issue in the next section of the chapter).

Poverty in Poland is becoming *long-term poverty,* and it forms another important trait. Although World Bank experts describe it as rather shallow and transient (Milanovic 1996; Topinska 1996), other evidence shows that it is increasingly long-lasting. The percentage of the poor population living in poverty for at least two years is growing. Among the population with an income below the social minimum level in 1990–1991, 11.6% remained in poverty for two years; in 1991–1992, 18.6%; and in 1993–1994, over 20% (Golinowska 1996d:358). Sixty-nine percent of households that were poor in May 1995 were also poor in May 1996. One-fourth of the poor population in 1996 had been poor since 1993 (Beskid 1999a:45). The results of qualitative field research show prolonged poverty, *an inheritance of poverty* (Zalewska 1997:112), or *permanent poverty* (Osinska and Sliwinska 1997).

The most vulnerable to long-term poverty are families with many children, where the head of household has a low level of education, suffers from unemployment, and is a resident in a small town or village. In general, long-term poverty is also deeper than average poverty (*Poverty Indicators* 1997:48).

Another important characteristic of new poverty is its *concentration*, both in urban as well as in rural environments. Poverty in Poland was always associated with economic backwardness and thus is highest in rural areas, traditional branches of heavy industry, and particular regions. According to World Bank analysis, the lowest levels of poverty are found in the biggest cities (6%), while in a village the respective percentage is 22% (Topinska 1996:90–1). In 1996, 26.2% of people resident in the largest cities lived below the social minimum (1.2% below the subsistence minimum and 4% below the relative poverty line), but in small towns these percentages were, respectively, 51.1%, 4.6%, and 14.8% and in villages, 57.7%, 6.8%, and 21.2% (see Appendix).

In the 1970s and 1980s poverty was geographically and socially dispersed, whereas today poverty is both regionally and locally concentrated. Central to this issue is the rural nature of new poverty. This poverty is connected to high rural unemployment caused by the closure of state farms, on the one hand, and the lack of reform of the private agricultural sector (small, dispersed, nonproductive farms), on the other. The closure of state farms in the early 1990s affected about 500,000 people (2 million with their families). It is estimated that at this time the phenomenon of hidden unemployment in private agriculture was at the level of 900,000. These rural conditions have negative consequences for the standard of living.

The new regional concentration of poverty is seen in urban areas as well as rural areas. In the old centers of industrial cities, such as Lódz, Wroclaw, or Katowice, where the old infrastructure and substandard houses still exist, researchers observe the formation of ghettos of poverty (Warzywoda–Kruszynska and Grotowska–Leder 1998), the "social inheritance of poverty" in the poor enclaves (Zalewska 1994:53), and a concentration of poverty (Zalewska 1997:94–95). Kazimiera Wódz describes the old quarters of industrial cities of Upper Silesia as a fertile ground for the emerging underclass (Wódz 1994). These phenomena are similar to those observed on the former state farms (Polawski 1997a; Tarkowska 1998; Gorlach 1998). Thus, the rural areas of the former state farms (mostly in the northwestern and the northeastern parts of Poland) and the small towns affected by the closure of local labor market monopolists together form "communities of permanent poverty" (Osinska and Sliwinska 1997).

In many cases, the new rural poverty affects regions that were poorer before the transformation (the so-called eastern wall). The regional accumulation of negative phenomena—such as poverty, unemployment, low education levels, lack of opportunities for the younger generation, limited mobility, uneasy communication with the outside world, and relative isolation—increases the danger of the recurrence of poverty in line with the "vicious circle of poverty," "persistent marginalization" or "underclass formation" theses.

The Peculiarity of Polish Poverty in International Perspective

The most important features of the new poverty in Poland are, in contrast to the old poverty, that it is *concentrated* and *long-lasting* (or even *permanent*) and *visible, official, and institutionalized.*

Poverty in Poland manifests many similarities to poverty in other postcommunist countries, for instance, its rural character, the phenomenon of the working poor, and strong connections with unemployment and low levels of education. At the same time there are important differences, for example, different causes of poverty (*shock therapy* or its absence) and different tempos and dynamics to the rise and decline of poverty. Some researchers see the greater income differentiation and the lower average level of income (Beskid 1999b:19) as the cause of the peculiarity of poverty in Poland. According to Lidia Beskid's report, based on 1995 SOCO international comparative research in Poland, Hungary, Slovakia, the Czech Republic, and the former East Germany, poverty is greatest in Poland. In Poland a larger share of the population falls into the "low" or "very low" income categories than in the other former state socialist countries (see Table.4.2).

Table 4.2
Percentage of Households in "Low" or "Very Low" Income Categories

	50% of average income and below	60% of average income and below
Poland	18.3	25.0
Hungary	9.3	18.3
Slovakia	6.7	14.1
Czech	6.1	13.2
E. Germany	6.6	12.5

Source: (Beskid 1999a:48).

According to the same research, poverty in Poland is the deepest; the *poverty gap* (the increase of income necessary in order to break out of poverty) was in Poland 37%, while in the Czech Republic and Slovakia it was 16%, and in Hungary and East Germany, 20%.[9] Also in Poland the extent of the subjective feeling of economic deprivation is the greatest (Beskid 1999a:49; 1999b:20).

Another international research project, also carried out in 1995 in Poland, the Czech Republic, and Slovakia, suggests that although there are positive economic trends in Poland, the bad economic condition of many households persists (Pelczynska–Nalecz 1998:392).

In more global perspective, Polish poverty is interesting. In respect to the phenomenon of child poverty and the relatively good material circumstances of the retired and pensioners, poverty in Poland looks similar to poverty found in Western Europe. The main differences are (1) the rural character of this poverty, (2) the poverty of working people, (3) according to some researchers, for example, Irena Topinska (1996), a weaker degree of discrimination against women, and (4) an absence of the ethnic dimension of poverty. The last two factors—gender and ethnicity—which shape contemporary poverty in the

Western world, are discussed in the next sections of this chapter.

GENDER AND POVERTY IN POLAND

Feminization is one of the main characteristics of contemporary poverty. Some research shows that this phenomenon is also found in Poland (Grotowska–Leder 1995; Warzywoda–Kruszynska and Grotowska–Leder 1996; Zalewska 1997).

Under state socialism a fight against sex discrimination was part of the official ideology. Gender equality was promoted in different spheres of life: education, labor, leisure, family life, and so on. In some areas, such as the labor market and education, these policies succeeded. The percentage of women with university degrees increased between 1950–1951 and 1973–1974 by 12.5%, and by 1979 it slightly exceeded the percentage for men. In the period between 1955 and 1974 the number of working women increased by 235.8% (men by 152.3%), reaching a level of 42% of all women in 1975 (Siemienska 1990:263).

However, it should be stressed that women remained concentrated in low-paid occupations. As Renata Siemienska shows, in 1979 women were in the majority only in financial and insurance institutions, health and social welfare, education, trade, and public administration (1990:264). The percentage of women in political elites (Parliament, government, the membership of the Polish United Workers' Party) or in the scientific or other elites was very modest. Even in institutions with largely female workforces, such as schools or hospitals, the executives tended to be men. In addition, a gendered division of labor and traditional model of what was a women's role remained prevalent within the family.

Thus, I would like to underline that in postwar Poland the status of women and their situation in many spheres of life profoundly changed. However, some traditional values and patterns of sex discrimination survived all transformations. This lasting discrimination, both on a macro- (or national) scale as well as in the microenvironment of the household, is well expressed in the phenomenon of the feminization of poverty.

In this section I discuss four areas in which gender is a relevant dimension of poverty in Poland: (1) women and the labor market (the unemployment question), (2) gender and income, (3) women and social assistance, and (4) single-mother families.

As the household, not the individual, is the elementary object in analyses of poverty completed under the auspices of the Central Statistical Office or by the Institute of Labor and Social Studies, these analyses do not provide a good base for a discussion of the impact of gender on poverty; gender differentiation is not estimable. Analysis by Irena Topinska for the World Bank showed that women are slightly poorer than men. Members of families headed by women are in a materially worse situation than members of households headed by men; the poverty rate in female-headed households (15.3%) is a little higher than in male-headed households (14.0%) (Topinska 1996:85). However, she states that "from a statistical point of view, it seems that the sex of the head of the household is not very important" (Topinska 1996:77). Nevertheless, other research focusing on women, rather than households, may speak more directly to this issue.

The *feminization of poverty* can be understood in many ways. According to Jolanta Grotowska–Leder, we can speak about the feminization of poverty when the extent of poverty is greater among women than among men; more women than men receive social benefits[10]; more single mothers than fathers are poor; the extent of poverty is greater among single-mother households than single-father households; the extent of poverty is greater among female-headed households than in those headed by men; the number of poor people is higher in the households of single mothers than in others; and the depth of poverty is greater in female-headed households (Warzywoda–Kruszynska and Grotowska–Leder 1996). This multiplicity of meanings contained in the phrase *the feminization of poverty* is important to keep in mind.

Women and the Labor Market

Researchers state that women have borne more of the costs of the transition toward a market economy than men. Women in the labor market have faced a situation of "relative deprivation" (Reszke 1995:137–138). "The young, women and people with few skills are in the worst labor market position," writes Jolanta Grotowska–Leder (1995:74). While there is a global trend toward increased female occupational activity, in Poland the opposite trend is occurring. The rate of female labor force activity decreased from 57% in 1988, to 46% in 1995 (Kotowska 1997).[11]

Central to the issue of female poverty is women's situation in the labor market because, as was stated before, poverty in Poland is now closely associated with unemployment. The feminization of unemployment is synonymous with the feminization of poverty, and there is now an overrepresentation of women among the unemployed. There is considerable evidence that it is harder for women to find work than it is for men. First, women make up a majority of the unemployed. In December 1995 they were 55.1% of the unemployed population, and it is estimated that by 1997 this had increased to 71% (Montgomery 1998). Second, women are more frequently exposed to long-term unemployment. In 1995, 42.9% of unemployed women had been outside the labor market for more than one year, and 22.3%, for more than two years. These proportions for men are, respectively, 30.5% and 12.1% (Kotowska 1997:99). Third, although unemployed women are, on average, more educated than unemployed men, they have to wait longer for jobs than men. Thus, education does not protect women from job loss or necessarily help them to find a new job.[12] Fourth, the special temporary public works' programs, designed to maintain labor market activity and provide an entitlement to social benefits, have a 95% male participation rate. In addition, because women usually have responsibility for the family (especially childcare), they have to coordinate this responsibility with a job search, making the latter more difficult. Lastly, unemployment benefits themselves are a source of inequality as women receive them much more rarely than men (Kotowska 1997). Thus, the first dimension of the feminization of poverty in Poland springs from women's discrimination in the labor market.

Gender and Income

Characteristic of poverty in the postcommunist countries is the phenomenon of the *working poor*. In Poland not only the unemployed but also employees, receiving low wages, are poor. Women are more likely than men to suffer from this form of poverty.

In Poland, as in other countries, there have always been inequalities between the wages of men and women (Domanski 1992; 1999). Today this differentiation is growing. In 1991 the average salary of a woman was equivalent to 70.2% of the average salary of a man. In 1995 it decreased to only 64.9% (Kotowska 1997:102). There are other indicators of lower salaries of woman, such as a large share (75%) of women whose salaries are below the national average salary (Knothe 1997:14) or a very small percentage of women in top positions connected with the best salaries (Knothe 1997; Domaski 1999). Under state socialism the low-paid occupations were feminized, and today women remain concentrated in the low-paying state sector (the so-called *budget sphere*: education, health service, social assistance, etc.).

Women and Social Assistance

The feminization of poverty in Poland is also connected with social assistance, as the receipt of social benefits is, generally, a good indicator of poverty. Jolanta Grotowska–Leder's research in Lódz and Katowice on social assistance recipients confirms the hypothesis that the feminization of poverty in large Polish cities is taking place. In both cities in the study—in Lódz and Katowice—there is a large overrepresentation of women among the social assistance recipients and among the poor; it seems that women are more vulnerable to impoverishment. Again, higher levels of education and higher levels of labor force activity do not provide protection against poverty (Warzywoda–Kruszynska and Grotowska–Leder 1996:159).

Compared to men, women receiving social benefits are younger, better educated, more often nonmanual workers, more often employed, more likely to have used social assistance before 1991 (which means that they are in long-term poverty), more likely to have a stable income (a salary and/or pension), and more likely to have a passive attitude toward life. Households headed by women are poorer, their incomes are lower, and they receive less social assistance (Warzywoda–Kruszynska and Grotowska–Leder 1996:162–163).

Single-Mother Families

In Western European and American cities single-mother families are an important dimension to the feminization of poverty. In the past in Poland single-mother families lived in especially difficult conditions, and today they remain some of the poorest households. In 1994, 4.85% of households headed by a single mother (40,000 households) lived below the subsistence minimum, whereas for families generally this percentage was 4.5% (Kolaczek 1996:295).[13]

In Poland, as elsewhere, there has been an increase in the number of single-parent families. Between 1988 and 1995 in those countries that belong to the Organization for Economic Cooperation and Development (OECD) there was a 30–50% rise in the rate of single-parent families; however, Poland had only an 11.3% rise in the rate of single-parent families during the same time period (Graniewska 1997:20). In 1995, 15.4% of families were single-parent; 13.6% were single-mother families, and only 1.8%, single-father families (Kolaczek 1996: 294). The feminization of families seen here is caused by the tendency of the Polish courts of justice to consign children to the care of divorced mothers and not divorced fathers (e.g., in 1993 divorced mothers were given responsibility for child care in 66.5% of cases, and divorced fathers in only 3.5% (Graniewska 1997:29)). It is also the product of a high male death rate (a trend that was strong at the end of 1980s and the beginning of the 1990s, especially for men 35–64 years old) and, lastly, is due to an increasing birthrate for illegitimate children (illegitimate children accounted for 5.7% of all births in 1988, 6.1% in 1990, and 8.2% in 1993 [Graniewska 1997: 21]). In 1988, 88.7% of single-parent families were headed by women; in 1995, 89.2% of single-parent families were headed by women. These women were widows (43.9%), divorced (21.6%), and unmarried (8.8%) (Graniewska 1997:19, 21).

During the transition period, with the development of mass unemployment and as the position of women (especially women with children) in the labor market became more difficult, the situation of single-parent families worsened. At the same time the social assistance previously distributed through the workplace and forms of social infrastructure based in the workplace (such as day-care centers, kindergartens, and subsidized vacations) diminished. Thus, the nonconflictual combination of a job and family obligations became more complicated. Although this was of importance to all women, it was critical for single mothers.

Generally speaking, the households of single mothers are characterized by a lower than average *per capita* household income; however, their material situation is not as bad as that of families with many children. For instance, in 1994, 6.0% of the family members in single-mother households lived below the subsistence minimum, while this percentage for members of families with many children was 20.4%. Consistent with this, 12.8% of the people living in single-mother families were below the relative poverty line, whereas 38.8% of the members of families with many children were, and 56.5% of members of single-mother families lived below the social minimum, as compared to 85.7% of members of families with many children (Golinowska 1996d:360).

The difficult material situation that is produced when one person's income is the basis of the whole family's existence turns into a catastrophe with unemployment, and single parents are more often unemployed than married people. In the years 1991–1994 there was a gradual decrease of the number of employed single parents (Kolaczek 1996).

According to the Institute of Labor and Social Studies research, in 1991, 91% of single-parent families affected by unemployment had an income that fell below the social minimum. In 1996, 45.5% of all members of single-parent families were situated below the social minimum level, and 4.0%, below the subsistence minimum (in families with many children the respective percentages are 80.0% and 16.0%). Of members of single-parent households, 11.1% are below the relative poverty line, while in the population at large the figure is 14%, and in families with many children, 38.2% (see Appendix).

The threat of poverty increases with an increase in the number of children in a single-mother family. For instance, 14.3% of single-mother households with six or more members live below the subsistence minimum, whereas this proportion is only 4.8% for all single-mother households (Kolaczek 1996:299). The threat of poverty in single-mother households is twice as great in villages as in cities. There is also a strong correlation between the level of education of the head of household and single-parent poverty. However, better-educated and working single mothers are also at risk of poverty. Employed women are overrepresented among poor single mothers. Wielislawa Warzywoda–Kruszynska notes that "in spite of fixed employment an adult woman is not able to financially secure her children" (1996:195).

Single-father families are in a better situation due to the better social and occupational position of men in society and the generally lower number of children in families headed by single fathers (Graniewska 1997).

I would like to mention here one more dimension of the feminization of poverty, which is of a cultural nature. Studies into the lives of poor families show that in a difficult financial situation women characteristically become pillars of the family. Wives take on their husbands' former roles, in particular, securing the means of survival by applying to social assistance for help, borrowing money, or purchasing on credit (Polawski 1997b; Tarkowska 1997). Thus, their obligations are doubled; they have their previous family duties (cooking, cleaning, taking care of children, etc.) as well as these new responsibilities. This microlevel dimension of the feminization of poverty is also visible in other Eastern European countries (in Hungary or Romania, according to *Country Reports*), where traditional cultural patterns persist.

The feminization of poverty in Poland has many forms. At the macrolevel it is associated with the situation of women in the labor market, with unemployment, and with income discrimination against women. At the microlevel the feminization of poverty has a cultural character. The peculiar economic, social, and cultural legacy of state socialism has given the Polish version of the feminization of poverty certain features common to all postcommunist countries. These include the poverty of working women and inequality within households. At the same time this means that the feminization of poverty in Poland is different from phenomena known in Western countries. This is especially true of the situation of single-mother families. Unwed teenage mothers or *welfare mothers*, so typical of ghetto poverty in American or Western cities, do not (yet?) constitute an important problem in Poland. However, these differences in the shape of the feminization of poverty in Poland do not alter its discriminatory character.

ETHNICITY AND POVERTY IN POLAND: THE ROMA ISSUE

Contemporary poverty has an ethnic flavor—so much so that some describe the ethnicization of poverty as the *differentia specifica* of poverty at the end of twentieth century. The correlation of poverty and ethnicity and association of the phenomenon of poverty with ethnic minorities constitute an example of the phenomenon of the accumulation of strangeness stigmas (Kurczewska 1999).

In contrast to other countries in both Western and Eastern Europe, there is a very weak ethnicization of poverty in Poland. This is mainly because of the small size of minority populations in Poland. Whereas in prewar Poland the non-Polish population constituted about 35%, it does not now exceed 4%.[14] Ukrainian, German, and Belorussian minorities are among the largest groups. Roma, as well as Lithuanians, Slovaks, Czechs, and Jews, are among the medium-sized minorities. Karaites, Tartars, Armenians, and Bulgarians form the smallest minority groups. The Roma population (Table 4.3) numbers about 20,000, according to the Ministry of Culture and Art's estimation, and about 30,000–50,000, according to Roma organizations (Kusmierz 1995:20; Bojar 1997:406; Sicinski 1997:395; Mirga 1998a).

Table 4.3
Estimates of Roma Population

1945–1946	10,000
1961–1962	12,000[a]
1978	15,000
1989–1990	20,000–30,000

Notes: [a]According to other estimates, the Roma population in 1961–1962 numbered 18,000 people (Bartosz 1994:189).

Source: (Sakson 1991:187).

The Polish Roma are not homogeneous but are deeply differentiated across many dimensions. The Roma population is composed of four groups (kin groups or tribes) with different pasts, cultures, dialects, and customs, as well as different past and present economic situations. The Carpathian Roma (Bergitka Roma) is a long-settled community in the southern part of Poland (in Nowy Sacz voivodship). Other groups, such as the Polska Roma, Chaladytka Roma, and Kelderasz or Lovari, practiced a nomadic way of life until the 1960s. When in 1964 the administration forbade the nomadic way of life and introduced forced settlement, the Roma dispersed to different regions and towns, settling in small groups of 100, 300, or 500.

The poverty of the Roma in Poland, which had always existed, became proverbial ("ragged as a Gypsy"). They were always at the bottom of the social ladder—the poorest, most marginalized, and most socially isolated group. Antipathy to the Roma was "an antipathy to somebody lower in social hierarchy, somebody inferior but at the same time unfortunate; tolerated without fear as a part of folklore" (Giza–Poleszczuk and Poleszczuk 1992:15).

The Carpathian Roma always were, and still are, extremely poor. For example, in a mountainous parish (Bukowina Tatrzanska) in 1997, social assistance protected 53% of the Roma population, while in the community as a whole this proportion was 13%, according to the documentation collected by Slawomir Lodzinski (1998). The Roma newspaper *Rrom p-o Drom* (1995, nos. 3-4) documents that 80% of Roma in Poland do not have social insurance, live in poverty and sickness, and are without medical aid. Roma activists alert people to the dramatic rise of unemployment that has taken place among the Roma. Ewa Nowicka, a sociologist from the University of Warsaw, describes Roma settlement at the peripheries of mountainous villages as life in the *culture of poverty* (Nowicka 1998).

But, of great importance to the Roma population in Poland is its deep differentiation. According to Andrzej Mirga (1998a), Roma activist and former president of the Polish Romani Association, "on average," Roma in Poland live relatively well. However, this is due to the effect on the average of the Roma elite ("Roma aristocracy"), for example, the group Polska Roma. According to him, the wealth of the "Roma aristocracy" dates back to the 1980s, when, after martial law, Poland faced economic crisis and shortages of everything. This became a period of prosperity for the group of Roma who, owing to their international kin relations, could import merchandise to Poland (Mirga 1998b:165). The wealth and fortunes gained by the Roma in this fashion were then sometimes manifested in demonstrative ways (with rich villas and palaces in Pabianice or Mlawa, luxurious cars, etc.).[15] Today the prosperity of some Roma is often connected with the shadow or illegal economy (e.g., car smuggling).[16]

The prosperity of these Roma resulted in a radical change in the mutual economic positions of Poles and Gypsies in the second part of 1980s and, especially after the rapid and coterminous impoverishment of the Polish population, became a source of conflict. In 1991 in Mlawa there was a pogrom against Gypsies. Mlawa was at this time a town experiencing a rapid increase in unemployment and poverty (the unemployment rate in Mlawa was then 35%, as compared to the national average of 10%). A tragic car accident caused by a young Roma who escaped from the site of the accident provoked riots. These then led to large-scale aggression directed against Gypsies and their settlements. In-depth analysis by sociologists from the University of Warsaw (Giza–Poleszczuk and Poleszczuk 1992) uncovered economic, rather than ethnic, roots of the conflict. Extremely important was the rapid transformation of the preexisting social order—a social and economic hierarchy in which Gypsies had always been located at the bottom.

It should be mentioned that during postwar Polish–Roma coexistence there, were a few pogroms and attacks against Roma in Poland: in Luków (August

1976), in Klodawa (August 1976), in Konin (September 1981), in Oswiecim (October 1981), and in Mlawa in 1991. Recently, there were also some attacks on Romanian Roma.[17] Andrzej Mirga connects these incidents with the social and economic crisis leading to the deepening of the ethnic conflict (Mirga 1998b:164).

The low educational level of Polish Roma exacerbates their poverty and marginalization. The absence of an educational tradition in Roma culture, together with the practice of enforced education (seen by many Roma as a form of forced assimilation, destructive of their ethnic identity), has left a legacy of high illiteracy rates among older generations, a low proportion of students completing primary-level education, poor school attendance, and a high dropout rate (Mirga and Gheorghe 1997). Andrzej Mirga, a Polish Roma activist, is afraid that during the transition period financial pressures have further limited the educational prospects of Roma (Mirga 1998a). A low level of education is marginalizing, especially in present-day Poland, where there is a strong negative correlation between education and poverty.

Jacek Kuron, head of the Parliamentary Committee for National and Ethnic Minorities, argues that Poland urgently needs a general governmental program to resolve the problems faced by the Roma population in such spheres as education, work, and housing (Kuron 1998). Yet it should be noted that the transformation in Poland has created new opportunities for Roma. For instance, they are now politically emancipated. Whereas during state socialism the Roma in Poland were marginalized both socially and politically, today they have their own organizations for representation and protection.

The mutual relations of Poles and Roma are not good. On the Polish side there are prejudices, stereotypes, feelings of strangeness, and a complete lack of knowledge of Roma culture, customs, and values. This is even the case for local officials and close neighbors in the Carpathian villages (Nowicka 1997). During the period 1974–1991 the level of Poles' antipathy toward the Roma almost doubled, and in 1991 they were the least respected minority in Poland (Bartosz 1994:49). In local communities, where they form small and poor groups, Roma are tolerated (Nowicka 1995), but any numerical or economic advance brings the possibility of open conflict. "Even today, every manifestation of Gypsies' 'good coping' strategies (their supposed wealth) is a source of envious antipathy, however in Ochotnica and Jurgów [names of villages] this problem does not exist because the Roma are a relatively poor group" (Nowicka 1995:375).

Thus, the Polish Roma are a relatively small population and are economically stratified. Except for the wealthy strata, the majority of Roma (unfortunately, there are not statistics in this field) live in poverty or in real destitution: without work, qualifications, or opportunities, in social isolation and contempt. "As an underdeveloped community with low educational and professional skills, the Roma were unable to maintain or compete for jobs in the emerging market economy" (Mirga and Gheorghe 1997:11). This development has left the Polish Roma in real danger of permanent marginalization and "ethno-class or underclass" (Mirga and Gheorghe 1997:35) formation. The term *underclass* is not generally applied to the Roma population[18]; instead, the lifestyle of poor Roma communities is framed in the language of the *culture of poverty* (Lewis 1966). However, as far as I am aware, this minority has not been studied exclusively from a poverty perspective. Because of the small size of the Roma population in Poland, the problem of the ethnicization of poverty is small. This differentiates the Polish case from both West and Central European ones.

UNDERCLASS FORMATION IN POLAND

Do We Have an Underclass in Poland?

Describing Polish poverty as relatively shallow, a World Bank economist stated that "there is not in Poland a numerically strong, marginalized group, forming a separate 'underclass' of extremely poor people" (Topinska 1996:76). "Poland shows no evidence of a distinct underclass," briefly asserts the World Bank report (Polawski 1997a:112). The opinion of researchers from the International Child Development Centre (ICDC) is similar: "In spite of the rapid increase of poverty, until now there is lack of evidence of permanent poverty in the region and of a so-called underclass emerging, understood as affected by many-sided deprivation" (ICDC 1996:99). Branko Milanovic describes poverty in Central Europe as "shallow and transient" (1996:66).

However, Polish sociologists take an opposing position, identifying both longlasting poverty and its reproduction. They generally state that in Poland economic privileges, as well as economic deprivation, are strongly inherited (Zaborowski 1998:76). Summing up the results of the research *Poles '95*, Wladyslaw Adamski and Andrzej Rychard are explicit: "In Poland the margin of poverty reproduces itself relatively more often than the margin of wealth" (1998:376). Other researchers present empirical evidence of emerging urban ghettos in the big cities (Wódz 1994; Zalewska 1994; 1997; Warzywoda–Kruszynska and Grotowska–Leder 1998) or an emerging underclass in the former state farms (Tarkowska 1998; Gorlach 1998). Sociologists agree that the people living downtown in old, substandard houses in big cities, as well as groups of former state farms laborers, are "the best candidates for the Polish underclass" (Polawski 1997a:110). The new poverty in Poland has found the social, cultural, and mental grounds for its consolidation and reproduction. But the underclass in Poland does not have an ethnic character. The feminization of poverty is evident in urban and in rural (formerly state farm) ghettos, but its character is distinct in the two places, and it is not the same as the feminization of poverty seen in the West. An important part of the new poverty in Poland is the situation of the families of former state farmworkers,[19] my focus in the final part of this chapter. Before that I comment on the conceptualization of the term "underclass."

I am fully aware that the term *underclass* is subject to strong criticism in poverty-related discussions, but I find it useful and agree with the Polish sociologist Wojciech Zaborowski that there is an urgent need "to consider the usefulness of the term *underclass* for the analyses of Polish society" (1998:67). As was mentioned in the first part of this chapter, the social sciences in Poland lack and need a serious debate about poverty, underclass formation, marginalization, and social exclusion. At present, the term "underclass" tends to be used in a loose, metaphorical way, with the aim of denominating poor, marginalized social groups, located at the bottom of the social ladder.

The empirical researchers cited earlier use this term to indicate the geographical concentration of poverty, a peculiar depth of poverty, or the accumulation (or coincidence) of many poverty-related phenomena (such as long-term unemployment, associated with low levels of education; prolonged dependence on welfare benefits; and a lack of opportunities for the young), which contribute to the reproduction of conditions of impoverishment from one generation to the next. The association of these conditions with spatial isolation sanctions the attempt to identify an underclass.

The critics of the term *underclass* argue that it is "mistakenly overloaded with stereotyped deviant behaviours" (Mingione 1996:VI); a "value-laden, increasingly pejorative term" related to the *undeserving poor* (Gans 1990:271); and associated more with "the issue of blame and responsibility rather than with systemic empirical inquiry" (Nolan and Whelan 1996:154). Most criticized are the behavioral (or cultural) definitions of the underclass (as opposed to the structural ones belonging to the Myrdalian tradition).

Conservative scholars and journalists (who criminalize poverty) make ethical strictures about the *underclass*. Conversely, Zygmunt Bauman stresses the need to "separate the 'problem of the underclass' from the 'issue of poverty'" and states that the failure to do this leads to an underestimation of the crucial (i.e., economic) dimension of poverty (Bauman 1998:70).

Herbert J. Gans, one of the most severe critics of the term "underclass" states that the underclass is an "umbrella term," and "the umbrella is open to anyone who wishes to place new meanings, or a variety of stereotypes, accusations and stigmas under it" (1996:151).

William Julius Wilson is very critical of a "value-laden use of the term by some journalists and conservative intellectuals," "blaming of the victim," and "simplistic distinction between culture and social structure" (1991). This last point is especially important from a sociological point of view. Sociological research, in opposition to economics, needs to search for the social and cultural content hidden by a bad or very bad economic situation; it should not be limited to the economic dimension. Taking into account the social and cultural dimensions of poverty does not necessarily lead to "connotations of undeservingness and blameworthiness." Wilson's empirical analysis of the "ghetto poor" (1991) is an excellent sociological approach to the issue of poverty and shows the need for an underclass approach. He takes into account the social contexts (social milieu, impoverished neighborhoods) that reinforce the effects of joblessness and influence young people's socialization. Wilson's conceptualization of "concentration effects" (the effects of living in a poor neighborhood) is useful in the study of poverty because it emphasizes *the need for discussion about the social and cultural content of economically understood poverty*.

I fully agree with Wilson's statement that "any crusade to abandon the concept underclass, however defined, could result in premature closure of ideas just as important new studies on the inner-city ghetto, including policy-oriented studies, are being generated" (1991:6). This statement seems especially apt in light of the discourse on poverty that is presently taking place in the Polish social sciences.

When I use the term *underclass* in my empirical studies, I take into account three main aspects of the phenomenon: (1) the accumulation of some economic, social, and cultural correlates of poverty (such as long-term unemployment, a low level of qualifications, or prolonged contact with social assistance institutions) in certain social places (milieus); (2) the spatial concentration and (a degree of) social isolation of these communities; (3) the risk (or the fact) of the perpetuation of these conditions and their transmission to the next generation. Defined as such, we can find an underclass in the settlements of the former state farms.

Why State Farms?

The former state farms deserve the attention of researchers studying poverty (and not only poverty). The particular milieu of the state farms, its culture, subculture, and the lifestyle of workers and other inhabitants are important elements in a sociological summary of the social, cultural, and mental legacy of socialism. In many respects, the legacy of state farms is a quintessence of attitudes, habits, and lifestyles shaped under "real socialism," for instance, a "learned helplessness," a lack of responsibility, and demanding behavior.

In the People's Republic of Poland there were more than 1,600 state farms, on which 500,000 people worked and lived with their families (a total of about 2 million people). After the closure of state farms, with economic transformation from 1991 to 1993, about 100,000 people became unemployed—a number that has now decreased to about 47,000 (Wilkin 1997). In *The Transformations of State Farms* by Jerzy Wilkin (1997), 72% of respondents, who were the former workers (and former inhabitants) of state farms, state that they are now worse off than before (and 52% say that they are much worse off than before the transformation).

For many years state farms fulfilled the functions of a real welfare state (with all the positive as well as the negative consequences). Patronalism was one of the most important characteristics of relations between the state plant and its workers (Halamska 1998). People adjusted their behavior to the vast system of different benefits and profits and secured satisfaction for their basic needs (although at a very low level). This understanding of the state farm as welfare-provider makes the study of its changing role of generalizable interest.

From the earliest days work on state farms (the unproductivity of which soon became evident) lacked any social prestige and attracted poorly-qualified workers (Mycielska 1966; Buchowski 1996). The state farm populations were characterized by atomization, conflicts, and alcoholism (Zadrozynska 1983). Living there was a form of marginalization and was perceived in this way. State farmworkers' families were among those with the highest number of children (32% of their families consisted of six or more members, while this figure for workers' families in general was 3% [Dzun 1991:124]). They also had a low level of work activity (in state farm families there was only one working person for every 2.6 nonworking family members, while in peasant families this proportion was 1 to 1.8), a low level of education (and a large proportion of unskilled workers), and weak professional ambitions (Dzun 1991).

In spite of the social and cultural marginalization of the state farms, they remained attractive to workers in many respects: the eight-hour working day offered on the state farms was a luxury in agriculture, and everybody understood it as such; there was pay sufficient[20] to cover the needs of large families; jobs were secure, and there were possibilities for other members of the family to earn extra money. Moreover (and importantly) work on a state farm brought with it a series of benefits: free accommodation that belonged to the enterprise, a plot of land, the possibility to raise a few farm animals on one's own, special allowances and price cuts (e.g., on milk or meals), free transportation, and the opportunity for various "arrangements" (i.e., the easy theft of fodder for pigs or cattle). It is important to emphasize both the formal and informal, legal and illegal nature of these benefits.

The closure of the state farm was a turning point and a catastrophe for many laborers. With the disappearance of the state farm, which had been a monopolist on the local labor market and the only source of family income, an entire lifestyle broke down. Since the farm was not only the employer but also a social and cultural environment, employees were particularly hit by its closure. They became helpless when faced with the difficulties of everyday life (and life in general). The *learned helplessness* and related phenomena of self-restraint and lack of self-preservation (Perepeczko 1994) are the result of many years of living on a state farm. Former employees are not effective at searching for new jobs. They are passive and prefer to let events take their course. They wait for someone else to make their vital decisions (Lapinska–Tyszka 1993:170; Buchowski 1996:37). Some researchers describe a "syndrome of the former state farm worker," which includes a lack of independence, passivity, and alcoholism.[21] Economist Jerzy Wilkin describes the situation of the "state farms' people" in terms of anomie, marginalization, and learned helplessness (Wilkin 1998).

Supplying employees with a rich social infrastructure, state farms helped to instill strategies for taking advantage of social property. These strategies, habits, and attitudes became useless and dysfunctional in a changed economic situation (Lapinska–Tyszka 1993:170). Thus, it seems justified to call those people "the victims of a social experiment" (Korab 1997). It was a double experiment, first, in what would happen when this form of agriculture was created (for ideological and political reasons), and second, in what would happen when it was finally ended (for economic reasons). In the second phase, people who were unable to undertake an active, independent life were left to themselves.

The "state farm poverty" (as it is described in our research) is a good example of new poverty in Poland as it is due to factors characteristic of new poverty (such as unemployment, a low level of education, large family size, and residence in the countryside). The central aspects of poverty on the former state farms include, first, a large disjuncture between the level of peoples' needs and the possibilities for their satisfaction. This particular form of poverty is caused by the newness of the phenomenon, connected with the recent closure of state farms and termination of income. Second, this poverty is not yet very deep; basic needs are still satisfied, although at a very meager level, and therefore a modest and limited existence is possible. Thus, this poverty is not as dramatic as prewar rural poverty was (where there were both hunger and the exploitation of children), but it is dramatic in another way because of the real danger of its recurring in the next generation. This danger is a third characteristic of this poverty. It is caused by a continuing lack of jobs and resulting total dependence on social benefits, which then limit the spirit of activity.[22] *This prolonged dependence is the product of habits formed while working and living on state farms.* In the past, all family life was dependent on the state farm infrastructure; now it depends on social assistance. "Maybe social assistance will not let us die," states one interviewee in research. "Old and New Forms of Poverty," mentioned earlier, clearly express their philosophy of life, hopes, and plans for the future.

Fourth, there are some pathological phenomena connected with the situation on the former state farms. There is a high level of participation in the shadow economy (30% of respondents in Wilkin's research were working in the second economy [1997:61]). This form of activity, of course, alleviates poverty and may sometimes be a way of escaping it. Alcoholism is also prevalent. Alcoholism was always the most characteristic feature of the state farm culture or subculture (Zadrozynska 1983). Now, presenting results of his research, Jerzy Wilkin is clear: "They do not work, they steal and drink." Field research recently by Maria Halamska in 10 former state farms shows the problem of alcoholism as one of the main social problems of these communities (Halamska 1998).

A fifth feature of this lifestyle, perhaps the most characteristic, is pervasive uncertainty. This uncertainty is found in all the basic dimensions of life. There is uncertainty over income, housing, food, work, and even the rhythm of the day. Uncertain conditions of everyday life foster a temporary, immediate, and short-term perspective and the feeling of a lack of influence over one's own life. In both the sociology of time and research into poverty it is argued that this time perspective is a direct derivative of poverty. It is also the legacy of many years of life and work at the state farm, where plans and long-term thinking were useless; everybody lived on a day-to-day basis, not caring for the future.

A sixth feature of poverty on the former state farms is the especially difficult situation of the young, living without prospects. With a low level of education and without jobs they have no possibility of escaping the vicious circle of poverty and have no prospects for a better future. For financial, cultural, and other reasons (e.g., uneasy communication with the outside world) these young people have no possibilities of getting more than an elementary, compulsory education. Thus, they become candidates for social exclusion, and the danger of the recurrence of poverty, social marginalization, and underclass formation is quite real.

The role of the woman as the pillar of the family is a seventh characteristic of these areas. The woman takes on the role that was her husband's during almost all of their previous life together—she secures the financial means of survival by borrowing, purchasing on credit, and so on. The woman, of course, retains her former duties such as cooking, doing everything in the home, working in the garden, taking care of the cattle; her everyday life is a permanent bustle, an interesting expression of the feminization of poverty, Polish-style.

An eighth important feature of this lifestyle is people's lack of interest in politics and social problems on a macrolevel. This is real political marginalization. There is a lack of proportion between the influence of politics on the lives of former state farmworkers and their families and these people's complete indifference toward politics (shown in a low voter turnout) and social change. In this context their dream of the return to state farms (very often expressed in research studies) is fully understandable.

Finally, it is worth noting another form of marginalization on state farms. This is spatial or territorial isolation, imprisonment in the locality, and ascription to the place of residence (attachment to the soil). Enforced localization is an important obstacle to entering the labor market and escaping poverty and marginalization. According to Zygmunt Bauman, in the world of globalization, imprisonment in the locality excludes the poor from the world (1997).

In summary, I suggest that the claims that an underclass does not exist today in Poland need to be tested against the poverty found on the former state farms. Social and cultural analysis of this poverty reveals many of the features of an underclass as defined earlier. Maybe there is not yet an underclass, but there are definitely conditions favoring its formation. In particular, the local concentration and relative isolation of poor people reinforce the effects of joblessness in an especially dangerous fashion.

CONCLUSION

Past and present poverty in Poland is complex and multidimensional and is studied from different perspectives. To show this complexity, as well as the multiple approaches that are taken in the study of it, was impossible in a short chapter such as this. Thus, the final picture remains incomplete in many respects. Second, because the history of poverty research in Poland is both long and rich but was the subject of a period of "ideological embargo" during state socialism, the reconstruction of past poverty is an especially difficult problem. Additional difficulties are caused by a lack of theoretical or conceptual discussion in Polish sociology about poverty itself, the underclass, social exclusion, or marginalization and the possibilities and limitations inherent in their application to Polish society. Third, poverty is among the most important problems in Poland today and is approached in different ways by economists, sociologists, psychologists, and social policy specialists (as well as the very different approaches taken by politicians and journalists). A complete reconstruction of the particulars of these different positions was not possible here, and certain simplifications have been inevitable.

Because changing poverty in contemporary Poland is such a large and complex issue, many general questions concerning its nature, historical sources, and a comparison of it with poverty in other countries need long and detailed explications. These would not be limited to the state socialist period but would need to delve more deeply into Poland's social history. Without this depth of research much will remain simplified or unaddressed.

Nevertheless, to conclude this chapter, I present what I see as the main characteristics of poverty in Poland. Poverty in Poland today is different, both from past poverty and from poverty found in other countries (either postcommunist or Western countries). At the same time there are many processes similar to those known from other industrial societies (such as growing "modern social conflict," increasing cleavage between the poor and the wealthy parts of the population, permanent marginalization, and a ghetto poor or underclass formation). Apart from the scope of contemporary poverty in Poland (twice as big as before transformation) and its dynamics (its stabilization over the last two or three years), one of the most notable features of current Polish poverty is its permanence (how it is "reproduced" across generations).

Other phenomena characterize Polish poverty today: the concentration of poverty (and other negative phenomena) in some regions (in particular the northeaster and northwestern parts of Poland) and in isolated social milieus (urban ghettos and former state farm settlements); the accumulation of poverty and factors conductive to its persistence and reproduction in particular places and among particular groups (i.e., the process of underclass formation that in Poland involves the concentration of unemployment, households headed by young people, large families, low educational levels, and residence in villages or small towns).

Some researchers, for example, Lidia Beskid (1999b:20), suggest that in some respects poverty in Poland is worse than in other Central European countries; it may be that the process of underclass formation is also more advanced. This is an important issue to investigate.

Poverty in Poland is mostly rural and in this respect differs from the poverty found in Western European countries (with the exception of Ireland). On the other hand, Polish poverty predominantly affects young people rather than the old, and in this respect it is similar to poverty in Western countries, where the economic situation of pensioners is also relatively good. However, the extent of the phenomenon of the *working poor* makes the Polish case more similar to other postcommunist countries than to Western ones.

The evidence suggests that the phenomenon of the feminization of poverty does exist in Poland but is different from the feminization of poverty witnessed in Western countries; there are not a large number of unwed teenage mothers, or *welfare mothers*, and women are not a culturally separated category of poor people. The working poor woman and the different forms of gender inequality she faces (both on macrolevel and inside the household) are characteristic of the Polish version of the feminization of poverty.

The Roma in Poland are a marginalized ethnic group. However, the significant economic stratification of this group as well as their small number (about 20,000–30,000) mean that the phenomenon of the ethnicization of poverty is virtually nonexistent in Poland. On the other hand, the poor Roma villages and settlements and the new phenomenon of Romanian Roma begging on the streets of Polish cities are worth investigation.

The process of underclass formation (involving the prolonging of, or making permanent, marginalization) in Poland is advanced. Its roots are in the fertile ground of the communist legacy that promoted passivity, helplessness, and dependence on welfare. The phenomenon of underclass formation in Poland is extremely important, both from a practical (or policy) perspective and from an academic one. It may be an opportunity to delve deeper into the legacy of "real socialism" and could provide the empirical material for a contribution to the theoretical debate on the underclass.

APPENDIX

Table 4A.1
Percentage of People in Households Below Social Minimum Level and Below Subsistence Minimum by Socioeconomic Factors in 1996

	Below social minimum	Below subsistence minimum
In general:	46.7	4.3
By socioeçonomic groups:		
Employees	48.2	3.2
Farmers	55.4	5.9
Employees-farmers	52.3	5.4
Self-employed	32.4	0.7
Retired and pensioners	36.8	3.9
Living on unearned resources	77.8	21.0
By number of members in household:		
1 person	23.3	1.5
2 persons	23.4	1.4
3 persons	34.9	3.0
4 persons	48.3	2.8
5 persons	61.1	5.7
6 or more persons	72.5	12.3
By biological type of household:		
Couple without children	19.8	1.1
With 1 child	31.6	1.6
With 2 children	47.1	2.4
With 3 children	63.0	5.3
With 4 or more children	80.0	16.0
Single parent	45.3	4.0
By type of locality:		
Towns, total	39.6	2.8
500,000 and more	26.2	1.2
200,000–500,000	36.0	2.3
100,000–200,000	37.8	2.0
20,000–100,000	43.1	3.0
Below 20,000	51.1	4.8
Village	57.7	6.8
By age of head of household:		
Up to 34 years	52.4	5.6
35–44	53.3	5.0
45–54	44.6	3.5
55–64	33.2	2.6

Table 4A.1 continued

	Below social minimum	Below subsistence minimum
65 years and above	33.0	3.7
By level of education of the head of household:		
University	14.1	0.3
Secondary	36.0	1.5
Vocational	56.2	5.0
Elementary and lower	57.2	8.0

Source: Poverty Indicators 1997:22–23.

Table 4A.2

Percentage of People in Households Below the Relative Poverty Line (50% of the Average Household Expenditure Per Capita)

In general:	14.0
By socioeconomic groups:	
Employees	11.3
Farmers	20.8
Employees-farmers	17.8
Self-employed	5.0
Retired and pensioners	12.5
Living on unearned resources	44.9
By number of members in household:	
1 person	5.3
2 persons	5.1
3 persons	7.3
4 persons	11.0
5 persons	19.9
6 or more persons	32.3
By biological type of household:	
Couple without children	4.0
With 1 child	5.7
With 2 children	9.6
With 3 children	19.8
With 4 or more children	38.2
Single parent	11.1
Others	17.0
By type of locality:	
Towns, 500,000 and more	4.0
200,000–500,000	7.5
100,000–200,000	8.0
20,000–100,000	10.6
Below 20,000	14.8
Village	21.2
By age of head of household:	
Up to 34 years	16.8
35–44	15.7
45–54	12.8
55–64	9.7
65 years and above	10.7
By level of education of head of household:	
University	1.5

Table 4A.2 continued

Secondary	6.7
Vocational	16.9
Elementary and lower	22.1

Source: Poverty Indicators 1997:33–40.

NOTES

An earlier version of this chapter was delivered at the international seminar "Racialization and Feminization of Poverty in Central and Southern Europe," Budapest, Hungary, on April 25, 1998. I would like to thank all participants for the discussion and especially Rebecca Emigh, Eva Fodor, and Iván Szelényi for their valuable comments. Special thanks to Joanna Sikorska for her assistance in preparing this chapter.

1. The Polish economists and statisticians apply nine poverty line measures: *absolute poverty*: (1) subsistence minimum, bundle of commodities essential to subsist (assuring subsistence); (2) fixed value of income or consumption in hard currency; (3) fixed sum equal to the average wage in a given year; *relative poverty*: (4) 50% of the average household expenditures per capita (equivalent unit); (5) minimum retirement pension (35% and 39% of the average wage in economy); (6) 60% of the average household expenditures per capita (equivalent unit); *subjective poverty*: (7) Leyden Poverty Line; estimate of essential income for one's own household; (8) estimate of essential income in society; *threatened with poverty* (repeated poverty): (9) social minimum; bundle of commodities essential for participation in social life (assuring integration) (Golinowska 1996b:68).

2. In Czechoslovakia the term "population with limited possibilities of consumption" was officially accepted for poverty and poor people (Mares and Mozný 1995).

3. This is the case of Piotr Glinski's excellent Ph.D. dissertation (1983) on "Economic Conditions of the Lifestyle of Urban Families in Poland in the 70s," containing a chapter on the "Lifestyle of the Poor People." Due to censorship, this study was never published.

4. A good example is the collected volume on *The Nature and the Question of Poverty*, edited by Witold Toczyski and published in 1991. The book contains the results of research started in the early 1980s and presented at a conference organized in 1984.

5. An excellent analysis of the discussion on the *culture of poverty* concept, made by Piotr Glinski (1983) was never published.

6. Of course, the Roma population was then a good example of the *culture of poverty*. Due to small size, on one hand, and their political, social, and cultural marginalization, on the other, this case was not taken into account in the public discourse. One can say that Roma were under state socialism twice marginalized: as Roma and as poor.

7. The analysis of poverty in Czechoslovakia reveals similar phenomena (Mares and Mozný 1995).

8. For details, see Appendix.

9. According to the World Bank estimates, Polish poverty is rather shallow: any minimal improvement of income will diminish the statistical image of poverty (Milanovic 1996:66).

10. Receiving social benefits is in this case an indicator of poverty.

11. This section of the chapter is based on articles by Reszke (1995) and Kotowska (1997).

12. The level and type of this education (12 grades of general secondary education)

are not profitable from the market economy point of view.

13. This part of the chapter is based on articles by Kolaczek (1996) and Graniewska (1997).

14. Due to the lack in Polish legislation of the category *nationality* (we use only citizenship), there is not in official documents, statistics, and so on any information concerning nationality. All data on nationality are approximated. Under the communist regime, all data on minorities were collected by the Ministry of Internal Affairs (a political repression institution). In 1990, the special Section for National Minorities was created in the Ministry of Culture and Art (from April 1992: Bureau for National Minorities), collecting all data and preparing estimates (Lodzinski 1992:92). The size of the minority population estimated by its organization is, in general, higher (Sicinski 1997).

15. I would like to underline that in Poland there are no data available concerning the numbers of wealthy Roma, as well as poor Roma, the levels of their education, the estimates of their unemployment, and so on. We also do not have statistics concerning demographic fertility or mortality of Roma population. Available data are fragmentary; the main source of information is ethnographic case studies or journalistic publications. Research on the Roma communities in Poland is done by many researchers, mostly by ethnographers and sociologists from the University of Warsaw (Lech Mróz, Ewa Nowicka, Slawomir Lodzinski); they have a qualitative, anthropological fieldwork and case studies character.

16. Andrzej Mirga (ethnographer and Roma activist) and Ireneusz Krzeminski (sociologist) discussed this problem at the seminar in the Institute of History of the Polish Academy of Sciences, February 27, 1998. They agree that it is not easy to speak about this problem because the supposed criminality of Roma was the reason of their extermination by Nazis. Stereotypes concerning Roma, their supposed well-being, the imagined sources of their well-being, and so on are another obstacle in such a discussion.

17. The poverty of Romanian Roma, who beg on the streets of Polish cities, reinforces the negative stereotypes, of both a poor Romanian as well as a poor Gypsy. This phenomenon is very visible but, according to estimates, not numerous. They do not constitute (yet?) an important part of ethnic poverty in Poland.

18. As far as I know, Pawel Polawski takes only Polish Roma into account when he discusses the question, Does the Polish underclass exist? But he states that "there is no reliable data concerning material situation and economic position of the Polish Roma" (Polawski 1997a:109).

19. This analysis is based on the results of empirical research "Old and New Forms of Poverty" directed by me, made within the international project *Social History of Poverty in Central Europe*, directed by Julia Szalai. The Polish part of empirical research was sponsored by the State Committee for Scientific Research (grant no. HOIF 015 13). The research has a qualitative character; it consists of reconstructions of family histories through in-depth interviews made with family members—representatives of three generations. During field research 27 differentiated cases of families living in poverty were collected. Seventy-two large interviews concerning different aspects of poor families' everyday life in the past and present were gathered. First results of the research were presented in collective volumes prepared by Julia Szalai (1995) and Zuzana Kusá (1997), as well as at the conference "Poland: Social and Cultural Paradigms" (Berlin, November 6–8, 1997) in my paper "Old and New Forms of Poverty in Poland."

In this analysis I also take into account results of studies made by eminent specialists of the state farm problems, such as Jerzy Wilkin, Barbara Perepeczko, Maria Halamska, and Anna Zadrozynska.

20. For instance, since the beginning of the 1970s there was a rapid growth of wages at state farms; for example, in 1975, the average wage was higher there than in the rest of

the state economy, and this lasted until 1983, a year of relative worsening of wage conditions (Dzun 1991:119–121). At the same time we have to keep in mind that state farms' laborers belonged to the worst-paid social category.

21. It is Maria Mydlak's analysis (Staszewski 1997).

22. In Gorzów voivodship, 25% of unemployed former state farmworkers do not want to work; they prefer to get social benefits (Wilkin 1997).

REFERENCES

Adamski, Wladyslaw, and Andrzej Rychard. 1998. "Zakonczenie, czyli głównie o dynamice kontestacji i partycypacji w procesach zmiany ustrojowej" [Conclusion, or Mostly on Dynamics of Contestation and Participation in the Processes of Systemic Change]. Pp. 369–382 in *Polacy '95. Aktorzy i klienci transformacji* [Poles '95. Actors and Clients of Transformation], edited by Wladyslaw Adamski. Warsaw: IFiS PAN.

Bartosz, Adam. 1994. *Nie bój si   Cygana* [Don't Be Afraid of Gypsy]. Sejny: Pogranicze.

Bauman, Zygmunt. 1997. "Glokalizacja, czyli komu globalizacja, a komu lokalizacja" [Glocalisation, That Is, for Whom Globalization and for Whom Localisation?]. *Studia Socjologiczne* 3(146): 53–69.

———. 1998. *Work, Consumerism and the New Poor*. Buckingham and Philadelphia: Open University Press.

Beskid, Lidia. 1999a. "Oblicze ubóstwa w Polsce" [Face of Poverty in Poland]. Pp. 38–53 in *Zmiany w zyciu Polaków w gospodarce rynkowej* [Changes in Poles' Life in Market Economy], edited by Lidia Beskid. Warsaw: IFiS PAN.

———. 1999b. "Wygrani/przegrani w procesie transformacji" [Winners and Losers in Transformation Process]. Pp. 15–27 in *Zmiany w zyciu Polaków w gospodarce rynkowej* [Changes in Poles' Life in Market Economy], edited by Lidia Beskid. Warsaw: IFiS PAN.

Bojar, Hanna. 1997. "Mniejszosci narodowe—nowe formy uczestnictwa w zyciu III Rzeczypospolitej" [National Minorities—New Forms of Participation in the III Republic Life]. Pp. 403–418 in *Elementy nowego ladu* [Elements of New Order], edited by Henryk Domanski and Andrzej Rychard. Warsaw: IFiS PAN.

Buchowski, Michal. 1996. *Klasa i kultura w okresie transformacji. Antropologiczne studium przypadku spolecznoci lokalnej w Wielkopolsce* [Class and Culture in the Period of Transformation. An Anthropological Study of a Local Community in Wielkopolska]. Berlin: Centre Marc Bloch.

Curtin, Chris, Trutz Haase, and Hilary Tovey. 1996. "Understanding Rural Poverty." Pp. 1–58 in *Poverty in Rural Ireland. A Political Economy Perspective*, edited by Chris Curtin, Trutz Haase, and Hilary Tovey. Dublin: Oak Tree Press.

Deniszczuk, Lucyna. 1972. *Wzorzec konsumpcji spolecznie niezbednej (minimum socjalne)* [Pattern of Socially Essential Consumption (Social Minimum)]. Warsaw: IPiSS.

Domanski, Henryk. 1992. *Zadowolony niewolnik. Studium o nierównociach miedzy mezczyznami i kobietami w Polsce* [The Grateful Slave. Inequality between Men and Women in Poland]. Warsaw: IFiS PAN.

———. 1999. *Zadowolony niewolnik idzie do pracy. Postawy wobec aktywnoci zawodowej kobiet w 23 krajach.* [The Grateful Slave Enters Labor Market]. Warsaw: IFiS PAN.

Dzun, Wlodzimierz. 1991. *PGR w rolnictwie polskim w latach 1944–1990* [State Farms in Polish Agriculture in 1944–1990]. Warsaw: IRWiR PAN.

Falkowska, Macieja. 1997. "Spoleczna definicja biedy, jej zasieg i przyczyny." [Social Definition of Poverty, Its Range and Causes]. *Serwis Informacyjny CBOS* 3:113–125.

Frackiewicz, Lucyna. 1983. *Sfery niedostatku* [Spheres of Deficiency]. Warsaw: IWZZ.

———. 1993. "Ubóstwo jako problem w okresie transformacji gospodarki" [Poverty as a Problem in the Period of Economy Transformation]. Pp. 41–49 in *Ubóstwo jako problem polityki spolecznej* [Poverty as a Social Policy Problem], edited by Lucyna Frackiewicz. Katowice: Uniwersytet Slaski.

Frieske, Kazimierz W. 1996. "Bieda—miary i interpretacje" [Poverty—Measures and Interpretations]. Pp. 226–238 in *Polska bieda. Kryteria. Ocena. Przeciwdzialanie* [Poland's Poverty. Criteria. Valuation. Counteracting], edited by Stanislawa Golinowska. Warsaw: IPiSS.

Frieske, Kazimierz W., and Joanna Sikorska. 1994. "Marginalizacja—partycypacja: pobocza oficjalnego porzadku spolecznego" [Marginalization versus Participation: At the Margin of Official Social Deal]. Pp. 35–56 in *W biegu czy w zawieszeniu? Ludzie i instytucje w procesie zmian* [In Motion or in Suspense? People and Institution in the Process of Change], edited by Kazimierz W. Frieske and Witold Morawski. Warsaw: IS UW.

Gans, Herbert J. 1990. "Deconstructing the Underclass: The Term's Danger as·a Planning Concept." *Journal of the American Planning Association* 56 (Summer): 271–277.

———. 1996. "From 'Underclass' to 'Undercaste': Some Observations about the Future of the Post-Industrial Economy and Its Major Victims." Pp. 141–152 in *Urban Poverty and the Underclass. A Reader,* edited by Enzo Mingione. Oxford: Blackwell.

Giza-Poleszczuk, Anna, and Jan Poleszczuk. 1992. *Cyganie i Polacy w Mawie. Konflikt etniczny czy spoleczny?* [Gypsies and Poles in Mawa. Ethnic or Social Conflict?]. Warsaw: CBOS.

Glinski, Piotr. 1983. "Ekonomiczne uwarunkowania stylu zycia. Rodziny miejskie w Polsce w latach siedemdziesiatych" [Economic Conditions of the Lifestyle of Urban Families in Poland in the 70s]. Ph.D. dissertation, Institute of Philosophy and Sociology, Polish Academy of Sciences, Warsaw.

Golinowska, Stanislawa. 1996a. "Badania nad ubóstwem. Zalozenia i metoda" [Studies on Poverty. Assumptions and Methods]. Pp. 7–17 in *Polska bieda. Kryteria. Ocena. Przeciwdziaanie.* [Poland's Poverty. Criteria. Valuation. Counteracting], edited by Stanislawa Golinowska. Warsaw: IPiSS.

———. 1996b. "Poverty in Poland in the 1st Half of 90s. Synthesis of Research Findings." Pp. 67–82 in *Social Policy towards Poverty. Comparative Approach,* edited by Stanislawa Golinowska. Warsaw: IPiSS.

———. 1996c. "State Social Policy and Social Expenditure in Central and Eastern Europe. Synthesis." Pp. 229–238 in *Social Policy towards Poverty. Comparative Approach,* edited by Stanislawa Golinowska. Warsaw: IPiSS.

———. 1996d. "Ubóstwo w Polsce w pierwszej polowie lat dziewiecdziesiatych. Synteza wyników badan" [Poverty in Poland in the First Half of 90s. Synthesis of Research Findings]. Pp. 349–365 in *Polska· bieda. Kryteria. Ocena. Przeciwdzialanie* [Poland's Poverty. Criteria. Valuation. Counteracting], edited by Stanislawa Golinowska. Warsaw: IPiSS.

———, ed. 1996e. *Polska bieda. Kryteria. Ocena. Przeciwdzialanie* [Poland's Poverty. Criteria. Valuation. Counteracting]. Warsaw: IPiSS.

Gorlach, Krzysztof. 1998. "Glos w dyskusji" [A Comment]. Pp. 132–134 in *Wielkoobszarowe gospodarstwa rolne, ich zaogi i nowi gospodarze* [Big Farms, Their Personnel and New Farmers], edited by Barbara Fedyszak–Radziejowska. Warsaw: IRWiR PAN.

Graniewska, Danuta. 1997. "Rodziny niepene. Wspólczesne tendencje i zagrozenia" [Incomplete Families. Present Trends and Threats]. Pp. 18–33 in *Rodzina polska w okresie kryzysu i oywienia gospodarczego* (1990–1995) [Polish Family in the Time of Crisis and Economic Boom], edited by W. Rakowski. Warsaw: PTD and IGS SGH.

Grotowska–Leder, Jolanta. 1995. "Sytuacja kobiet lódzkich—problem feminizacji biedy." [Situation of Women in Lodz—Problem of Feminization of Poverty]. Pp. 69–82 in *Poverty, Social Resourcefulness, Social Change*, edited by Danuta Zalewska. Wroclaw: IS UWr.

Halamska, Maria. 1998. "Spoleczne problemy osiedli popegeerowskich" [Social Problems of the Former State Farms Settlements] (mimeo).

Hirszowicz, Maria and Elzbieta Neyman. 1997. "Panstwo opatrznosciowe i jego ofiary" ["The Providence State and Its Victims"]. *Studia Socjologiczne* 3(146):71–100.

ICDC UNICEF. 1996. "Z badan ICDC UNICEF nad ubóstwem w krajach Europy Srodkowej i Wschodniej" [From International Child Development Centre Studies on Poverty in Central and Eastern Europe]. Pp. 92–100 in *Polityka spoleczna wobec ubóstwa. Ujecie porównawcze* [Social Policy towards Poverty. Comparative Approach], edited by Stanislawa Golinowska. Warsaw: IPiSS.

Jarosz, Maria. 1984. *Nierównosci spoleczne* [Social Inequalities]. Warsaw: KiW.

Knothe, Maria Anna. 1997. "Kobiety i praca. Problemy polskiego rynku pracy dla kobiet w okresie przejscia do gospodarki rynkowej" [Women and Labor]. Pp. 10–18 in *Kobiety wobec przemian okresu transformacji* [Women Encountering Changes of Transformation Period], edited by Krystyna Faliszek, Elisabeth McLean Petras, and Kazimiera Wódz. Katowice: Slask.

Kolaczek, Bozena. 1996. "Rodziny niepelne—prawdopodobienstwo zagrozenia ubóstwem" [Incomplete Families: Probability of Threat of Poverty]. Pp. 294–334 in *Polska bieda. Kryteria. Ocena. Przeciwdziaanie* [Poland's Poverty. Criteria. Valuation. Counteracting], edited by Stanislawa Golinowska. Warsaw: IPiSS.

Korab, Kazimierz. 1997. "Spoleczne ofiary eksperymentu ideologiczno-naukowego" [Social Victims of Ideological and Scientific Experiment]. Pp. 173–176 in *Ludzie i ziemia po upadku pegeerów. Analiza socjologiczna i ekonomiczna* [The People and the Land after a Collapse of the Former State Farms. Sociological and Economic Analyses], edited by Kazimierz Korab. Warsaw: SGGW.

Kotowska, Irena E. 1997. "Równosc kobiet i mezczyzn na rynku pracy" [Equality of Women and Men on the Labor Market]. Pp. 85–105 in *Wokól zawodowego równouprawnienia kobiet i m zczyzn* [On Occupational Equality of Rights of Women and Men], edited by Renata Siemienska. Warsaw: Scholar.

Kraczla, Roman. 1993. "Bezdomni w miastach slaskich" [The Homeless in Silesian Towns]. Pp. 29–52 in *W kr gu ubóstwa. Próba analizy psychospolecznych aspektów zjawiska* [In the World of Poverty. An Analysis of Psycho-Social Aspects of the Phenomenon], edited by Kazimiera Wódz, Katowice: lask.

Kurczewska, Joanna. 1999. "Contemporary Europe—Ethnicization of Poverty." *Polish Sociological Review* 1(125):73–83.

Kuron, Jacek. 1998. "Rola Parlamentarnej Komisji ds. Mniejszosci Narodowych i Etnicznych w zwalczaniu nietolerancji i ksenofobii" [The Role of the Parliamentary Committee for National and Ethic Minorities in Combating Ethnic Intolerance and Xenophobia]. Paper presented at the Conference on *Problemy nietolerancji i ksenofobii w Polsce* [Combating Ethnic Intolerance and Xenophobia in Poland], European Commission against Racism and Intolerance, Warsaw, May 5.

Kuron, Jacek, and Jacek Zakowski. 1997. *Siedmiolatka czyli kto ukradl Polske?* [Seven Years or Who Has Stolen Poland?]. Wroclaw: Wydawnictwo Dolnoslaskie.

Kusá, Zuzana, ed. 1997. *Past and Present Poverty*. Bratislava: Institute for Sociology and SPACE.

Kusmierz, Jacek. 1995. "Zarys problematyki mniejszoci etnicznych w Polsce" [Ethnic Minorities in Poland. Outline of Problem]. *Mniejszosci Narodowe* 4:16–22.

Ladányi, János. 1998. "Country Report—Hungary." Paper presented at the Conference *Racialization and Feminization of Poverty in Central and Southern Europe*, Budapest, April 24–26.

Lapinska–Tyszka, Krystyna. 1993. "Bezrobocie w gminie wiejskiej" [Unemployment in the Rural Community]. Pp. 165–180 in *Syndrom bezrobocia* [The Syndrome of Unemployment], edited by Ryszard Borowicz and Krystyna Lapinska–Tyszka. Warsaw: IRWiR PAN.

Lewis, Oscar. 1966. "The Culture of Poverty." Pp. 67–80 in *Anthropological Essays* by Oscar Lewis. New York: Random House.

Lodzinski, Slawomir. 1992. "Struktura narodowosciowa Polski i polityka panstwa wobec mniejszosci w latach 1989–1992" [Polish Ethnic Structure and the Policy of the State towards Ethnic Minorities in 1989–1992]. *Kultura i Spoleczenstwo* 3:85–98.

———. 1998. Research collection of documents concerning Roma.

Mares, Petr, and Ivo Mozny. 1995. *Poverty in the Czech Republic: Transformation or Transition*. Research Papers. Praha: Foundation for Research on Social Transformation.

Milanovic, Branko. 1996. "Income, Inequality and Poverty during the Transition: A Survey of the Evidence]. Pp. 52–66 in *Social Policy towards Poverty. Comparative Approach*, edited by Stanislawa Golinowska. Warsaw: IPiSS.

Mingione, Enzo. 1996. "Preface." Pp. xiii–xix in *Urban Poverty and the Underclass. A Reader*, edited by Enzo Mingione. Oxford: Blackwell.

Mirga, Andrzej. 1998a. "Elity cyganskie w Europie" [Romani Elites in Europe]. Paper presented at the seminar in the Institute of History of the Polish Academy of Sciences, Warsaw, February 26.

———. 1998b. "Romowie—proces ksztaltowania sie podmiotowosci politycznej" [Roma—Process of Political Subjectivity Formation]. Pp. 110–179 in *Mniejszosci narodowe w Polsce* [National Minorities in Poland], edited by Piotr Madajczyk. Warsaw: ISP PAN.

Mirga, Andrzej, and Nicolae Gheorghe. 1997. *The Roma in the Twenty–First Century: A Policy Paper*. Princeton: Project on Ethnic Relations.

Montgomery, Katarzyna. 1998. "Seksbomba w kuchni" [Sex Bomb in the Kitchen]. *Gazeta Wyborcza*, March 7–8.

Mycielska, Dorota. 1966. "Problemy zyciowe pracowników Panstwowych Gospodarstw Rolnych" [Vital Problems of the State Farmworkers]. *Kultura i Spoleczenstwo* 3:179–188.

Nolan, Brian, and Christopher T. Whelan. 1996. *Resources, Deprivation and Poverty*. Oxford: Clarendon Press.

Nowicka, Ewa. 1995. "Rom jako swój i jako obcy. Zbiorowosc Romów w swiadomosci spolecznosci wiejskiej" [Roma as "Our Own" and "the Other." The Perception of Gypsies by Rural Community]. *Lud* 78:357–375.

———. 1997. "Polityka oswiatowa wobec osiadlych Romów w Polsce. Wielokulturowosc jako wartosc" [Education Policy toward Settled Roma in Poland. Multiculturalism as a Value]. Pp. 246–256 in *U progu wielokulturowosci. Nowe oblicza spoleczenstwa polskiego* [At the Threshold of Multiculturalism. New Faces of Polish Society], edited by Marian Kempny, Alina Kapciak, and Slawomir Lodzinski. Warsaw: Oficyna Naukowa.

————. 1998. "Biedni w palacu—bogaci w chatynce. O biedzie i bogactwie Romów w Polsce" [Poor in a Palace—Rich in a Hut. Poverty and Wealth of Roma in Poland]. *Res Publica Nowa* 4(115):43–47.

Ochocki, Andrzej. 1997. "Skala ubóstwa rodzin w Polsce" [Range of Families' Poverty in Poland]. Pp. 126–134 in *Rodzina polska w okresie kryzysu i ozywienia gospodarczego (1990–1995)* [Polish Family in the Time of Crisis and Economic Boom], edited by W. Rakowski. Warsaw: PTD and IGS SGH.

Osinska, Katarzyna, and Anna Sliwinska. 1997. "Spolecznosci permanentnego ubóstwa" [Permanent Poverty Communities]. Pp. 139–147 in *Polskie badania nad mniejszosciami kulturowymi. Wybrane zagadnienia* [Polish Research on Cultural Minorities], edited by Grzegorz Babinski, Janusz Mucha, and Andrzej Sadowski. Bialystok: Filia UW.

Pelczynska–Nalecz, Katarzyna. 1998. "Polska na tle Czech i Slowacji: podstawowe wskazniki statystyczne" [Poland, Czech and Slovakia: Basic Statistical Indicators]. Pp. 389–392 in *Polacy '95. Aktorzy i klienci transformacji* [Poles '95. Actors and Clients of Transformation], edited by Wladyslaw Adamski. Warsaw: IFiS PAN.

Perepeczko, Barbara. 1994. "W strone normalnosci. Refleksje z badan nad prywatyzacja panstwowych gospodarstw rolnych" [Toward Normality. Remarks from Research on Privatization of the State Farms]. *Wies i Rolnictwo* 3–4 (84–85):70–77.

Polawski, Pawel. 1997a. "Kulturowe znaczenie underclass. Spór o sens terminu a polska transformacja" [Cultural Meaning of Underclass. Sense of the Term and Polish Transformation]. Pp. 99–116 in *Ofiary sukcesu. Zjawiska marginalizacji spolecznej w Polsce* [Victims of the Success. Social marginalization in Poland], edited by Kazimierz W.Frieske. Warsaw: IS UW.

————. 1997b. "Rodzina i instytucje w sferze ubóstwa. Procesy spolecznej marginalizacji" [Family and Institutions in the Sphere of Poverty. Processes of Social Marginalization]. Pp. 17–98 in *Kontrola spoleczna procesów marginalizacji* [Social Control of Marginalization Processes], edited by Jerzy Kwasniewski. Warsaw: Interart.

Poverty Indicators (in View of Household Budget Survey). 1997. Warsaw: GUS.

Radicová, Iveta and Michal Vesecka. 1998. "Slovakia Report." Paper presented at the Conference *Racialization and Feminization of Poverty in Central and Southern Europe,* Budapest, April 24–26.

Rajkiewicz, Antoni. 1993. "Minimum socjalne wobec procesów pauperyzacji" [Social Minimum and the Processes of Impoverishment]. Pp. 51–55 in *Ubóstwo jako problem polityki spolecznej* [Poverty as a Social Policy Problem], edited by Lucyna Frackiewicz. Katowice: Uniwersytet Slaski.

Reszke, Irena. 1995. "Bezrobocie kobiet—stereotypy i realia" [Unemployment of Women—Stereotypes and Reality]. Pp. 135–154 in *Co to znaczy byc kobieta w Polsce* [What Does it Mean to Be a Woman in Poland?], edited by Anna Titkow and Henryk Domanski. Warsaw: IFiS PAN.

Sakson, Andrzej. 1991. "Mniejszosci narodowe w Polsce ze szczególnym uwzglednieniem mniejszosci niemieckiej" [National Minorities in Poland: German Minority]. *Kultura i Spoleczenstwo* 4:185–203.

Sicinski, Andrzej. 1997. "O stosunku wspólczesnych Polaków do 'innych'" [Attitudes of Contemporary Poles toward "Others"]. Pp. 393–402 in *Elementy nowego ladu* [Elements of New Order], edited by Henryk Domanski and Andrzej Rychard. Warsaw: IFiS PAN.

Siemienska, Renata. 1990. "Poland." Pp. 261–265 in *Gender Inequality. A Comparative Study of Discrimination and Participation,* by Mino Vianello, Renata Siemienska, Natalia Damian, Eugen Lupri, Renato Coppi, Enzo D'Arcangelo, and Sergio Bolasco. London: Sage.

Staszewski, Wojciech. 1997. "Gdzie ja, sierota do sklepu?" [I, an Orphan, to a Shop?]. *Gazeta Wyborcza,* April 19–20.

Szalai, Julia, ed. 1995. *The Social History of Poverty in Central Europe. Working Papers.* Budapest: Max Weber Foundation.

Tarkowska, Elzbieta. 1996. "Unequal Distribution of Time: A New Dimension of Social Differentiation in Poland." *Polish Sociological Review* 2:163–174.

————. 1997. "Old and New Shapes of Rural Poverty in Poland: The Former State Farm Worker's Family." Pp. 44–57 in *Past and Present Poverty*, edited by Zuzana Kusa. Bratislava: Institute for Sociology and SPACE.

————. 1998. "Ubóstwo w bylych PGR-ach. W poszukiwaniu dawnych zróde nowej biedy" [Poverty in the Former State Farms. In Search of Past Sources of the New Poverty]. *Kultura i Spoleczenstwo* 2:91–104.

Tarkowska, Elzbieta, and Joanna Sikorska. 1998. "Social History of Poverty: Polish Experiences and Research Perspectives." *East Central Europ—L'Europe du Centre-Est* 20–23, parts 3–4 (1993–1996):171–188.

Thomas William I., and Florian Znaniecki. [1918]1958. *The Polish Peasant in Europe and America.* New York: Dover.

Toczyski, Witold, ed. 1991. *Natura i kwestia ubóstwa* [The Nature and the Question of Poverty]. Gdansk and Warsaw: Osrodck Badan Spolecznych.

Topinska, Irena. 1996. "Ubóstwo w Polsce na podstawie badan Banku Swiatowego" [Poverty in Poland according to the World Bank Studies]. Pp. 67–110 in *Polska bieda. Kryteria. Ocena. Przeciwdzialanie.* [Poland's Poverty. Criteria. Valuation. Counteracting], edited by Stanislawa Golinowska. Warsaw: IPiSS.

Tulli, Renata. 1978. *Jednoosobowe gospodarstwa domowe* [Single Households]. Warsaw: IFiS PAN.

Tymowski, Andrzej. 1973. *Minimum socjalne. Metodyka i próba okreslenia* [Social Minimum. Methodology and Attempt to Define]. Warsaw: PWN.

Warzywoda–Kruszynska, Wielislawa, and Jolanta Grotowska–Leder. 1996. *Wielkomiejska bieda w okresie transformacji (zasilkobiorcy pomocy spolecznej)* [Poverty of a Large City in the Period of Transformation (Recipients of Welfare)]. Lodz: IS UL.

————. 1998. "Concentration of Poverty in Polish Large City: The Example of Lódz." *East Central Europe—L'Europe du Centre-Est* 20–23, parts 3–4 (1993–1996):79–93.

Wciórka, Bogna. 1999. "Ludzie biedni w Polsce" [Poor People in Poland]. *Serwis Informacyjny CBOS* 2:84–116.

Wilkin, Jerzy. 1997. "Przeksztalcanie sektora PGR-ów w Polsce w opinii wladz lokalnych i mieszkanców 'osiedli pegeerowskich'" [Transformations of State Farms in Poland in View of Local Authorities and Inhabitants of "State Farms Settlements"]. Pp. 44–75 in *Ludzie i ziemia po upadku pegeerów. Analiza socjologiczna i ekonomiczna* [The People and the Land after a Collapse of the Former State Farms. Sociological and Economic Analyses], edited by Kazimierz Korab. Warsaw: SGGW.

————. 1998. "Przeksztalcanie panstwowych gospodarstw rolnych—procesy racjonalizacji i marginalizacji" [Transformations of State Farms—Rationalization and Marginalization Processes]. Pp. 43–55 in *Wielkoobszarowe gospodarstwa rolne, ich zaogi i nowi gospodarze* [Big Farms, Their Personnel and New Farmers], edited by Barbara Fedyszak–Radziejowska. Warsaw: IRWiR PAN.

Wilson, William Julius. 1991. "Studying Inner-City Social Dislocations: The Challenge of Public Agenda Research." *American Sociological Review* 56 (February):1–14.

Wnuk–Lipinski, Edmund. 1981. *Budzet czasu—struktura spoleczna—polityka spoleczna* [Time Budget—Social Structure—Social Policy]. Wroclaw: Ossolineum.

Wódz, Kazimiera. 1994. "Underclass w starych dzielnicach przemyslowych miast Górnego Slaska" [Underclass in Old Quarters of Industrial Towns in Upper Siłesia]. Pp. 193–198 in *Stare i nowe struktury spoleczne w Polsce* [Old and New Social Structures in Poland], edited by Irena Machaj and Józef Styk I. Lublin: UMCS.

Zaborowski, Wojciech. 1998. "Stara i nowa struktura spoleczna—aktorzy zmian" [Old and New Social Structure—Actors of Transformations]. Pp. 49–95 in *Polacy '95. Aktorzy i klienci transformacji* [Poles '95. Actors and Clients of Transformation], edited by Wladyslaw Adamski. Warsaw: IFiS PAN.

Zadrozynska, Anna. 1983. *Homo faber i homo ludens. Etnograficzny szkic o pracy w kulturach tradycyjnej i wspólczesnej* [Homo Faber and Homo Ludens. An Ethnographical Essay on Work in the Traditional and Contemporary Cultures]. Warsaw: PWN.

Zalewska, Danuta. 1994. "Sfera ubóstwa we Wroclawiu" [Sphere of Poverty in Wroclaw]. *Acta Universitatis Wratislaviensis* 1549: 50–54.

———. 1997. *Ubóstwo. Teorie, badania* [Poverty, Theory, Research]. Wroclaw: UWr.

5

The Social Construction of Romanian Poverty: The Impact of Ethnic and Gender Distinctions

Nándor L. Magyari, Enikö Magyari-Vincze, Livia Popescu, and Troian Rotariu

INTRODUCTION: THE ROMANIAN TRANSITION

The Romanian political situation prior to 1989 was somewhat different from the situation of other societies in the region. Similarly, unlike in other countries, the new regime, which came to power after December 1989, had little legitimacy. In order to solve these problems of legitimacy, early governments tended to adopt populist measures.

In communist Romania the distribution of power was exceptionally unequal. The political "class" (recruited on the basis of loyalty to the "ruling family") held absolute power, and as a result civil society was even weaker than elsewhere in the Soviet bloc. Individualistic values were not widely shared; most people expected that solutions to their problems would come from the state. The Romanian society was socially "homogenized," at least in terms of "material capital." Cultural capital remained a source of social differentiation and reproduction. However, unlike countries in the region where the "intelligentsia" within the party apparatus came to control a significant part of social activity, in Romania intellectuals played a more limited role. The Romanian Communist Party remained essentially a "workers' party." The leaders did not trust either social or technical intellectuals.

Romania at the end of the 1980s was a totalitarian regime. It was also an impoverished country. Its citizens had adapted to various forms of economic and political survival within the system, but they lacked social or economic initiative. It was a country with a political class made up of those who had come directly (or indirectly) from the "working class." This country was not ready for the changes that began in December 1989.

Not surprisingly, the "transition" in Romania is also slower. Due to the lack of skill and will of the country's leaders, the difficult transition period is prolonged.

ECONOMIC TRANSFORMATION, INEQUALITIES, AND POVERTY

Transition to the Market Economy

The oscillating reforms of the 1990–1996 governments have resulted in poor economic performance. In terms of gross domestic product (GDP) and the rate of inflation, Romania has constantly been behind the Visegrad countries (Hungary, the Czech Republic, and Poland). GDP declined between 1989 and 1993 and afterward recovered slowly, remaining at only 84.5% of the 1989 level in 1995 (its best postcommunist year) (Table 5.1). The acceleration of reform in 1997 has so far led to further decline in GDP (National Commission for Statistics 1997:1; 1998).

Table 5.1
The Annual Rate of GDP Real Change (%) (Year/Increase)

1990	1991	1992	1993	1994	1995	1996	1997	1998
-5.6	-12.9	-8.8	1.5	3.9	7.1	4.1	-6.6	-5.1

Source: National Commission of Statistics 1998.

The rate of inflation increased and peaked in 1992–1993 (256.1%). In 1994 it declined to 136.8% but increased again to 54.8% in 1997, to drop to 51.7% in 1998. Foreign debt kept growing after 1990, reaching 8 billion USD in 1997.

Privatization and the move toward markets were slow in Romania. Between 1992 and 1996, 41.0% of companies and 15.0% of former state capital stock were privatized. The majority (96.8%) of privatized companies were small or medium-size. The industrial giants were left out of the privatization. Private sector participation in GDP formation increased from 16.4% in 1990, to 52.0% in 1996 and then to 58% in 1997 (Radocea 1996; National Commission for Statistics 1997; Georgescu 1998). In 1996, 49.2% of the population was engaged in the private sector; 46.5% of them were self-employed (mostly individual farmers), 26.1% were unpaid family members, 22.6% were employees, and 4.8% were employers (National Commission for Statistics 1996a:56).

Romania was not seen as an attractive site for foreign investments. Foreign capital investment had reached only 2.57 billion USD (or 130 USD per capita) in July 1997 (Georgescu 1997). Whereas foreign investment increased in 1997, it began to decline again in 1998 due to increased political instability.

Illegal privatization is widespread and the informal economy keeps expanding. According to the Romanian Information Service, the "underground" or "black" economy produces about 40% of GDP. The Ministry of Labor and Social Protection estimates the "black" labor force to be 20% of the economically active population.

Land was privatized in 1991 (Popescu 1998). After 1990 the state housing stock was sold to tenants at the cost of the original construction and with favorable mortgage conditions. Very little housing now remains in the public sector, as both the state building industry and housing policy are minimal. Until 1999, public rents were frozen at the 1989 level (less than the price of a pack of cigarettes in 1997), while private rents reached a level that exceeds the average monthly earnings.

The decline in state industry and agriculture led to sizable unemployment after 1991. In 1991 unemployment was 3.0%; it grew to 8.4% in 1992, 10.4% in 1993, and 10.9% in 1994. Following a 1994 peak, unemployment decreased to 6.3% in 1996. The decline in official figures of unemployment between 1994 and 1996 cannot be interpreted as signs of economic recovery. Low unemployment during these years reflected a slowdown in the transition toward a market economy. When economic restructuring was resumed in 1997, a new increase in the unemployment rate followed: 8.8% in 1997 and 9.3% in May 1998. Unemployment varied significantly between regions throughout the period 1991–1997: eastern counties have a rate 1.5% higher than the national rate, while in Bucharest and some western counties unemployment is as low as half of the national rate (National Commission for Statistics, 1997:xix).

The number of people eligible for unemployment benefits decreased significantly. Between 1993 and 1996 the proportion of registered unemployed people eligible for benefits declined from 91.5%, to 72.0%. Such a trend indicates the rise of long-term unemployment (*Human Development Report in Romania* 1996:15).

The groups most severely impacted by unemployment are manual workers (who made up 75.9% of the unemployed in 1997) and people under 25 (44.1% of the unemployed in 1995). Women were consistently overrepresented among the unemployed between 1991 and 1996; 61.8% of the unemployed were women in 1991—this proportion declined to 54.1% in 1996 and finally to 48.6% in 1997. However, women continue to be a majority (53.3%) of the unemployed whose benefit eligibility has expired (*Human Development Report in Romania* 1996:15; National Commission for Statistics 1997:xix).

The Social Protection System

The welfare system has not changed radically since 1989. Yet, although its basic components have been maintained (a public health fund; old-age pension insurance; child-care allowance), and new ones have been added (unemployment benefit; social benefit), social security provision is far from adequate.

Child allowance became a universal benefit only in 1993. Before this, full-time employment in the state sector was the eligibility criterion. Since its extension, coverage has become available to the children of individual farmers, the unemployed, self-employed, and privately employed families, who had been excluded from the benefit provision both during the communist regime and during the first two postcommunist years. Eligibility for school-age children is still tied to school attendance. In 1996 a *supplementary child allowance* was introduced in order to alleviate the economic problems faced by families with more than one child.

The share of GDP allocated to child allowance declined from 2.7% in 1990, to 0.9% in 1994, to 0.7 % in 1995, and to 0.6% in 1996. The allowance was not adequately protected against inflation; thus, the allowance for one child represented 25.5% of its 1989 value in 1994, 28.8% in 1995–1996, and 65.0% in 1997 (UNICEF 1993; Zamfir 1997:22–31).

The insurance system, which has been in place since the 1970s, has two major parts: *State Social Insurance* and *Farmers' Social Insurance*. The State Social Insurance is based on a compulsory employer contribution. Starting with 1999, the contribution varies between 40% and 30% of the total wage. State Social Insurance provides benefits for a variety of situations, apart from old age, including temporary incapacity to work (due to accidents, illness, or maternity), infant care, and the need for rest or cure. Part of the pension scheme is a compulsory employee contribution (3% of gross wages) to the Supplementary Pension Fund.

Farmers' Social Insurance provisions cover the same range of situations as State Social Insurance, but the cash benefits are substantially different. The budget of Farmers' Social Insurance is based on small, compulsory contributions paid by agricultural employers and on the insured person's voluntary contribution (7% of declared monthly income).

Compensation for unemployment is paid through the *Unemployment Fund,* also part of the insurance-based system. Unemployment compensation is provided in the form of unemployment benefits for a period of 270 days. Following this, if still unemployed, a person is entitled to support allowance for another 18 months. Both unemployment benefits and support allowance have a workfare component and a means-tested element.

The Unemployment Fund also funds the professional integration allowance that is provided to noncontributors. Among the groups eligible for this allowance are drop-outs or graduates, at least 18 years old, who have no personal income sources that surpass half the national minimum wage and are unable to get employment within the 60 days after they leave school or graduate (*Human Development Report in Romania* 1996).

The "social safety nets," which were critical under the communist regime, became utterly inadequate during the transition to the market economy. Growing unemployment, falling wages and pensions, and other difficulties in coping with changes have caused a surge of poverty that none of the existing provisions were able to alleviate. Zamfir (1994:126) argued that, as the eligibility criteria for social aid are very restrictive (in terms of goods and ownership), the law would represent a "poverty trap" for the poor, who would be tempted to sell their property in order to receive the benefit. Over time the criteria have become more restrictive, and the workfare component of the scheme has been enhanced. The modest share of social expenditure and GDP allocated to social aid benefit (0.38% in 1996) resulted in limited coverage for people in real need. In 1996 the new government acknowledged that there were disparities in the coverage and (in the absence of an appropriate evaluation of the scheme) decided to extend it by 11% and adjust the amount of the benefit to the increase in the cost of living (*Romania libera* 1997). However, not only did its value remain very low, but important delays in the actual payment of the benefit became almost general since 1998.

A *National Solidarity Fund* was enacted in 1999, aimed at alleviating the poverty condition of people in extreme difficulty. The targeted recipients are either persons   excluded   from the existing social benefits (especially unemployed people who are not covered by the unemployment benefit) or those receiving benefits   below a specified level. The solidarity allowance will be provided to persons having an income below 50% of the minimum national wage and belonging to specific categories such as unemployed persons, families with dependent children, orphans or abandoned children, young adults who have been in residential care as orphan children, children attending school, disabled persons, and pensioners.

Among all Eastern European countries, Romania had a low, if not the lowest, allocation of GDP to social expenditures—14.2% in 1989. A slight increase in 1990 was followed by new cuts of up to 11.2% in 1993. Subsequent improvements in the proportion could not compensate for the decline in the GDP itself (Zamfir 1995:426; 1997:23).

Understanding Poverty

In postcommunist Romania the state continues to be the main employer. Workers in extractive industries, production of energy, petrol, and railway transport, and the communication industry are better off than in other sectors. Not only was the average wage in these sectors 20–50% higher than the national average, but the gap between the two has increased steadily since 1990. At the bottom of the salary hierarchy are workers in education, medical care, and personal social services. Here the average salary is 15–20% lower than the national average. The earnings differentiation in Romania today reinforces the pattern established during communist rule. "Productive," mainly manual, activities are privileged in comparison with "nonproductive," mainly nonmanual, ones. The only exception to this is the banking sector, where the average salary is now 248% of the national average (National Commission for Statistics 1996b, 1997; Popescu 1998).

After a general increase in 1990, real wages started to drop (Table 5.2).

Table 5.2
Index of Real Earnings—All Employees

Years	1991	′92	1993	1994	1995	1996
Increase reported on previous year (%)	-18.2	-12.7	-16.8	+0.1	+11.9	-13.7

The minimum wage has been continuously eroded. The minimum wage as a percentage of the average wage has dropped steadily, from 65.3% in 1989, to 30.1% in 1996 (a further decrease, to 24.5%, is the estimate for 1997) (Zamfir 1997:23).

Between 1990 and 1994 the real value of pensions dropped more steeply than the real value of wages (Table 5.3). In 1994 pensions were at 58.1% of their 1989 level, while the real value of the average wage was 62.4% of its 1989 level (Zamfir 1997:22). Despite an increase in the real value of supplementary pensions, the ratio of average pension/average wage oscillated. In 1990 the average pension was 45.4% of the average wage. After an important depreciation in 1992 (of 39.0%), the value of pensions began to increase, reaching 54.5% in 1994 and 50.5% in 1995 (Zamfir 1995:428; National Commission for Statistics 1996b:64).

Table 5.3
Income Dynamics (Average 1989 Income = 100%)

	1990	1991	1992	1993	1994	1995	1996	1997 (Mar.)
Net average wage	105	87.7	73.6	57.0	62.4	70.2	77.0	68.7
Net min. wage	-	-	-	-	33.4	33.9	35.6	25.8
Average pension	-	-	-	-	58.1	63.1	65.0	-
Family cash benefits	96.9	49.6	29.2	22.9	21.9	22.0	-	-

Source: Zamfir 1997: 22–24.

Whereas the inequality between average and minimum wages has increased, pensions have followed the opposite route. In fact, due to one specific policy, the adjustment and the compensation for the increase in the cost of living benefited the low-end pensioners disproportionately. The difference between the minimum and average decreased between 1990 and 1995, at which time the minimum pension reached a peak of 88.5% of the average pension (it had been only 53.5% in 1990). Thus, the majority of pensions (87%) are within +10% and -10% of the average pension (National Commission for Statistics 1997).

In 1995 the average unemployment benefit was 97.4% of the minimum (National Commission for Statistics, 1996b).

The negative effects of a decreasing real wage on household income have been somewhat compensated for by the increased role played by nonsalary income sources. In 1997 the average income of an employee household could be broken down as 78.1% monetary income and 21.9% food consumption from the household's own resources (National Commission for Statistics 1997:xxvii). Differences between types of household are important. While employers' households receive 2.7 times the average income, unemployed households manage only 71.1% of this average (National Commission for Statistics, 1996b:4).

Measuring Poverty

There is no official definition of poverty. Several attempts has been made to establish poverty thresholds, and indirect measures have been used to estimate the scale of the problem in the 1990–1997 period.

The main source of data on the structure and distribution of incomes and on patterns of consumption is the Family Budget Survey. In 1995 this was modified and became the Integrated Household Survey (IHS). These surveys chart self-declared incomes. The Family Budget Survey offers a relatively accurate picture of the general features of income distribution and consumption (Plesca and Rata 1996). Five categories of households are distinguished in the data: employees, employers, peasants, unemployed persons, and pensioners. The type of household is based on the self-declared occupational status of the household head (National Commission for Statistics 1996b).

Consumption expenditures are often considered an adequate approximation for a household's standard of living. A common approach to the study of changes in the extent of poverty is to focus on the structure of consumption, namely, on "food shares"—the share of expenditures devoted to foodstuffs. In the period 1990–1996 there was a considerable increase in expenditures on food as a proportion of total consumption expenditures. Table 5.4 shows the evolution of this proportion for three types of household: employees, peasants, and pensioners.

Table 5.4
The Evolution of Food Expenditures as a Percentage of Total Consumption Expenditures for Three Groups of Households: Employees, Peasants, and Pensioners

1990			1991			1992		
1	2	3	1	2	3	1	2	3
49.4	67	58.2	51.4	71.4	63.6	55.9	75.1	66.9

1993			1994			1995		
1	2	3	1	2	3	1	2	3
58	78.1	67.1	61	78.1	70.2	60.68	68	65

Note: 1 = Employees; 2 = Peasants; 3 = Pensioners.

Source: National Commission for Statistics (1991–1996).

The decrease of the food share, which started in 1995, continued in 1996. According to the survey that was carried out between July 1996 and June 1997, food expenditures were 57.8% of total expenditures in employee households (National Commission for Statistics 1997:xxvii).

Surveys show that in Romania an important proportion of food is self-produced. This became even more pronounced in the period 1992–1994 (National Commission for Statistics 1996b). The transition from a traditional subsistence economy to a modern market economy thus had not yet occurred (Popescu 1998).

World Bank estimates of the level of *absolute poverty* in Romania are made using both the caloric method and the food share method. The World Bank charts a slight increase in absolute poverty between 1995 (when 19.4% of the population was "very poor," and 25% were "poor") and 1996 (when the figures were 19.6% and 25.4%, respectively). In both years rural poverty was found to occur with greater frequency. In 1995, 24.1% of the rural population was very poor, and 30.3% was poor (United Nations Development Program 1997: 58).

The Research Institute for the Quality of Life has established a basket of goods (food and nonfood) and of services considered necessary for the preservation of health and for social participation. It calculates the poverty threshold per household and uses two types of households—households with four members (two adults and two children under 14) and households with two members above 60 years old—to calculate the goods and services basket and build up an equivalence scale. Two versions of the poverty threshold are presented: (1) *the decent minimum—DM* (equal to the monthly income corresponding to the whole basket of goods) and (2) *the subsistence minimum— SM* (the food component of the basket diminished by 20%) (Zamfir 1995a).

A third poverty threshold has also been used. Known as the *Ministry of Labor and Social Protection Minimum—Official Minimum,* this is the entitlement level for social aid benefit. It catalogs a situation of severe poverty or misery. The ratios between these three poverty levels—all of which rely on a form of the "normative method" of calculating poverty—for the standard family (two adults and two children) are as follows: SM = 59.9% of the DM; Official Minimum = 31.5% of the DM; Official Minimum = 52.6% of the SM (Zamfir 1995a:16–19). The Research Institute for Quality of Life estimated that in 1994 absolute poverty affected 25% of the households in the sample and 27% of the individuals (Zamfir 1995a:21).

Estimates of the incidence of poverty vary to some extent depending on the methodology adopted. Table 5.5 gives recent evaluation of the literature.

Table 5.5
Percentage of Households and Individuals Suffering from Absolute Poverty as Determined by Different Poverty Lines

World Bank *Poverty level*			
Very poor		Poor	
Household	Individual	Household	Individual
13.9	19.4	18.4	25.0
Research Institute for Quality of Life *Poverty level*			
Subsistence		Decent	
Household	Individual	Household	Individual
21.5	27.3	43.4	50.0

Source: United Nations Development Program 1997:59–60.

An attempt to capture changes in inequality and patterns of *relative poverty* using data provided by the Family Budget Survey can be found in *Welfare in Romania during Transition: Analysis of Family Budget Survey Data* (1989, 1992, 1993) (Plesca and Rata 1996). The authors use different computational methods and assess their respective strengths in accounting for either social inequality or poverty.

Relative poverty increased between 1989 and 1992 but decreased between 1992 and 1993 (Plesca and Rata 1997:16–19). The ratio of the income of the poorest 10% to the richest 10% changed significantly, an indicator of increased social polarization between 1989 and 1993 (the ratio was 1:6.71 in 1989, 1:7.87 in 1992, and 1:8.49 in 1993). This suggests that the poor become even poorer, while the rich become even richer (Plesca and Rata, 1997:12).

The UNICEF Regional Monitoring Report makes estimations using the Organization for Economic Cooperation and Development (OECD) method, applied to the 1989 average wage. The data show a decline in the incidence of poverty in 1990 and a steady increase after this. If the poverty line is considered to be 45% of the 1989 average wage, the percentage of the population living in poverty decreased from 27% in 1989, to 18% in 1990 and, following the start of economic reform in 1991, rose continuously to 51.1% in 1992 (UNICEF 1993:8).

Methods based on average income (or wage) are useful but not considered relevant for the situation in Romania (Zamfir 1995a).

In 1995 the National Commission for Statistics developed a new approach for measuring relative poverty. The poverty threshold is taken as 60% of average adult expenditures. The relative poverty rate produced by this method is presented in Table 5.6.

Table 5.6
The Relative Poverty Rate (% of the Sample) Estimated by the National Commission for Statistics

	Household	Individual
1995	17.7	25.2
1996	16.3	23.4

Source: United Nations Development Program 1997:61.

The overall deterioration in living standards also has an important subjective dimension. Categories that have been used in the opinion polls are not exactly equivalent to those used in the normative approach, but some comparisons can be made.

Since 1994, surveys documenting opinions on poverty have been carried out on a regular (quarterly) basis by independent teams. Over this period perceptions about living standards have been relatively stable (Metro Media Transylvania 1999).

The 1996 *Human Development Report* deals with the issue of poverty under the section "Social Equity and Stability. Limiting Social Tensions." The authors took into consideration the "perception of standard of living" using a scale that ranged from poverty (1) to wealth (10). The average level perceived was located at 4.25 on the scale, indicating that the majority of respondents perceive their own conditions as closer to poverty than wealth (*Human Development Report in Romania* 1996:46).

The poverty risk of a household is highly dependent on occupational status. The most at-risk groups are people without occupational skills (who are also not eligible for unemployment benefits), unemployed people, housewives, children (both preschool and school age), and peasants (Table 5.7).

Table 5.7
The Incidence of Poverty (Percent Impoverishment According to Various Definitions of Poverty) in Different Groups of the Population, 1994

	Below Official Minimum	Between Official Min. & SM	Between SM and DM	Total below DM
Total population	**11.8**	**27.5**	**38.9**	**78.2**
Employers	1.7	10.2	23.7	35.6
Pensioners	5.8	21.9	40.2	67.9
Employees	4.1	24.4	45.0	73.5
Peasants	20.9	21.3	39.7	81.9
Students	13.4	35.1	36.0	84.5
Preschool children	19.3	34.3	33.7	87.3
Housewives	20.3	35.9	31.4	87.6
Unemployed people	21.0	39.1	30.5	90.6
Without occupation	40.1	31.0	21.9	93.0
Urban	6.3	31.0	43.3	80.6
Rural	13.1	18.3	35.1	66.5
General/vocational educ.	14.8	32.6	35.1	82.5
Secondary/post-secondary educ.	6.4	27.1	41.7	75.2
High school/university educ.	1.6	13.4	49.9	64.9
Couple without children	5.8	12.1	38.2	56.1
Couple with one child	7.6	22.8	47.2	77.6
Couple with two children	6.9	35.5	42.7	85.1
Couple with three or more children	30.2	39.5	22.5	92.2
Single family with one child	11.1	40.7	33.0	84.8
Single family with two children	40.0	36.0	16.0	90.0

Source: Zamfir 1995a:57–61.

Can research data provide the empirical criteria for differentiating "new" poverty from "old" poverty? The answer is rather hypothetical since there are no reliable data from the communist period.

During the final 10–15 years of the communist regime standards of living worsened, and the situation of some low-income groups, affected by hidden unemployment and too many children, was particularly serious. According to

1989 macroindicators, Romania was behind most other Central and Eastern European countries (National Commission for Statistics 1996b; Zamfir 1997:98). Subsequently, in the aftermath of the revolution, the country was facing serious problems. These economic conditions partially explain the first post-totalitarian government's so-called reparable policy, decided in 1990, which called for a decrease in the prices for several consumption goods, the creation of new jobs, an increase in social expenditures, and so on. However, the postponement of structural economic change has been rewarding only for the powerful and unionized sectors of the labor force in the short term and has prevented none of the "evils" associated with "shock therapy" transition: hyperinflation, unemployment, the increased vulnerability of weaker social groups, and an overall deterioration in the standard of living (Popescu 1998).

The acceleration of reforms, which tentatively began in 1997, brought about a decline in the standard of living in comparison with 1996. The values of the 1997 and 1998 indicators show a deterioration of both the economic performance and the standard of living, but the consequences of this in terms of different types and levels of poverty have not yet been rigorously evaluated.

THE ROMA (GYPSY) PEOPLE AND POVERTY IN ROMANIA

Without concrete and reliable data about the size of Roma poverty, the discussion on the relation between poverty and ethnicity may appear risky at least.

Ethnicity and the social system are interrelated aspects of reality (Barth 1969: 10, 1996). According to some analysts, nearly 80% of the Roma population belong to the poor or the very poor. We believe that Roma poverty is connected or related to the "culture of poverty" (Lewis 1969). In terms of social anthropology, poverty is inherited generation by generation as a part of socialization and results in cultural divergence/differentiation that links the specific ethnic features of the Roma with their social consciousness. The historical location of Roma among the lower classes led to an identification of Roma lifestyle, culture, and behavior with the culture of poverty. This process lasted from slavery until 1856, 500 years until the formation of the present urban Roma underclass. The social institutions of Roma slavery are characteristic of the Romanian principalities only outside the Carpathians (Moldavia, Tara Romaneasca), not of the historical Transylvania. In the regions where there was Roma slavery it was so typical that until not long ago the word "Roma" (*tzigan* in Romanian) was synonymous in common language with the word "slave" (*rob* in Romanian).

Because of the geographical dispersion of the Roma population, case studies are very important.

Typical Roma Poverty? What Kind of Underclass Exists in Romania?

We would like to reiterate what Gans (1996:151) wrote about the terminology, "underclass": "Underclass and undercaste are umbrella terms, and the umbrella is open to anyone who wishes to place new meanings, or a variety of stereotypes, accusations and stigma under it." We suggest that the postcommunist underclass differs somewhat in its history, scope, and nature from the new urban poor of the West (especially the United States). We strongly believe that in Bucharest and in other "big cities" there are groups that, after losing their social functions, not only became redundant but also failed to integrate over the long run. The underclass made by socialism has many similarities to the one established in the West, but also some differences. For now, its peculiarities may be accessible only through our impressions and field experience and only in a hypothetical way.

Undoubtedly, in Romania a relatively large underclass is in formation. There are increasing numbers of individuals and groups whose sociological traits may be described in the following manner:

- urban inhabitants who are members of what we call "pre-urban" (Bíró, Bodó, and Magyari 1991:71) families
- unskilled or low-skilled workers who were made redundant on a massive scale during the transformation process
- rootless people who immigrate to the cities and settle in housing estates because they have no place in the rural work distribution system, especially after the liquidation of agricultural cooperatives. It is almost certain that the Roma are among this group and are overrepresented among the urban poor, becoming a permanent part of the underclass in formation. However, there are no data on the extent of this process.

The American underclass (and the ethnic groups that constitute it) fell out of the labor market. They were marginalized after being left out or losing position in a situation of market competition. This did not occur in Romania since the rules governing the new market mechanisms are not yet developed, and the parameters of competition are undefined, and therefore it is impossible to be "left out." If the "underclass" generally means that groups of people are for their lifetimes or for more than one generation living in a situation close to absolute poverty and are isolated in social and cultural (and sometimes even in spatial) ghettos, then in our case the definition is not very useful.

Linking the problems facing the Roma and the phenomenon of poverty is suggestive of a social-political approach. It suggests that the Roma issue should first mean social and political responsibilities and tasks for the government, local administration, and the civil society. This would mean additional burdens for the present government, which, apparently, it is not ready to accept. Any possibility of aid or social benefit being given to the Roma brings unpopularity to politicians. Negative attitudes toward the Roma mean that aid for them is generally perceived as positive discrimination, and hence it becomes a cause of tension and conflict.

Second, the Romanian political elite in the period after the change of regime almost constantly builds on nationalist and ethnocentric discourse, on a discourse of late nation-building, and on the development of the Romanian national consciousness and imagined community. In answer or counterreaction to this, minorities are also involved in discourses about identity and formulate all their problems in such terms (especially the Hungarians—the policy of the Democratic Alliance of Hungarians in Romania is one example of this type of formulation). Thus, the Roma "political entrepreneurs" apply the same type of discourse to their needs to create political capital. This means that, in most cases, they do not refer to poverty, relative deprivation, or marginalization but to human, cultural, and historical rights and satisfactions, to the correction of ethnic grievances and the meeting of expectations. Third, the multiethnic and multicultural situation in Romania changes the perception of the Roma problem. It is almost impossible to view the Roma issue as a "purely" social challenge while considering the Hungarian issue in terms of minority/national/ cultural/legal spheres of authority! Obviously, the Roma issue in Romania is also a Romanian issue, and a Hungarian issue.

In the period following the 1989 change of regime the differences between social strata became more pronounced, meaning that rapid stratification began. However, we believe that this process was quickly contained, and, as a result of the pauperization that occurred after the first two or three years of the 1990s, it has slowed down. Unstable economic empires are in decline, many such empires are going bankrupt or have become entangled in corruption scandals, and the generalization of poverty is wiping away differences between social classes and strata.

Many political analysts are talking about the "import" of a Russian or South American model of Peronism (see the recent discussion by Brucan 1998:13–18). Brucan gives the following figures for the size of the middle class in Eastern European countries: in the Czech Republic, 30% of the population; in Slovakia, 25%; in Hungary, 20–25%; in Poland, 15%; in Romania and Bulgaria, 5%; and in Albania and Russia, 1%. Brucan considers this form of marketization process and the social developments involved in it "the new Russian way of class-development." It is important to note that this form of class development differs from earlier Western development in its absence of a middle class (and of everything linked to this class, such as a particular economic structure, a free market, a democratic and liberal value system, pluralistic political options, the stratification of society and particular foreign polities, etc.). Obviously, these theoretical ideas are no more than hypotheses, but the diffuse political attitudes observable in postsocialist Romania and the agenda of the native political class suggest that it is very reasonable to think seriously about the fit of this model to the particularities of Romanian development.

Ethnic and Identity Policies after 1989

In the years after 1989, ethnic segregation has become rather common; it affects others besides the Roma, yet they have been the most negatively affected by it.

The "newly created segregation" of the Romanian Roma is forced, built on Roma marginalization, experiences of discrimination, and their rejection from the majority society. Their segregation leads them to escape into an old lifestyle, with its language, behavior, and occupations, much of which was long forgotten. Losers in recent reforms, they are put under (sometimes even physical) pressure and withdraw into an "old" state of separation. This is the case regardless of the "ethnic renaissance" of a very small Roma elite in the field of politics (the most effective speaker for the ethnic emancipation of Romas is Nicolae Gheorghe; see his report, written in cooperation with Jean-Pierre Liegeois, *Roma/Gypsies: A European Minority* [Liegeois and Gheorghe 1995:40]). The present reconstruction of Roma culture is mainly a "cultural response to constraints and limited opportunities that have evolved over time" (Wilson 1996:xviii). The "myths of marginality" and the knowledge and feeling of exclusion, have, for centuries, been components of the Roma cultural response. Thus, they continually reproduce their own segregation and exclusion, at the same time (perhaps) producing a Roma underclass or even undercaste. This process is emphasized by the spatial segregation of the Roma. There has been a slow creation of a "Roma line" (isolating Roma in rural areas) and of Roma estates (or ghettos) in cities.

There are an insignificant number of other minorities in Romania. The once-strong German (Saxon and Swabian) community has almost entirely emigrated; only the (very) old members of the community remain. Their presence is now that of a "folklore ethnic group" with political representation and cultural customs.

What Happened and Is Now Happening to Ethnic Groups, Especially the Roma?

It is a paradox that socialist conditions in Romania proved relatively advantageous to the Roma. Full employment, industrialization, socialist urbanization, the housing policy, "free" health care, and mass education all worked to incorporate the Roma more fully in society. This process—the history of the Roma from slavery until the present day—is characterized by Nicolae Gheorghe as a slow, but steady, process of acculturation, during which (among other changes) the original Roma culture has been reduced and the language has been lost (N. Gheorghe 1990:32).

In Romania following the fall of the socialist regime (and especially the downsizing of industrial giants) the phenomenon of "re-agriculturalization" (meaning a slight increase in the number of those employed in agriculture) is observable (Table 5.8).

The first generation of the urban "rootless" have moved back to rural areas and perform agricultural activities with "premodern" tools on small pieces of land, what they obtained from the land reform. This is a temporary solution, adopted for lack of a better one. The escape to older lifestyles, occupations, and family and social structures also characterizes the lives of urban Roma over the last few years. While the processes of "reruralization" and "renomadization" are observable among the Roma, we know little about the extent of these processes because currently extant empirical examples primarily focus on Roma families experiencing forcible expulsion, impoverishment, and then aimless, nomadic lives. There are data describing Roma immigration to Western Europe (mainly West Germany) and their expulsion, but again they are descriptive of only a small percentage of the Roma who have been forced to return to a "premodern" (or more precisely, "presocialist") way of life. Readoption of a nomadic lifestyle after being driven out of cities and into rural suburbs is clearly visible in studies of Roma repopulation of German Saxon villages and the transformation of these villages into "ghettolike" places.

Table 5.8
Number of Employees in Agriculture, 1990–1996

	1990	1991	1992	1993	1994	1995	1996
Number - (1000 Persons)	3,055	3,116	3,362	3,567	3,561	3,189	4,037
% of Total Employed	28.1%	28.8%	32.1%	35.3%	35.5%	33.5%	37.1%

Prior to 1989 the rural Roma population was employed by agricultural cooperatives in animal husbandry. The Roma were almost completely left out of the land distribution that resulted from the liquidation of agricultural cooperatives and application of the land law. This population was therefore unexpectedly "superfluous" and unemployed.

The "socialist-type" resolution of the specific problems of the Roma papered over the cracks; the apparent economic, cultural, and social integration was actually only "marginal integration." Most Roma are not dissimilar from the several million Romanians who were relocated into cities and transformed into a "lumpen proletariat" during the 1960s and 1970s (thus increasing the preurban population living in the socialist cities and subsistent on salaries, wages, unemployment benefits and social security). A clear sign of the marginal integration of this group or stratum of new city dwellers is that small alterations quickly highlight their vulnerability; the smallest economic and social changes disintegrate, and cause extreme deprivation for, the formerly "invisible" urban Roma population. This process has occurred to a greater extent among the Roma than among members of the majority group or other minorities (Hungarians, Germans, etc.). The first to be made redundant in industry are unskilled workers and the Roma; see Chelcea (1995:125–130); Zamfir and Zamfir (1993); or other surveys detailing attitudes toward Roma.

Public Attitudes Toward the Roma: Evidence from Survey Data

Only a few sociological surveys seriously focus on the form and intensity of public attitudes toward the Roma. Besides a few nationwide pieces of research and one or two regional surveys, this field has been dominated by local case studies. This is probably related to an issue to which we will return, that there exists a specific, Romanian, service-favoring "science policy."

In 1992 the CURS (Center for Urban and Regional Sociology) conducted two surveys (in May and August) in which respondents were asked questions about the Roma issue. The survey found that the great majority of the population has strong negative feelings about Roma. This situation is persistent; in

December 1997 the CURS repeated its survey and found that in the period since the last survey public perception of Roma had hardly improved. The results of this survey are presented in Table 5.9.

Table 5.9
Public Attitudes Toward the Roma (% of Respondents)

Institute/Date	No Answer	Very Negative	Negative	Positive	Very Positive
CURS 1992	5	40	34	19	2
CURS 1997	6	67		27	

Most Roma organizations talk even about the preceeding (along with a few other movements directed against the Roma) as a *"pogrom."* However, Roma-related interethnic conflicts are analyzed differently by those involved in them, the authorities, and "official" authors. These people talk about lifestyle conflicts, on the one hand, or ethnic conflict and tensions as a social issue, on the other.

"Lifestyle Conflicts"

The Hadrév/Hadareni case study proved that Etienne Balibar was right: the lifestyles and traditions characteristic of underdeveloped cultures are incompatible with the modern, civilized lifestyle of Romanian rural communities (M. Băcanu 1996:185). In other cases ethnic prejudices and social differences are simply seen to arise out of antipathy toward other ethnic groups' lifestyles. There is an assumed incompatibility between the culture and lifestyle of "the hard-working, modest, patient, welcoming. . . . etc." Romanians and the culture and lifestyle of the "criminal, lazy, aggressive. . . .etc." Roma.

"Social Conflicts, Yes; Ethnic Conflicts, No!"

Research findings do not fully substantiate attempts to give an ethnological explanation to conflicts in Transylvania (in March 1990 there was a violent conflict in Targu–Mures between Romanians and Hungarians) or to violent altercations involving Roma groups (Kogalniceanu, Bolintin, Ogrezeni, and Hadrev/Hadareni in September 1993). Hence, we cannot talk about a mass social space and even less about Romanian ethnic space in treatments of ethnocentrism. Marian Preda writes, in her analysis of the Roma–Romanian conflict in the village of Kogalniceanu, that "the conflict had a purely selective character, the target was not the ethnic group as such, but certain smaller ethnic concentrations which were not defined using ethnic criteria" (Preda 1993: 200).

Interethnic Conflicts

These conflicts involving Roma are described by participants as lifestyle conflicts, echoing the opinions of "official" analysts. Differentiating social from ethnic-cultural issues is, however, basic to the work of those formulating the Roma issue from a political, civil, legal, and moral perspective. Zamfir and Zamfir (1993:19) argue that in Romania "confusion between the ethnic and social dimensions, often together with ignorance/disregard toward social traits, leads to an inadequate definition of the nature of the situation, therefore having serious consequences for the identification of solutions."

The Number of Roma in Romania

There is a consensus that census data always give a minimum tally of the number of Roma in Romania. While censuses are based on self-identification, there are several good reasons for Roma not to identify as such. This means that we have no trustworthy data on the "real number" of the Roma population. Discovery of the exact size of the Roma population is a difficult task because this is both a question of definition and methodology and a question of (social and identity) policy. Table 5.10 gives census figures for the size of the Roma population.

Table 5.10

Size of the Roma (Gypsy) Population According to Romanian Population Censuses over the Twentieth Century

	1930	1956	1966	1977	1992
Number	242,656	104,216	64,197	227,398	409,723
Percent of inhabitants	1.7%	0.6%	0.34%	1.05%	1.8%

In 1992, the year of the national census, the ICCV (Research Institute for Quality of Life), led by Catalin Zamfir, conducted an extended survey of the Roma issue (see Zamfir and Zamfir [1993]). The survey was administered to a representative sample of 1,804 families. It attempted to estimate the size and relative weight of the Roma population. This survey considers not only official and informal self-identification in attempting to classify the Roma population but also "hetero-identifications." It should be mentioned here that ethnic affiliation is inherently based on "evaluative" opinions, attempting (for whatever reason) to create a Roma social strata. The authors of the survey conclude that "we can estimate, on the basis of the various data available to us, that the Romany population, characterized in different degrees by traditional ways of life, or by ways of life close to their traditions, is at present approximately: 1,000,000—that is 4.6% of the total population" (Zamfir and Zamfir 1993:206).

Projection of the Number of Roma in Romania

Vasile Ghetău (1996) makes a projection of the number of Gypsies in Romania, basing his study on the corresponding data from the 1992 ICCV research. This projection is made by starting with an estimate that takes into consideration both the 1992 official census (which says that there are 409,723 Roma people) and the figure of 2.5 million, found in the statements of some Roma leaders. It results in the figure of 1.5 million (a second version), situated somewhere between the two. However, this projection is an attempt to estimate the number and percentage share of the Roma population over a period that is long-term (1992–2025). This leaves open the question of what year's demographic data are used by the author.

Table 5.11
Fertility (Live Births per 1,000 Women) in Different Ethnic Groups, 1992

Age/Cohort	Total	Romanians	Hungarians	Roma/Gypsies
15–49	1,467	1,452	1,418	2,449
15–19	67	60	57	362
20–24	647	632	582	1,607
25–29	1,513	1,488	1,428	3,001
30–34	1,967	1,942	1,883	3,744
35–39	2,140	2,119	2,052	4,002
40–44	2,287	2,274	2,172	4,035
45–49	2,343	2,348	2,136	3,873

To make a population estimate for the Roma, it is important to know the mortality rates for different ethnic groups, but these data are not available. In 1994 Romanian life expectancy at birth was (A) 65.5 years for men and (B) 73.1 years for women. Ghetău bases his calculations on these national findings and on Roma mortality rates, estimated to be 5 years shorter than the national averages; therefore, (C) life expectancy for Roma men = 60.5 years, and (D) life expectancy for Roma women = 68.1 years. Ghetău's projection does not take into account the external migration rate of the Roma population, as we also do not have reliable data about this. Ghetău's results are summarized in Table 5.12.

We can compare the preceding data with less "scientific" projections. Roma sociologist and human rights politician Nicolae Gheorghe estimates the number of Roma in Romania to be between 1,800,000 and 2,500,000 (Liegeois and Gheorghe 1995:42).

QUESTIONING THE "FEMINIZATION OF POVERTY"

Because of the shortcomings of empirical—sociological and anthropological—research on the condition of women and on the gendered aspects of poverty in Romania, we must stress the preliminary nature of this chapter. Accordingly, our endeavor in the following paragraphs is, first, the elaboration of a theoretical/methodological framework that will be useful in future social and cultural empirical research and, second, the review of some interpretations of the socialist legacy and of the challenges of postsocialist transformations aiming to reconstruct the formation of the gender order from Romania.

Table 5.12

Romanian Inhabitants According to Census from 1992 by Nationality and the Conditional Projection for 2025

First Variant: 1992 Roma population = 1,000,000 (1,000s people)					
	Total	Romanians	Hungarians	Roma	Other
1992	22,810.0	19,851.0	1,583.6	1,000.0	375.4
2025 1. B.	20,427.7	17,271.9	1,225.8	1,644.3	285.7
2025 1. D.	20,348.0	17,271.9	1,225.8	1,564.6	285.7
Second Variant: 1992 Roma population = 1,500,000 (1,000s people)					
1992	22,810.0	19,385.5	1,549.1	1,500.0	375.4
2025 2. B.	20,644.4	16,705.5	1,186.7	2,466.5	285.7
2025 2. D.	20,524.7	16,705.5	1,186.7	2,346.8	285.7

The Present State of Research into the Condition of Women by Romanian Social Sciences

Existing statistics treat only some phenomena by sex, such as the country's population, the internal migration due to permanent residence change, the structure of employment, the sectors of the national economy, and the registered unemployed. But we are without data on issues like family income by race, sex, and household status; gender differences in rates of poverty; and proportion (in the population and in poverty) of female-headed households and of single-mother households.

Turning our attention to the local *qualitative investigations*, we may observe that these are dominated by some militant and some philosophical, historical, and media studies. These conceptualize women's problems through themes such as reproductive rights and health, sexual education, women's sexual life, abortion, sexual minorities, social equity, power distribution and participation, the presence of women in politics, the negative attitude toward feminism among women and men, the Romanian historiography on male and female identities, and the image of femininity in the media (see, e.g., Babeøi 1996; Bãban and David 1995; Bucur 1996, 1997; Constantinescu 1997; Manolescu 1996; Miroiu 1994; 1995; 1996; 1997; Nicolaescu 1996; Popescu 1997). These categories have become the main entry points into what might be called in Romania "women's studies," a new and hardly established discipline in this country.

Conceptualizing the Feminization of Poverty in the Context of Broader Social Inequalities

Following the proposal presented in Chapter 1 in this volume, we discuss the feminization of poverty in the context of substantially *increasing inequality and poverty* during the Central and East European postcommunist transition. We treat the social construction of poverty, emphasizing that it is not only an economic process but also a classificatory struggle around positions in the new social and cultural order (Chapter 1 in this volume). Our starting point is the hypothesis that in the processes of postcommunist social and economic differentiation, gender (as well as ethnicity) is used as an instrument in the construction of distinctions between the poor, not-so-poor, and rich and to legitimate newly established hierarchies. Specifically in terms of gender, we hope that the conclusion of the proposed research project will bring answers to the following types of questions. To what extent is poverty feminized (or, is there a gender gap in the newly emergent poverty)? Is feminization an important aspect in explaining the peculiarities of postcommunist poverty? Which characteristics of the feminization of poverty can be attributed to the postcommunist reforms, and which, to the communist heritage? How do racialization and feminization interact in the classificatory struggle around the definition of poverty? Whether discussing the use of ethnic and/or gender identities in the construction of poverty, one has to bear in mind the economic and political mechanisms through which the postcommunist order has emerged (and produced certain social inequalities) but also the ways and terms in which different social groups and individuals are experiencing their new conditions and the rearranged social hierarchies.

We conceive *social stratification* as one form of a more general phenomenon, social differentiation, that "emerges prominently once a society achieves a degree of economic surplus, which is translated into prestige and power and is transmitted intergenerationally" (Rossides 1997:11). Social stratification is a matter of power because it involves the process by which particular rights, duties, and attributes are ascribed to some members of a society in order to assign them to certain social positions.

With regard to *gender stratification*, several studies have found that sex (as well as age and kinship) was used as a classificatory criterion even in "simple" societies and that the differentiation of social tasks on this basis led to certain forms of inequality (Rossides 1997:11–12). If social stratification is the process whereby groups or individuals in a society are located in a hierarchical arrangement, then gender stratification is nothing else than the hierarchical distribution by gender of society's economic and social resources (Andersen· 1997:109). Related to the issue of gendered social stratification are also the analyses of "gender segregation" (the phenomenon whereby women and men are situated in different occupational categories and/or jobs) and of "sexual discrimination," understood as an institutionalized process whereby women are disadvantaged on the basis of their presumed "natural" traits (see Andersen 1997:114–124).

A concern with the reconstruction of the social and cultural order after the collapse of socialism and with the emergence, formation, and consolidation of new inequalities and systems of oppression makes it necessary to interpret *how race, class, and gender interact* in these processes, how they affect the experiences of all groups (women and men of different ethnicities and classes), their opportunities and chances, and their abilities to control available social and economic resources. Following Linda Lindsey, we contend that the goal is to understand how gender, race, and class as social categories simultaneously work together, how power relations construct difference, and how the multitude of forms of oppression affect, and are affected by, diversity of all kinds (see Lindsey 1997:10–11). In whatever way class, race, and ethnicity interact, people may experience their social identity differently in particular contexts, for example, more in the terms of class than of race or gender, or vice versa. Therefore, as Harriet Bradley points out, a very flexible approach is needed to cope with the complexities of social divisions (see Bradley 1996). We would like to add that the approach adopted has to include an awareness of the political and cultural dynamics underlying the perception of people's complex social identities and be sensitive to the diverse social cleavages conveyed by different terms.

The Gender Perspective and Gender Regimes

In introducing the *gender perspective* to the discussion of poverty, we have to be aware of its theoretical, methodological, and critical potentials and limits. While we question the ways gender is used in the classificatory struggles around rich and poor, it is important not to reify gender differences but to consider them, in turn, as constructed by certain processes in which the meanings and significance of gender are created. As Nancy Chodorow stresses (1995:48), "It is crucial for us feminists to recognize that the ideologies of difference which define us as women and as men, as well as inequality itself, are produced, socially, psychologically, and culturally, by people living in and creating their social, psychological, and cultural worlds."

A *gender analysis* of poverty views women and men in terms of their culturally constructed social roles and compares women and men, rather than looking at women as an isolated group. Central to this discussion is the task of deconstructing the homogeneous perspective of women and identifying the differences within in order to explain how women's poverty functions and how it is experienced by them. Thus, links between different types of identities should be deconstructed, and an attempt has to be made to understand the phenomena (at either an individual or a collective level) that are located at the crossroads of different subjectivities. Among others, a gender analysis should investigate how gender relations are a class phenomenon but are also power relations in their own right. Therefore, it is important to differentiate between inequalities to which men and women are both subject and inequalities that pertain only to women—or only to men (cf. Rossides 1997:17).

The investigation of poverty and social inequality through the perspective of gender means questioning the *gender regime(s)* of a society. In the view of R. W. Connell, the gender regime is the state of play in gender relations in a given institution. Gender relations are present in all types of institutions; however, family and kinship have been, until now, studied most as the bearers of gender and sexuality. The analysis of a gender regime has to take a closer look at the division of labor, power structure, and structure of cathexis in these institutions, as well as the relationship between gender regimes in different institutions. Connell illustrates how the domestic gender regime (that assigns most child care and housework to the wife-and-mother) and the labor market gender regime (that offers low-paid, low-status, part-time jobs to married women) support each other. So it happens that "this pattern of recruitment is justified by employers on the grounds that married women only want part-time work because of their domestic responsibilities and only need low pay because theirs is a 'second wage,'" while at the same time "at home the much heavier domestic work of women is justified by husbands because their wives can only get part-time jobs" (Connell 1995:38).

The Condition of Women in Romania in the Light of the Legacies of Socialism

Many research results on *the general condition of women in Romania* may be useful in interpreting (1) the links between the economic, social, political, and cultural aspects of women in poverty and (2) the cultural categories through which women's positions are defined and naturalized in the public and private sphere.

First, we very briefly mention some of the characteristics of women's economic condition *before socialism*. As Doina Pasca Harsanyi (1993), among others, stresses, Romania was a rural country before becoming a member of the socialist bloc in that, in 1938, 80% of the working population was employed in agriculture and patriarchal practices. The picture, in terms of numbers, changed a lot during socialism, and by 1989 only about 28% of the labor force worked in agriculture, although 46.2% of the population still lived in the countryside. Thus, the new problems faced by women were tied to the development of a type of agrarian small town, not the complete urbanization of villages (see Pasca Harsanyi 1995).

The interwar period also saw the appearance of feminist movements in Romania, especially among the aristocratic and upper-class, Westernized elite. These movements were committed to obtaining legislative improvements in women's social protection and their right to vote (this was a period when the level of women's education and their involvement in certain public domains were beginning to grow; see Arbore 1912; Cancea 1976; Catargi 1927; Dumbrava 1912; Stratilescu 1911). However, at this time, the proportion of economically dependent women in the population was huge, and cases of an independent female were very rare exceptions.

In *rural, presocialist Romania* a woman's position was produced and shaped by her agricultural role, by her stature in the family, kin group, and neighborhood, and by various public and private rituals that significantly contributed to the cultural construction of rural, gendered social hierarchies.

Analysis of *the legacies of socialism* in terms of the position of women in Romanian society leads to the conclusion that, despite its promise, state socialism did not emancipate women; it even produced a series of new conflicts and unresolved paradoxes. As was mentioned, the fact that Romanian society is a male-dominated, patriarchal society, without any strong commitment to full female social and economic equality, is not peculiar to this country. This is why analysis is needed that will investigate what is distinctive about the patriarchy that exists in the particular conditions of Romania and whether and to what extent this male-dominated society can (in the future) respond to egalitarian norms (see McIntyre 1985).

As Barbara Einhorn (1993) observes, the link between socialist revolution and women's emancipation produced the reductive concept of labor force participation as not only necessary but also sufficient for women's emancipation. By proclaiming women as equal with men, early constitutions in state socialist societies granted women legal rights but did not recognize broader gender issues, such as the domestic division of labor and sex discrimination.

Another contradiction in the socialist definition of a woman's role appeared in the relationship between her productive and reproductive (and child-raising) functions. In the context of socialist industrialization and extensive economic development, women were viewed by the state primarily in terms of their productive potential and, by households (through their work in the state-owned economy), as adding a necessary component to the family income. But recognition of a potential labor shortage (which threatened the Communist Party's long-term plans for economic development) led to an intensive pro-natalist campaign starting in October 1966. This campaign made it virtually impossible to obtain abortions and divorces and increased the taxes on childless adults, married or unmarried (see Fischer 1985).

While women in communist Romania were mobilized to join the paid labor force in large numbers, the sectoral segregation of men and women that is typical of noncommunist societies continued under Communist Party rule and has been a legacy of that time. As Mary Ellen Fischer and Doina Pasca Harsanyi (1994) show, the sectors where women most often worked received less investment and were less well remunerated than more "masculine" areas (yet men still tended to hold positions of power in these "female" sectors). In addition, within any sector, women were concentrated in low-prestige jobs with poor remuneration.

In discussing the inferior labor-market position of women, it is important to note that one of the legacies of socialism was that the work of women was evaluated as of lesser economic importance and social prestige than that of men. In the literature on this aspect of socialism there seems to be a consensus that, besides its own, independent contribution to the production of gender inequalities, the socialist regime reinforced the patriarchal character of traditional Romanian society (albeit under the guise of an egalitarian ideology).

Doina Pasca Harsanyi suggests that the gender gap was increased by drawing a line between easy work (in fields like textile and food processing, services, education, and health care) that was suitable for women and hard, better-paid work (in fields like metal processing, construction, and mining) that was legitimate for men. As a result, although most women worked during this period and were educated to have a profession and spend their active years in the workforce, they were clustered in the feminized economic sectors and at the bottom of the occupational hierarchy. They earned less and could derive less prestige from their jobs.

Barbara Einhorn (1993) suggests that one of the great paradoxes lived by women under socialism was that they became "emancipated" without being evaluated properly as such. In contrast, they were likely to be "punished," to carry a double burden as worker-mothers. She emphasizes that the socialist state undervalued the private sphere in relation to the public sphere of work. Despite socialist ideology that praised the double heroism of women (celebrating them as "heroine workers" and "heroine mothers"), the system exhorted them to participate in the labor market while officially according their work a lower status than men's. Far from exposing gender divisions in the family, the (low) value attributed to the private sphere in state socialist countries both strengthened the public/private divide and solidified practices within the private sphere. In this way socialism failed to highlight either woman's rights or gender inequalities and instead discredited any public commitment to the equality of women.

The "Feminization of Poverty" as Cultural and Economic Process

As Linda Lindsey stresses, in the contemporary world "the 'feminization of poverty' theme reverberates throughout the social sciences, has been picked up by the media, and has become a defining characteristic of national and global poverty." At the same time, she states, since the birth of black feminism in the 1960s, "the gender-class-race construct . . . has been incorporated into the discourse of all the social sciences and has offered many interdisciplinary leads for theory building" (Lindsey 1997:10). Examining the feminization of poverty, Western scholars investigate problems like the proportion of women among the poor or sex differences in poverty; median family income by sex and household status; earnings in particular occupations by sex or the pay gap by sex; changes in labor force participation by gender; occupational segregation by gender; the rate of single-parent (single-mother and single-father) families; and unemployment rates of women and of men. For example, Andersen (1997:142–143) concludes her analysis with the statement that "the causes of poverty for women are their status in the labor market, their roles in child rearing, and the rising rate of the divorce." While she does stress that "the experience of women workers in the paid labor force is further complicated by the intersection of race, class, and gender," her general point remains, that "poverty is increasing among women, especially among those who head households" (142).

Discussing possibilities for future research on the feminization of poverty in today's Central and Eastern Europe, Chapter 1 in this volume suggests that the phenomenon has different causes and a different shape in this region than it does in Western societies. At one point it is contended that differences within the region are strictly related to general stages of marketization and democratization and the variation in these across Eastern European countries.

Earlier in this section, using works by Doina Pasca Harsanyi, Mary Ellen Fischer, and Barbara Einhorn, we focused on how the policies of *state socialism* assumed that labor force participation was a sufficient condition for female emancipation and, in making this assumption, reproduced a patriarchal gender regime. Considering this, Katherine Verdery argues that the very (inbuilt) qualities (and inequalities) of *patriarchal gender regimes* favor the occupants of masculine gender roles (see Verdery 1994, 1996). Gail Kligman (1988) stresses that this form of social organization constructs hierarchies according to age and sex. It locates men in the public sphere and women in the private sphere and defines men's power in the family as formal and delegates them to positions that control, in public, interfamily relationships. It considers women to be administrators of unofficial family problems and the private mediators of the links between different families. It limits the social space and the liberty of female mobility and, generally speaking, ascribes to kinship and family ties the important social role of solving, by different informal means, the problems of everyday life (see Kligman 1988). Using these analyses, one may conclude that socialism privileged male roles and implicitly assigned women to inferior social positions. In addition, economic sectoral segregation increased the gender gap, contradictions between the productive and reproductive functions of women went unquestioned, and, despite the fact that the system exhorted women to participate in the labor market, their work was undervalued. Through its aggressive politics of urbanization, industrialization, and emancipation, socialism reinforced (in various ways) the naturalized, taken-for-granted inequalities between men and women and even produced experiences that relegitimated a "traditional" cultural and social (gendered) order, thereby, willy-nilly, producing negative attitudes toward the politics of women's emancipation. The cultural order of the gender regime, mentioned earlier, located women in positions that made them more vulnerable and defenseless (economically) and also enabled an easy definition of this condition as "acceptable" or "admissible" by both public opinion and officials.

Beside all these disadvantages and paradoxes, the positive aspects of the socialist system might be reiterated: women entering the labor market had the chance to gain economic independence from men, and legislation gave them the right to be full citizens. These changes must have had an impact on the redistribution of gender roles inside families and on people's understanding of women's participation in the public sphere and their authority in the private one. But, on the other hand, all this happened in a time when women, like all of Romanian society, were becoming dependent on a paternalist-ethnonationalist regime, the socialist parent-state, and the logic of the program of socialist development.

Turning to discuss the feminization of poverty during *the postsocialist transition,* one may observe that there are two main positions about this. One states that, at least, the first stage of transition was relatively beneficial to women (see Chapter 1 in this volume), and the other states that women have consistently borne most of the costs of this period (World Survey on the Role of Women in Development 1994). The first set of arguments emphasizes that at the beginning of the transition mainly sectors of the economy that were privileged during socialism (and that were masculinized) collapsed. On the other hand, the sectors where the majority of employees were (and are) women have enjoyed increasing privileges. The second set of arguments stresses that in the sectors most affected by reform women are laid off first and that (once unemployed) they face greater difficulties than men in obtaining alternative employment. Additionally, proponents of this argument emphasize that privatization favors those who had, in the previous system, access to capital, information, and markets—overwhelmingly men.

The gender regime, discussed earlier, is the context and the cultural logic within which the poverty of women in Romania occurs, and while turning to the statistical data this context should be borne in mind. The structure of employment by professional status (Table 5.13) shows differences in employment status between economically active women and men. These data should be evaluated with those in Table 5.14, which show that women work in the lowest-paid branches of the economy, leading to the reproduction of their economic dependence and inferior status in spite of their presence in the labor market, and with those of Table 5.15, which show that women's unemployment between 1991 and 1997 was consistently higher than the unemployment rate of the general population.

It is obvious by now that our starting point in *conceptualizing the feminization of poverty* is to locate it within the framework of the gender regime(s) of the society in question. It must be emphasized that the social and cultural analysis of a gender regime has to focus on the set of economic, social, political, and cultural mechanisms through which differences between men and women are transformed into social inequalities. If differences between the sexes are naturalized and explained in biological terms, then social inequalities built on these differences also begin to be legitimated with references to the "natural order of things." Analysis needs to consider gender identity as an instrument in the construction of social hierarchies, one of the tools by which the social organization of cultural differences is going on in a particular society.

Table 5.13
Percent of the Active Population by Employment Status, Women's Employment by Status, and Comparison with Men's Employment by Status, 1996

	Employment status				
	Employee	Employer	Own-account worker	Unpaid family worker	Member of agricultural company
Percent economically active population (men and women)	62.8%	1.4%	19.5%	15.8%	0.5%
Percent economically active women	58.4	0.6	15.6	25.0	0.4
Women as percent of all economically active with the same employment status	41.7	23.3	35.8	70.6	40.0

Source: *Quarterly Household Labor Force Survey*, fourth quarter 1996, p. 47.

Table 5.14
Number of Female Employees and Average Monthly Salaries by Economic Sector, 1996

Economic sector	Women % total employees	Monthly average salary
Agriculture	47.8%	211.479
Industry	39.9	322.979
Construction	15	261.202
Services	49.3	295.437
Publ. administration, defense	21	230.885
Education	72	244.212
Health, social assistance	78	201.406
Others	45.3	256.982

Source: Quarterly Statistical Bulletin 1997/3:10.

Table 5.15
Unemployment Totals and Rates for the Whole Population and for Women, 1991–1997

Year	Total Unemployed	Total Women	Unem. Rate	Unem. Rate, Women
1991	337,440	208,457	3%	4%
1992	929,019	563,065	8.2%	10.3%
1993	1,164,705	685,496	10.4%	12.9%
1994	1,223,925	693,342	10.9%	12.9%
1995	998,392	551,492	9.5%	11.4%
1996	657,564	355,345	6.3%	7.3%
1997	721,077	363,813	5.5%	-

On the basis of the preceding, the feminization of poverty means the economic and cultural processes through which the category of women (defined through certain "natural" characteristics) is linked to the category of poor and which naturalize this relationship (so that it becomes taken for granted). These processes are part of a broader context in which inequalities of class, gender, and race/ethnicity are generated culturally as well as economically.

We consider that research into the feminization of poverty should proceed on two levels: the microlevel of the household and the macrolevel of Romanian society. The following issues are pertinent to this methodological organization:

- feminization of poverty within the household. The focus here should be the identification and interpretation of women's positions inside the family (including their economic situations and cultural positions). Included in this research should be (1) households in poverty, (2) not-poor families where women do not participate in the labor market and cannot make decisions about family economic problems, and (3) female-headed households.
- feminization of poverty at the macrolevel of the society. The focus here should be the identification of "feminized" public spheres of activity (for instance, economic sectors and "feminized" jobs within other sectors) in order to examine their social prestige and cultural worth.

Besides investigating these issues (and issues previously discussed) with a nationally representative sample survey, we suggest that a qualitative case study of "female experiences of urban poverty" could be useful for providing insight into the situation of women living in a postsocialist gender regime. The aim of the proposed case study would be to identify and to interpret the nature and dynamics of the feminization of poverty within a well-defined social space, both to uncover the subjects' perspectives and to locate the cases within a broader social-historical framework.

Finally it is necessary to state that we assume a *feminist standpoint* in research on women in poverty. It might happen that this could result in overemphasizing the feminization of poverty in postsocialist processes of impoverishment, as well as stressing the sexist nature of oppression and gender stratification over other processes of social differentiation. But at least this self-location makes explicit our aim "to focus on power relations from the perspective of women located within a variety of social structures who are 'ruled' and who lack the resources to seriously challenge or alter the existing arrangement" (Lindsey 1997:12). It also enables us to question issues like sexual stratification, the division of labor, and the distribution of rights and duties in institutions where the patriarchal gender regime functions as a "natural" order. While recognizing that the extra-analytic values of the researcher have an impact on results, we subscribe to the position that states that "feminism involves opposition to the sexism and patriarchy inherent" in the society under scrutiny and that "feminist theory provides the ideological framework for addressing women's inferior position and the social, political and economic discrimination which perpetuate it" (Lindsey 1997:13).

NOTES

Corresponding author, Nándor L. Magyari, 3400 Cluj, Babes-Bolyai University, Department of Sociology, Kogalniceanu Street, No. 1-2, Tel. +40-654-194315 (ext. 125), Fax +40-64-191906, E-mail nmagyari@hera.ubbcluj.ro.

We are thankful for the contribution of Gabriel Troc and Alina Branda-Cuceu, teaching assistants on cultural anthropology at the Faculty of European Studies, and Laszlo Peter, assistant in the Sociology Department at our university.

REFERENCES

Andersen, Margaret L. 1997. *Thinking about Women. Sociological Perspectives on Sex and Gender.* 4th ed. Allyn and Bacon.

Anuarul Statistic al Romaniei (Statistical Yearbook of Romania). 1994, 1995, and 1996. *Comisia Nationala pentru Statistica* (Romanian Commission for Statistics), Bucharest.

Arbore, Ecaterina. 1912. *Femeia muncitoare în lupta spre dezrobire. Conferinta tinuta la Brila in ziua de 28 martie 1911.*

Băban, Adriana, and Henry P. David. 1995. *Voci ale femeilor din România. Aspecte ale sexualităøii, comportamentului de reproducere ši ale relaøiilor de cuplu în epoca Ceaušescu* (Voices of Women from Romania. Aspects of Sexuality, Reproductive Behavior and of Couple Relationships during Ceausescu). Bucharest.

Babeøi, Adriana. 1996. "Povešti cu amazoane" (Stories with Amazons). *Secolul 20*, 7–9.

Băcanu, M. 1996. *Øiganii—minoritate naþionalã sau majoritate infracøionalã?* (The Gypsies—National Minorities or Criminal Majority?). Bravo Press.

Barth, Fredrik. 1969. *Ethnic Groups and Boundaries: The Social Organization of Culture Difference.* Boston: Little, Brown.

Barth, Fredrik. 1996. *Régi és új problémák az etnicitás elemzésében* (Old and New Problems in Analyzing Ethnicity). In Regio, 1, pp. 3–26.

Biró, A. Zoltán. 1992. *A regionális identitás kialakitásának néhány vonásáról* (Some Aspects in Development of Regional Identities). In Regio, 4.

Bíró, A. Zoltán, Julianna Bodó, and Nándor László Magyari. 1991. *Térhasználati stratégiák beépített környezetben* (Space Using Strategies in Urban Areas). In Átmenetek 1, 65–77.

Bradley, Harriet. 1996. *Fractured Identities: Changing Patterns of Inequality.* Cambridge: Polity Press.

Brucan, Silviu. 1998. *De la party hacks la nouveaux riches—schimbarea sociala in Rusia si Europa de Est* (From the Party Hacks to the New Riches—the Social Transformation in Russia and Eastern Europe). In *Sfera Politicii*, 59, 13–18.

Bucur, Maria. 1996. "Între mituri, icoane ši tăceri. Femeile române în primul război mondial" (In Between Myths, Icons, and Silences. The Romanian Women during the First World War). In *Cine suntem noi?* (Who Are We?), coordinated by M. Nicolaescu. Bucharest.

Bucur, Maria. 1997. În cinstea mamelor bine crescute. *Sfera Politicii* 47.

Burtea, Vasile. 1996. *Marginalizare istoricã ši cooperare socialã în cazul populaøiei de rromi* (Historical Marginalization and Social Co-operation Concerning the Gypsy Population). Revista De Cercetari Sociale (RSC), 109–120.

Burtea, Vasile. 1997. *Pentru o egalizare a šanselor* (For Equal Opportunities). In Romathan, I, 35–38.

Cancea, Paraschiva. 1976. *Micarea pentru emanciparea femeii în România 1848–1948.*

Catargi, Micaela. 1927. *Feminismul. Conferina inut la edina festiv a seciilor "Astrei" în 5 decembrie 1927.*

Chelcea, S. 1995. Attitudes of the Romas. *Revue Roumanie de Psychologie*, no. 38, 151–159.

Chodorow, Nancy. 1995. "Gender, Relation and Difference in Psychoanalytic Perspective." Pp. 41–50 in *The Polity Reader in Gender Studies*. Polity Press.

Connell, R. W. 1995. "Gender Regimes and the Gender Order." Pp. 29–41 in *The Polity Reader in Gender Studies*. Polity Press.

Constantinescu, Lidia. 1997. "Consiliul naøional al statutului egal" (The National Council of the Equal Status). *Sfera Politicii* 47.

Countering Anti-Roma Violence. 1994. In the Snagov Conference and Related Efforts, PER Raport.

Dumbrava, Dinu. 1912. *Femeile vor s voteze! Câteva note asupra "micrii feministe."*

Einhorn, Barbara. 1993. *Cinderella Goes to Market. Citizenship, Gender and Women as Movements in East Central Europe.* Verso.

Evolutia economico-sociala a Romaniei in anul 1997 (Social and Economic Evolution of Romania in 1997). 1998. In *Revista Romana de Statistica* (Romanian Magazine for Statistics) 47,1–2, 1–41.

Feischmidt, Margit, Magyari-Vincze Enikô, and Zentai Violetta (eds.). 1997. *Women and Men in East European Transition.* Cluj: EFES.

Ferréol, Gilles. 1996. *Reprezentările sociale ale øiganilor: elemente de reflecøie* (The Social Reflection of the Gypsy: Elements for Reflection). In Minoritari, marginali, excluši, pp. 89–97.

Fischer, Mary Ellen. 1985. "Women in Romanian Politics: Elena Ceausescu, Pronatalism, and the Promotion of Women." In *Women, State, and Party in Eastern Europe*, edited by S. L. Wolwick and A. G. Meyer. Duke Press.

Fischer, Mary Ellen, and Doina Pasca Harsanyi. 1994. "From Tradition and Ideology to Elections and Competition." In *Women in the Politics of Postcommunist Eastern Europe*, edited by M. Rueschemeyer. M. E. Sharpe.

Friedmann, John. 1996. *O reconsiderare a sărăciei: autonomizarea ši drepturile cetăøenilor* (Reconsidering the poverty: Autonomy and the Citizen's Rights). In Minoritari, marginali, excluši, pp. 246–260.

Gans, Herbert J. 1996. "From 'Underclass' to 'Undercaste': Some Observations about the Future of the Postindustrial Economy and Its Major Victims." Pp. 141–152 in *Urban Poverty and the Underclass. A Reader*, edited by Enzo Mingione. Oxford: Blackwell.

Georgescu, I. 1997. Dolar la dolar trage. *Capital* 47, 63.

Georgescu, I. 1998. Privatizatul este baiat bun. *Capital* 3, 27.

Gheorghe, Nicolae. 1990. *Mit jelent cigánynak lenni?* (What Does It Mean to Be Roma?). In Átmentek 1, 31–35.

Ghetãu, Vasile. 1996. *O proiectare condiøională a populaøiei României pe principalele naøionalităøi (1992–2025)* (A Conditional Projection of Romania`s Population by Main Minorities, 1992–2025). In RSC 1, 77–106.

Grünberg, Laura. 1996. "Feminismul ca experienøă personală" (Feminism as Personal Experience). *Secolul 20*, 7–9.

Helsinki Watch. 1992. *Raport despre drepturile omului.* Document official, New York.

Human Development Report in Romania. 1996. Bucharest.

Human Rights Problems Faced by Roma-Gypsies. 1997. Work Document, MG-S-ROM, Strasbourg.

KAM-RAKK. 1995. *Változásban?* Elemzések a romániai magyar társadalomról (In Transition—Analysis about the Hungarian Society from Romania). Csíkszereda, Proprint.

KAM-RAKK. 1996. *Egy más mellett élés* (Living Next to Eachoher). A magyar-román, magyar-cigány kapcsolatokról, Csíkszereda, Proprint.

Kapcsolat-Környezet-Közösség Csikszeredai antropológiai írások. 1992. Budapest. Politika+Kultúra Alapitvány.

Kemény, István-Havas, and Gábor-Kertesi Gábor. 1995. *Beszámoló a magyarországi roma (cigány) népesség helyzetével foglalkozó 1993 októbere és 1994 februárja között végzett kutatásról.* (Manuscript) pp. 1–41.

Kligman, Gail. 1985. "The Rites of Women: Oral Poetry, Ideology, and the Socialization of Peasant Women in Contemporary Romania." In *Women, State, and Party in Eastern Europe*, edited by S. L. Wolchik and A. G. Meyer. Duke Press.

Kligman, Gail. 1988. *The Wedding of the Dead: Ritual, Poetics and Popular Culture in Transylvania.* University of California Press.

Ladányi, János. 1996. *Romák Közép-Kelet Európában.* In TÁRSADALMI SZEMLE, 4.

Ladányi, János. 1998. *Gettóügyek rendszerváltás elôtt és után.* In Mozgó Világ, 1, pp. 77–87.

Ladányi, Janos, and Ivan Szelényi. 1998. *Ki a cigány?* In KRITIKA, 3, 3–7.

Lewis, O. 1969. *La vida. On Puerto Rican Family in Culture of Poverty: San Juan and New York.*

Liegeois, Jean-Pierre. 1997. *Rromii ši comunitâøile nomade: cercetare-acøiune ši proiecte de intervenøie* (The Roma [Gypsies] and the Nomadic Communities: Research—action and Projects of Intervention). In Romathan, I, pp. 3–10.

Liegeois, Jean-Pierre, and Nicolae Gheorghe. 1995. *Rromii—minoritate europeanã* (Roma/Gypsies: A European Minority). London: Minority Rights Group.

Lindsey, Linda L. 1997. *Gender Roles. A Sociological Perspective.* 3d ed. Prentice-Hall.

Magyari, Nándor László. 1991. *"Marasztalnak, tehát megyünk" (Gondolatok válság(ok)ról és elvándorlásról).* In Regio, 4, pp. 110–121.

Magyari, Nándor László. 1995. *Civil társadalom, vagy amit akartok.* Korunk, 11, 58–69.

Magyari-Vincze, Enikö. 1997a. *Antropologia politicii identitare nationaliste* (Anthropology of Nationalist Identity Politics), EFES: Cluj.

Magyari-Vincze, Enikö. 1997b. "Politics as a Symbolic Fight with and over Nationalism." In E. Magyari-Vincze: Kísérletek kulturális elemzésre. Experimente în analiza culturalã. Experiments in Cultural Analysis, EFES: Cluj.

Magyari-Vincze, Enikö. 1997c. "Relaøii interetnice de-a lungul storiei Transilvaniei." In E. Magyari-Vincze: *Kísérletek kulturális elemzésre. Experimente în analiza culturalã. Experiments in Cultural Analysis*, EFES: Cluj.

Manolescu, Anca. 1996. "Antropologia creština ši conštiinøa de sine a femeilor" (The Christian Anthropology and the Self-Consciousness of Women). *Secolul 20*, 7–9.

McIntyre, Robert J. 1985. "Demographic Policy and Sexual Equality: Value Conflicts and Policy Appraisal in Hungary and Romania." In *Women, State, and Party in Eastern Europe*, edited by S. L. Wolchik and A. G. Meyer. Duke Press.

Metro Media Transilvania. 1999. *Barometrul de opinie publica.* Bucharest: Fundatia pentru o societate deschisa.

Miroiu, Mihaela. 1994. "Breaking the Spell." *Revista de cercetãri sociale* 2.

Miroiu, Mihaela. 1995. *Gândul umbrei* (The Thought of Shade). Bucharest: Alternative.

Miroiu, Mihaela. 1996. "Experienøele femeilor ši pericolul feminist" (The Experiences of Women and the Feminist Danger). *Secolul 20*, 7–9.

Miroiu, Mihaela. 1997. "Hrana conservatorismului: antifeminismul" (The Food of Conservatism: Antifeminism). *Sfera Politicii* 47.

Modalitâøi de prevenire a conflictelor interetnice prin cunoašterea multiculturalã a etniilor din Transilvania: 1997, (Prevention of Interethnic Conflicts Through the Understanding of Different Ethnic Minorities in Transylvania). Asociaøia pt Dialog Interetnic-Fundaøia pt. Dezvoltarea Societãøii, Civile, Cluj.

Moore, Henrietta L. 1988. *Feminism and Anthropology.* University of Minnesota Press.

Moore, Henrietta. 1995. "The Cultural Constitution of Gender." Pp. 14–22 in *The Polity Reader in Gender Studies*. Polity Press.

National Commission for Statistics. 1996a. Starea sociala si economica a Romaniei in anul 1995, Bucharest.

National Commission for Statistics. 1996b. *Veniturile, cheltuielile si consumul populatiei,* Informatii statistice operative, nos.1–2.

National Commission for Statistics. 1997. *Buletin Statistic Lunar,* no.12.

National Commission for Statistics. 1998. *Buletin Statistic Lunar,* no.12.

Neculau, Adrian, and Gilles Ferroél (eds.). 1996. *Minoritari, marginali, excluši* (Minority, Marginality, Exclusion). Polirom, Iaši.

Nicolaescu, Mădălina. 1996a. "Utopian Desire and Western Representations of Femininity." *Replika* (special issue).

Nicolaescu, Mădălina (coord.). 1996b. *Cine suntem noi? Despre identitatea femeilor din România* (Who Are We? On the Identity of Women from Romania). Bucharest: Anima.

Noraianu-Oancea. 1994. *The Legislative and Institutional Framework for the National Minorities of Romania*. Bucharest: Romanian Institute for Human Rights.

Pasca Harsanyi, Doina. 1993. "Women in Romania." In *Gender Politics and Post-Communism. Reflections from Eastern Europe and the Former Soviet Union*, edited by N. Funk and M. Mueller. Routledge.

Pasca Harsanyi, Doina. 1995. "Participation of Women in the Workforce: The Case of Romania." In *Family, Women, and Employment in Central-Eastern Europe*, edited by B. Lobodzinski. Greenwood Press.

Plesca, M., and C. Rata. 1996. *Welfare in Romania during Transition: Analysis of Family Budget Survey Data (1989, 1992, 1993). Technical Report,* Center for Economic Research and Graduate Education, Charles University.

Popescu, Liliana. 1997. "Šoapte fierbinøi ši fantezii romantice?" (Hot Whispers and Romantic Fantasies?). *Sfera Politicii,* 47.

Popescu, L. 1998. State and Market in Romanian Social Policy. In J. Hopps and D. Iatridis, *Privatization in Central and Eastern Europe: Perspectives and Approaches*. Westport, CT: Praeger, pp. 155–169.

Preda, Marian. 1993. *Studiu de caz. Conflictul din localitatea Mihail Kogalniceanu* (Case Study. The Conflict from Mihail Kogalniceanu Willage). In Elena Zamfir and Catalin Zamfir (eds.), *Øiganii între ignorare ši îngrijorare* (The Gypsies between Ignorance and Anxiety). Bucharest, pp. 175–201.

Radocea, A. 1996. *Evolutia sectorului privat in economia Romaniei* (Evolution of Private Sector in the Romanian Economy). In *Revista Romana de Statistica* (Romanian Magazine for Statistics), 45, 1, 1–14.

RCIRT. 1998. *Romanian and Hungarian in Postcommunist Transition (Mental Images and Inter-Ethnic Relation in Transylvania).*

Roma (Gypsies) in the OSCE Region. 1993. Official Document, Council of Europe.

Romania Country Profile. 1997–1998. Economist Intelligence Unit, London, U.K.

Romania libera. November 25, 1997.

România ši minoritãøile. 1997. (The Minorities from Romania, Collected Documents) Colecøie de documente, Ed. Pro Europa, Tg-Mureš.

Romanian Human Development Report. 1996. Bucharest.

Romas in Central and Eastern Europe. 1992. PER Document.

Rossides, Daniel W. 1997. *Social Stratification. The Interplay of Class, Race, and Gender*. 2d ed. Prentice-Hall.

Starea sociala si economia Romaniei in anul 1991 (Social Situation and the Economy of Romania in 1991). 1992. *Comisia Nationala pentru Statistica* (Romanian Commission for Statistics).

Stewart, Michael. 1993. "Gypsies, the Work Ethic, and Hungarian Socialism." In C.M. Hann, ed., *Socialism: Ideals, Ideologies, and Local Practice*. London: Routledge, pp. 187–203.

Stewart, Michael. 1994. *Daltestvérek—az oláhcigány identitás és kösösség továbbélése a szocialista Magyarországon* (Brothers in Song—the Persistence of Gypsy Identity and Community in Socialist Hungary). Budapest: T-Twins Kiadó.

Stratilescu, Eleonora. 1911. *Temeiul micrii feministe i scopurile pe care le urmrete. Precedat de un mic istoric al micrii feministe în România.*

Strobel, Pierre. 1996. *De la sărăcie la excludere: societate salarialã sau societate a drepturilor omului?* (From Poverty to Exclusion). In Minoritari, marginali, excluši, pp. 260–278.

Szelényi, Iván. 1997. *A Proposal for a Joint Program of Training and Research in Comparative Social Analysis in Central and Southern Europe* (manuscript).

Szelényi, Iván, and Rebecca Emigh. 1998. *Racialization and Feminization of Poverty During Market Transition—the Central and Southern European Case* (manuscript).

Trebici, Vladimir. 1994. Is There a Need for a Demographic Policy in Romania? In *Revista de Cercetari Sociale*, 2.

Trebici, Vladimir. 1996. *Minoritãøile naøionale din România: prezent ši estimaøie prospectivã* (National Minorities from Romania: Present and Forcasting). RSC 1,106–124 pp.

UNICEF. 1993. *Central and Eastern Europe in Transition. Public Policy and Social Conditions.* Regional Monitoring Report, 1, Florence: ICDC.

UNICEF. 1994. *Central and Eastern Europe in Transition—Public Policy and Social Conditions.* Economies in Transition Studies, Regional Monitoring Report, No. 2.

United Nations Development Program. 1997. Metode °i tehnici de evaluare a sărăciei (Research Report). Bucharest.

Verdery, Katherine. 1994. *From Parent State to Family Patriarchs: Gender and Nation in Contemporary Eastern Europe.* East European Politics & Society 8:225-255 pp.

Verdery, Katherine. 1996. "From Parent-State to Family Patriarchs: Gender and Nation in Contemporary Eastern Europe." In *What Was Socialism, and What Comes Next.* Princeton: Princeton University Press.

Wilson, W. J. (ed.) 1993. *The Ghetto Underclass.* Sage.

Wilson, W. J. 1996. *When Work Disappears. The World of the New Urban Poor.* New York: Vintage Books.

World Survey on the Role of Women in Development. 1994. *United Nations Publication.*

Zamfir, C. 1994. In centrul atentiei: Legea Ajutorului Social (In the Focus: The Draft of the Law on Social Benefits). In *Revista de cercetari sociale,* 3, 121–134.

Zamfir, C. (ed.). 1995a. *Dimensiuni ale saraciei.* Bucharest: Editura Expert.

Zamfir, C. (coord.). 1995b. Politica sociala în Romania în Tranziøie (Social Policies in Transitional Romania). In C. Zamfir and E. Zamfir (eds.), Politici sociale. Romania in Context Euopean, Bucharest: Editura Alternative.

Zamfir, C. (ed.). 1997. *Pentru o societate centrata pe copil.* Bucharest: Edit. Alternative.

Zamfir, Elena and Catalin Zamfir (eds.). 1993. *iganii între ignorare i îngrijorare* (The Gypsies between Ignorance and Anxiety, with English Résumé). Bucharest.

6

Redistribution's Role in Leveling Income: The Overgrown Slovak Welfare State

Iveta Radicová and Michal Vašecka

INTRODUCTION

The main goal of welfare reform in Slovakia was to prepare and adopt legislative and institutional regulations that would guarantee the social security of citizens who faced a new, previously nonexisting social threat, as well as to create a new system of labor relations and social security that would weaken the role of the state and would stimulate individuals to take responsibility for their own standard of living.

Results, however, indicate a failure to fulfill this goal. Expenditures on welfare are growing, a situation that indirectly reinforces the role of the state. The current conception of social policy, based on a shift of many responsibilities onto the individual and the family, applies to the social situation of overburdened and "tired" family networks. There is a risk that the family, being simply exhausted, will refuse to take over these responsibilities, sighing nostalgically for the past.

The basic trends of social policy are the following: a shift from the role of the state to the one of civil society; a shift from the system of public services to a system of private services; and a shift from universalism to particularism when providing services (to socially dependent groups). The risk factors of these processes are closely linked with the existing security. Access to social security benefits is determined by one's position in the labor market. The whole system of social securities is derived from labor and employment. An effective market and an efficient private sector are the underlying presumptions of such trends. The market is in danger in monopolism—any surviving monopoly negates the essence of the market operation. The system of health insurance, social insurance, retirement security, and housing is determined by one's placement in the labor market and by employment. This condition creates a phenomenon of a multiple disadvantage and, consequently, of risk. The multiple disadvantage of moving from the sphere of labor to the area of housing, health, and education thus can result in a risk of self-marginalization as a tool and strategy of survival.

This study is aimed at an analysis of problems and risk factors of the current concept of social justice, the character of which can be described as redistributive. Any decision to change such a concept takes place whenever relevant problems cannot be solved with the current formulation of the concept. Obviously, the identification of a problem situation should result in social change. The solutions to social problems are connected with the social goal. The social goal is a differentiation based on efficiency; prevention of marginalization, self-marginalization, and social exclusion; and prevention of social tension; formation of mechanisms to lower the number of socially dependent groups by enabling all members of such groups to achieve freedom from the existing situation.

Country Facts

The Slovak Republic was established as a separate state in 1993 after the split of the former Czechoslovak Federal Republic. During the years 1948–1989 Slovakia was under communist dictatorship. During this time there was a fully nationalized economy and rule by one political party—the communists. When this came to an end, change primarily involved political democratization (pluralization of the political scene and liberalization of the economy), the creation of a private sector (connected with decentralization), deregulation, and demonopolization. The political situation since the Velvet Revolution in November 1989 has been very dynamic, and the political climate has been unstable. Since 1989 there have been seven governments and four general elections. The heritage of the former regime and the transition to a social-market economy have been connected with phenomena such as increasing social and regional differentiation; the creation of, and further increases in, unemployment; a deteriorating standard of living; and the population's strong disillusionment with the social reality of transition (as compared to their original expectations for it).

Demographic Features

In 1996 the population was 5,378,932, and the percent of women in the population was 51.3%. The current aging of the population is a typical, yet nonlinear, demographic development. The process is based on two population waves—the first wave is of people born in the first half of the 1970s (who are now between 25 and 30), and the second, older wave occurred in the 1940s (involving people now aged between 45 and 55). As a consequence, the average age of the population is slowly going up, but there is a decline in the proportion of both children (at the preproductive age) and older (postproductive) people. Changes in the population at postproductive and preproductive ages, expressed in an aging index, show a constant rise.

Nowadays, more than half the population lives in towns. Forty years ago, two-thirds of the population lived in the countryside. Most adults in the population have a secondary school education, either with or without obtaining a secondary school-leaving exam (and including those people in the population who have what is known as an apprenticeship education). The proportion of university graduates among the economically active population is 10.7%, and it is 7.7% within the whole population (*Slovak Statistics and Demography* 1996).

The majority of adults in Slovakia have married at least once (only 17.98% of men and 10.43% of all women aged 20 or older are single), the majority of women have children, and the majority of children are born in wedlock (90%). Of all households, those composed of family members are the most common (77.8%, according to the 1991 population census); of these, nuclear families are a large majority (86.6%). Of all families, 13.4% are one-parent families (or 10.4% of all households). The remaining households comprise single individuals (21.8%) and other nonfamily households (0.4%). Most family households with dependent children are two-children families (46.2%) (*Statistical Analysis and Information in 1995*).

Demographic development will intensify the pressure on the labor market as the population of working age increases—this is of concern to men of 23 and over (considered to be their productive age range) and to women of 25 and over (considered their productive age range).

Ethnic Structure

Roughly 14% of the people living in Slovakia are members of national minorities. In this light, Slovakia is one of the most ethnically heterogeneous countries in Central Europe. The largest minority is Hungarian (567,300 people in the last, 1991 census, or 10.76% of the population), and the second largest is Roma (80,627 people; or 1.7% of the population). These major minority groups are joined by smaller groups of Czechs (59,300, or 1.1%), Ruthenians (17,200), Ukrainians (13,300), and several other minorities, including Germans, Jews, Poles, Bulgarians, and Russians (*Slovak Statistics* 1995).

In the 1991 census, when Roma had a chance to claim their ethnicity for the first time, only 80,627 citizens said that they were of Roma nationality. More realistic estimates of the number of Roma in Slovakia are based on data collected by city councils in 1989. These suggest that the number of Roma is 253,943 (4.8% of the total population of the Slovak Republic). However, experts' estimates suggest an even higher number—between 480,000 and 520,000—of Roma in Slovakia. There exist various explanations for the inconsistency in the data.

Multiculturalism should be the first aim of Slovak policymakers. Unfortunately, current policy shows no suggestion of overcoming an understanding of the state as tied to a single nationality. The danger of excluding different groups of people from the social and political discourse is increasing.

Main Social Problems

A "shock" for the population is a relatively new phenomenon—unemployment. Unemployment is a serious problem for citizens with few qualifications but also for secondary school and university graduates. In 1994 there was an increase in the number of unplaced graduates of secondary schools and universities and by 1995, 13.6% of the unemployed were graduates (*Report on Social Situation of the SR Population in 1995*).

The area seeing the largest growth in expenditure between 1989 and 1994 was social protection—here government expenditures increased as much as 233%. This growth was mainly caused by increased spending on social benefits (which is directly related to the growth of long-term unemployment), yet expenditures on social services grew only minimally (*Basic Figures in the Field of Social Security in the Development Series 1957–1994*).

The high inflation rate in 1991 was largely caused by a liberalization of the majority of prices, which had previously been administratively fixed (this liberalization was launched on January 1, 1991). The successful control of inflation, for which Slovakia ranks top among postcommunist countries, is founded on the National Bank of Slovakia's responsible and restrictive monetary policy (in 1997, 7%).

The real value of earnings at the end of 1994 was 23.2% lower than in 1989. Since 1989, the value of real wages has increased only twice: in 1992 and 1994. Whereas the average growth of real wages in 1994 was 4.3%, salaries increased by only 1% in budgetary organizations (state-financed organizations). By the end of 1994 the low level of reward in the budgetary sphere (education, health care) was, justifiably, considered a serious social problem (the minimum monthly wage in 1995 was SK2,700, or USD90; in 1998 it was SK3,000, or USD100) (*Indicators of Economic Development of the SR 1996*).

POVERTY

Poverty in Slovakia from a Historical Perspective

In comparing transformation processes in Slovakia and in other countries of Central Europe (especially in comparison with the Czech Republic), the worse starting conditions of Slovakia are often pointed to. These are suggested to be the result of a historic delay in modernization (including industrialization, urbanization, and the development of a democratic culture).

The slow progress of modernization in Slovakia over the nineteenth and first half of twentieth centuries can be seen in the slow development of industry, a continuing large majority of the population working in agriculture, continuous subdivision of the land (caused by a specific Hungarian law according to which all the children in a family had equal inheritance rights), and increasing village poverty. During this time there was a pauperization of the peasantry in Slovakia. According to the 1869 census (Sveton 1969:185) more than one-half of all fully employed agricultural workers were village poor people without ownership of the means of production. Slovakia, with its high proportion of rural inhabitants (62.5% in 1930), was, with Poland, Yugoslavia, and Bulgaria, among the most backward agrarian countries (Kusá, 1997).

The constant characterization of Slovakia as a country of limited opportunities is shown also by the data on rising emigration, recorded in all censuses of that time. During the period in which the census of 1857 was completed, 100,000 people had left their homes (Sveton 1969). Between 1869 and 1910 emigration absorbed nearly 60% of the natural population increase in

Slovakia. This was, with the exception of Ireland, the greatest relative migration loss in Europe. Even during the period 1926–1935, on average, nearly 13,000 people migrated from Slovakia every year. Of these, more than two-thirds were male and most were agricultural workers. It can therefore be said that the most usual strategy to escape poverty in Slovakia at that time was to escape the country. This meant transferring the demographic potential (mainly of the agricultural proletariat) from Slovakia to the United States, Canada, and those other countries where there was the industrial capacity to accommodate a growing labor force (Feglová, Kusá, Radicová, and Simunková 1995).

Although "poverty" was not among the key social science concepts in socialist Czechoslovakia (including what is today Slovakia), surveys of the part of the population with a "limited possibility of consumption" were regularly carried out after 1958 by research institutes in the Ministry of Social Affairs. Poverty, as in other countries, was classified two ways (less than the social minimum, or less than the subsistence minimum), using income criteria and minimum standards of living (until 1991).

Even in 1988 there were in Slovakia, where lived one-third of all citizens of the Czech and Slovak Federative Republic (CSFR), the majority (54%) of all of the poor people in the CSFR. However, the proportion of poor households in Slovakia had significantly decreased over the period 1958–1988 (Analýza 1992: 47); see Table 6.1 (Appendix).

The proportion of the almost-poor (with an income in the range of 56–62% of the average) was permanently about 6% of the population of Slovakia (Analýza 1992:47).

Present Study on Poverty

In analyzing the social situation in the SR (Slovakian Republic), we rely heavily on 1997 Microcensus results; this was a selective survey of the level and structure of household incomes in 1996. It was carried out in 19,301 households (2,287 of which did not respond) during the period March 12–21, 1997. Based on data from the Microcensus, the average annual income in 1996 was SK42,562 (or SK3,546.88 per month) per person (based on Radicová 1997); see Table 6.2.

The lowest-income group is made up of those households whose average income per person is below subsistence level. (The subsistence level is determined theoretically by normatively stating a subsistence level for a four-member household of two adults and two dependent children. In 1996 this equaled one-half of average net cash income per person.) Of the population, 8.8% lives below the subsistence level. On the contrary, 5.9% of the population is in the highest-income category, meaning a net monthly income per person of equal to, or greater than, twice the average net monthly cash income (SK6,944 and above per month); see Table 6.3.

Table 6.3 implies that the groups with the lowest incomes are housewives, the unemployed, and people who are economically inactive. In comparison to the whole population, economically inactive people are overrepresented among those with below-average incomes. Of economically active people, 77% have incomes between 0.5 and 1.5 times the average net income, and 9.3% have incomes that are below subsistence level (less than 0.5 times the average net income). The situation of pensioners, usually discussed (along with the unemployed) as socially endangered, is not as appalling as is the situation of economically inactive people. Nevertheless, pensioners' standard of living will deteriorate as the economically active become less able to make pension contributions.

Thus, the status of the weakest groups in society is a function of the weakness of the middle strata. Solutions to their problems do not lie in the realm of social policy alone but must also be sought in economic and employment policy.

Changes in Income Distribution

Changes in income distribution can be illustrated by comparing Microcensus results from 1992 and 1996 (Table 6.4). In order to make comparison possible, we recategorized the original income ranges using a single key. We look at the population as a whole because different subpopulations were identified in 1992 and 1996, making comparison of particular social groups impossible (Radicová 1997).

While in 1992, 87.5% of households had incomes between 0.5 and 1.5 times the average, in 1996 this figure was 75.7%. Of the 11.8% no longer in the middle-income bracket, half slipped to a lower-income range (below subsistence level) and half joined the group of people with incomes 1.5 or more times the average. Thus, heterogenization did not mean a movement of the population into higher income categories but the strengthening of extreme income groups.

The Relationship of Work Income and Social Income

By work income we mean income from full-time work, part-time work, agriculture, or a private business. Social income includes all kinds of pensions (e.g., retirement, disability, partial disability, orphanage, widow's, and widower's), sickness benefits and other related benefits (e.g., benefits for caring for a family member, maternity pay, and compensatory benefits paid during pregnancy and maternity), child benefits, parental benefits, and other state benefits (child delivery support, care benefits, compensation benefits for using a soldier's apartment, income compensation for military service and for civil military service, funeral benefits, spa care benefits), benefits for families with children (monetary and material benefits for parents with dependent children and pregnant women, child allowance, monetary benefit for children in their guardians' care, monetary benefit for parents who gave birth to triplets or to more than three children), benefits for severely handicapped people and for the elderly (single monetary benefits, single benefits for purchasing special aids, benefits for the adjustment of living spaces, benefits for individual trans-portation, benefits for increased living costs, benefits for war pensioners, war widows' benefits, benefits for the blind, benefits for looking after a close relative or other person), and unemployment support (*Social Policy in SR in*

1996 1997).

In 1996 work income accounted for 66.8% of the population's income, social income was 28.5%, and other income (e.g., income in kind, from the sale of agriculture products, or from abroad) was 4.7%. In 1992 the sources of the total population's income were work income (63.6%), social income (35.4%), and other income (1%). Thus, the share of total income that came from social income was 6.9% lower in 1996 than in 1992, a drop accounted for by increases in the shares from work income and from other income (which, respectively, make up an additional 3.2% and 3.7% of total income). The relative weight of these different types of income source differs across different income categories; see Table 6.5.

More than one-third of 1996 household income was social income. This share is not considerably lower in any income group except for income groups with incomes over 1.5 times the net average monthly income (or the top 15% of households by income).

The loss of social income is compensated for in various ways. Among groups that have average and above average incomes it mainly arises from, or is mainly compensated for with, an increase in other income, rather than work income. On the contrary, where groups below subsistence level have decreasing social incomes, it is mainly the consequence of an increase in work income.

Table 6.6 shows the relationship between receipt of social income and the social activity of household head. The collective means of social income (in the form of tax revenue) is accumulated from two groups: economically active people and economically inactive people with their own source(s) of subsistence.

A homogeneous, low level of income is only possible where strong and continuous devices of redistribution are at work. However, strong forms of redistribution weaken and demotivate those who produce the means of redistribution. These people seek escape mechanisms such as the gray economy, illegal (noncontributory) work, "official salary" decreases, high rates of employment disability (in comparison with 1996, this has increased, reaching 5.3% on average), an increased sharing of work costs, murky channels for obtaining income (in the formal, informal, and illegal sectors), and even economic crime (like asset-stripping). In essence, strong forms of redistribution push both economically active people and inactive people who have their own source(s) of subsistence into the same income category as other population strata. The determination of the amount of the minimum wage can either reinforce, or respond to, a homogenizing, low-income society. While it can be set at a high rate in order to increase overall income levels, its increase may result in increasing unemployment, thereby decreasing the total means of redistribution and the capacity to set high income levels. A comparison of the income sources of two social groups—the economically active and the unemployed—within the same income band demonstrates the role of redistribution (see Table 6.7).

Perceptions of Poverty

Subjective estimations of the number of low-income households (those with incomes up to SK7,000, or USD234) are prone to overestimation when compared to the number of households included in particular income intervals on the basis of summing individual household members' incomes. On the other hand, subjective estimations tend to produce underestimations of the number of households with high incomes. The error in both directions is approximately 3%.

There is a significant gulf between real household incomes and the income that is necessary to meet household needs. According to their statements, over 70% of households that were in deteriorating financial situations needed SK7,000 per month or more to survive. However, less than 30% of these households had this sum at their disposal.

In contrast to rather favorable "objective" findings about the socioeconomic situation of households, data on subjective attitudes indicate continuing large-scale poverty.

Research on a representative sample of 1,204 respondents (all with permanent addresses) enables us to identify the most endangered part of the adult population in terms of their ability (or lack thereof) to meet basic and "developing" needs. This research confirmed that most at risk are the unemployed, pensioners, and people with an elementary education or less. Almost one-quarter of all respondents consider their household to be poor, and one-quarter do not consider their household poor. However, more than two-fifths stated that they consider their household poor in certain situations. When questioned about the specific situations in which they consider their household poor, respondents gave various answers. The most frequent response (36%) was that they considered their household poor when spending a holiday away from home. In addition, more than one-fifth of citizens feel poor when they attempt to refurnish their household (when they buy furniture, electric appliances, or accessories). Every fifth citizen feels poor when contemplating the purchase of expensive things (such as a car, garage, or other immovable item) (Information Bulletin Názory 1996).

This research indicates that the ownership relations in the company or organization in which the respondent is employed significantly influence the respondent's living standards and propensity for poverty. Strengthening the private sector of the economy produces a gradual decline in the number of households below the poverty line, as there is a high correlation between the kind of firm ownership and income levels, with higher incomes in the newly established private sector than in the public, or state, sector (Statistical Figures and Charts 1995, 1996).

An inevitable part of market transition is the process of income differentiation. However, two aspects of this process are causing problems. First, differentiation is not occurring simultaneously with an improvement in the living standards of the majority of the population (as it tends to in developed countries); rather, there is a simultaneous deterioration in the average living standard. Second, the criteria used as the basis for differentiation are not generally accepted by society as just, nor do these criteria often accord with those in operation in market economies. Illustrative of the seriousness of present differentiation is the fact that today the legal definition of the subsistence minimum is about 66% of the average per capita income. The consequences are, on the one hand, social tension endangering the social consensus and, on the other hand, depriving groups with low incomes of the satisfaction of their "higher needs." A social structure typical of Latin America—in which the middle-income population stratum is absent—is starting to form. This course of development could lead to a deterioration in the intellectual level (and, ultimately, civilization) of future generations (Radicová 1995).

Explanation of Poverty before the Year 1988 and at Present

Data collected on poor households before 1988 suggest that there was a strong relationship between poverty and households with many dependent members (and thus that there was a close relationship between poverty and a certain phase in the family life cycle). Poverty was generally a temporary period in the life of the family: the group most prone to poverty (approximately 50% of the total poor) was children from two-parent families where only one parent was gainfully employed and that had a maximum of three children. As a rule those in poverty were young households in which the mother was taking care of children less than three years of age. Approximately one-fourth of all children in the Slovak Republic were not, at this stage in their lives, living at the social minimum level. Yet, in more than 90% of these families low incomes ceased to be a problem within three years as the mother began work again (Analýza 1992). Poverty as a "transition period"—connected with a certain stage in the life cycle—is in contradiction to the hypothesis that poverty is rooted in social-cultural factors that may be reproduced within the family. On the other hand, the tendency to enter marriage and have children regardless of economic conditions may signal a certain cultural tendency capable of transmission through the family.

Poor families before 1988 did have some distinguishing social characteristics. A comparison between the characteristics of families living in poverty in 1988 (Kusá 1997) and families presently in poverty suggests that there are some fairly permanent factors contributing to poverty in Slovakia.

The Demographic Structure of Households

In both periods families with dependent children constituted the largest share of poor households. In 1994, 82% of poor households were families with dependent children. Childless families were, in 1993, in the most advantageous situation (with only about 2% of these families below the subsistence-minimum level), and families with four or more children were in the least advantageous (with about 30% living below subsistence level) (Feglová, Kusá, Radicová, and Simunková 1995).

In 1988 the households most often in poverty were newly created families with a head aged 24 (regardless of the number of children). In the 1990s it was more likely for households with older heads to fall below the subsistence minimum. In 1992 about 43% of poor households had middle-aged heads (heads between 30 and 50). In 1994 the most critical period (in terms of the household's risk of impoverishment) was that time before the head reached 44. In households with an older head (from 45 to 65) the situation was relatively favorable, and the probability of sinking below the subsistence-minimum level was four (or even five) times lower.

Both before and since the transition in Slovakia a significant share of poor households is made up of pensioners over 70 years of age (in 1992, 29% of households had a member aged 60 or more).

The Number of Gainfully Employed Household Members and the Number of Dependents

The ratio of dependents to employed household members has had a significant influence on families' situations in both periods. In 1994 the proportion of low-income households among households with an unemployed woman ranged between 28.2% and 51.7%. In households with an employed wife these proportions dropped to between 9.8% and 21.9%.

Social Status of the Head of the Household

In 1988 among the sample of young families (with household heads age 24 or less), the groups most likely to live at or under the subsistence minimum were "others" (perhaps including married students), workers, and agricultural workers. In 1994 the households most frequently with low incomes were the families of workers and of agricultural workers. The occurrence of low incomes was approximately the same for families of employees and for families of the self-employed.

The Level of Education of the Head of a Household

Before 1988 there was no research dedicated to analyzing the educational level of household heads in relation to poverty. However, from the overrepresentation of workers' and agricultural workers' households among those living in poverty and from our knowledge of these workers as, in large part, possessing only vocational or primary school education, an association between poverty and the head's educational level can be deduced. In 1992 about 41% of poor households had heads who had only a primary education, but there were also about the same number (about 40%) in which the head had completed secondary school education. In 1994 the groups that were the worst off were households in which the head had either an incomplete secondary education (secondary education without graduation) or a complete vocational one. Although a significantly smaller share of low-income households had heads with higher or university education, 8.5% of all Slovak households in which the head had university education lived below the subsistence-minimum level.

Household Situation by Urban or Rural Settlement

According to 1988 data on the distribution of poverty by settlement size and region of the Slovak Republic (Feglová, Kusá, Radicová, and Simunková 1995), there were more households below the subsistence-minimum level in towns (70% of all impoverished households) than in villages and more in towns of over 10,000 inhabitants than in smaller ones. In 1994 the situation in larger settlements appeared more favorable; with increases in the size of the village comes a decreasing share of low-income households.

Type of Apartment and Household Facilities

The kind of accommodation (e.g., a family or rented house, the number of rooms) and the existence of particular household facilities (e.g., a washing machine, television set, refrigerator) did not in the past, and still does not, distinguish poor from rich households.

Regional Distribution of Poverty

In both periods low-income households were unevenly regionally distributed. The most impoverished regions were in eastern and southern Slovakia. More precise pictures of the distribution of poverty and its relation to characteristics of the social area (e.g., the kind of work opportunities available) are possible only on a district-by-district basis.

The preceding characteristics can be used to create a summary picture of the modal low-income household in the Slovak Republic today. This household includes a single breadwinner who is a worker either in agriculture or in industry. Its head's highest educational level is either vocational or incomplete secondary school. In the household live two or more children, and it is located in a village with less than 5,000 inhabitants.

THE POOR AND THE NOT-SO-POOR

Discussion and analysis of poverty in Slovakia are weak or, more precisely, are based on low-income families and on those in social need. Most statistics and analytical materials concentrate on those in need, not explicitly on poverty. In other words, analyses are based on poverty in relative, not absolute, meaning.

The change in the philosophy and practice of economic management also involved changes in state guarantees regarding the standard of living. With economic reform came violation of the continuity of the measurement system that had, throughout the period of state socialism, governed the development of the standard of living through the means of economic planning.

Before 1989 living conditions were relatively equal, life activities were uniform, and the emphasis was primarily on meeting fundamental needs. This led to intolerance toward differences in living standards, and thus people attempted to cover up potential differences or were demotivated to improve their qualifications. A family with two incomes was fixed as the standard in setting wages; however, real income fluctuation was caused by fluctuations in social income (maximum income limits, central regulation, and the tax system), which, in turn, was tied to the number of people being provided for. In practice, social incomes only partially compensated for cost-of-living increases found in families with a larger than average number of dependents.

Income differentiation emerged from government policy that rated different departments (sectors) of the economy differently. Thus, in the "productive" sectors (mining, the military, etc.), incomes continued to be pegged to standard-of-living estimates, whereas in the so-called non-productive sectors (health care, education) incomes have been, over the long term, kept at below-average levels (in 1994 the average monthly wage in mining was SK7,364; in education SK5,096; and in health care SK5,451). The average monthly wage was SK6,088 (*Statistical Review of the Slovak Republic* 1994, 1995). Below-average wages were found only in education, health care, public and social services, and agriculture. Important for achieving a specific standard of living have been both the development of family networks and participation in the second economy. In addition to social incomes, the second economy has made a relative increase in families' living standards possible, although at the price of an enormous expenditure of energy and the detriment of leisure time (Radicová 1996)

The main change in the state's attitude toward the standard of living is a shift from defining maximum normative limits, to defining a minimum normative limit, to the definition of a subsistence minimum (this can be defined using two methods based on either consumption or income distributions. In Slovakia the subsistence minimum, until 1998 or 1999, is defined as the last decile of households in the income distribution).

Subsistence Level

Law No. 463:1991 of the Collection on the Subsistence Level (amended by law No. 277:1993 of the Collection) and regulated by the Ministry of Labor, Social Affairs and Family (MPSVaR) according to law No. 243:1993 of the Collection on Social Dependency (social need) outlines the criteria for social dependence. A socially dependent citizen (a citizen in need of social care and/or social benefits) is one whose income does not total the sum necessary to meet sustenance and other basic personal needs as well as necessary household costs (as given by legal definitions of the subsistence level). Another condition for social dependence is that a citizen does not increase his income through his own efforts. This means that if she is unemployed, she must be registered in a labor office. Local offices give socially dependent citizens regular social benefits.

Individual benefits (e.g., to cover health expenses, or expenses consequent to the death of a member of a socially dependent family) can be provided by municipalities. However, their allocation depends on the municipal budget.

A citizen can obtain social assistance from the state if she or he applies for it. The process of receiving social benefits begins with an application to a local office, including proof of the applicant's social situation. A particular level of household furnishing is also used as a standard by which to evaluate applicants, and applicants' property assets are stated using a statutory declaration. Whether and how much social benefit will be given depend on the local office's department of social affairs and the health of the local office's budget. There are four social groups that are in need but do not apply for social benefits:

1.   people who do not apply because they do not fulfill conditions of application, such as holding a permanent address (as is the case for the homeless);

2. people who do not know that their income is lower than subsistence level and therefore do not know that they have a right to apply for assistance;
3. young people without income who live with relatives with incomes and who do not know that they can apply;
4. families where the relations between parents are not clearly legally defined do not apply for child allowance.

Because they do not come into contact with social benefit offices there is no information about how large these groups of people in need are.

The subsistence level is legally tied to low-income jobholder households' cost-of-living index (where the definition of a jobholder is not clear, it is possible to use an "average household" to determine the cost-of-living index). Valuation (regular increase of social income according to the rate of inflation) occurs only if the cost-of-living index has increased by at least 10% since a previous evaluation of the subsistence level. Based on data from family accounts, comparing levels of net monthly income in low-income households with levels of net monthly income in all households, it appears that there was an increase in the cost-of-living index by 10% (and so the first valuation of the subsistence level should have occurred) in 1991 and again in 1994 (valuation is, on average, also 10%).

However, in reality only one law on the subsistence level (No. 463:1991) was adopted in 1991. At the end of 1993 this was amended by law No. 277:1993, which made it pertinent to an independent Slovakian Republic. The subsistence level is based on relative income levels and differentiates between households on the basis of the number and age of people living in the household. The subsistence level consists of two parts: a sum to cover sustenance and other basic personal or individual needs and a sum to cover the necessary and inevitable costs of household upkeep. The sum necessary for sustenance and other basic personal needs is divided into five categories and set using concrete rates.

The law on the subsistence level does not serve as the basis for a claim to any benefits. Rather, it is a legal regulation on which other legal regulations rest, and it is on these that either a claim to a certain benefit or a particular allowance can be based. The law on the subsistence level serves to identify a circle of recipients (using income testing) and aids in the derivation of rates for certain social security benefits. Thus, it is understood that a package of goods and services is necessary if households below subsistence level are to be able to fulfill their needs at a level that is recognized by society (at any given time) as the minimum necessary for the maintenance of a reasonable consumption level and a normal social life. The subsistence level includes the costs of current consumption (sustenance, other basic personal needs, expenses connected with general household operation) but excludes expenses connected with the purchase and replacement of objects used over the mid- or long-term.

Recipients of Social Assistance—Socially Dependent Citizens or the Really Poor

At the end of 1995, 274,932 people (or 5.1% of the total population) were registered recipients of social assistance benefits. After including dependents (who are mentioned in social assistance claims), the number of socially dependent people in Slovakia was 408,507, or 8% of the total population (*Social Policy in SR in 1996* 1997). Despite a 1995 decrease in the number of people dependent on social assistance, there has been an increase in those with incomes on the borders of the social dependence level as legislation on the subsistence minimum has shifted the social dependence limit so that it encompasses a higher-income group (and enables more of the low-income population to claim social care benefit).

Social assistance benefits for families with dependent children are normally provided on a monthly basis to about 84,000 families (or 21% of all families with dependent children). This suggests that families with dependent children are, over the long term, in a disadvantageous social situation that is usually solved only with repeated injections of social assistance and benefits. An increasing number of families draw social benefits during disadvantageous economic periods as a consequence of one parent's, and in some cases both parents', persistent unemployment. This is particularly true of low-income, young families. Thus, the adverse situation faced by families with dependent children is the consequence of long-term unfavorable developments in the economic sphere and the effect of these on the labor market.

The "contribution granted to dependent children," where the court obliges someone to pay a sustenance allowance, has increased 580% since 1989. In 1995, 130,205 people received this "contribution" (*Report on Social Situation of the SR Population in 1995* 1995).

The group of people who draw "benefits for citizens in need of special care" is at substantial risk. In the majority of cases their only income is social assistance benefits (for other people these benefits merely complement existing income, bringing it to the social dependence limit). This group is over-whelmingly made up of the unemployed (registered as job applicants) who either live alone or are in other families without dependent children, or they are under-age job applicants. In 1995, 167,000 people depended on this kind of benefit (13.7% more than in the previous year) (*Social Policy in SR in 1996* 1997).

In 1995, a total of 4,875 socially unadjusted people were registered for, and received, the special "social assistance benefit for socially unadjusted citizens" (socially unadjusted people are those who are released from prison, detoxicants, dependent on alcohol or toxins, etc.).

Unemployment and Social Need

Central problems in the area of employment are:

- a large regional concentration and differentiation, in unemployment. In 1994, 15 regions out of a total of 38 in the Slovakian Republic had an unemployment rate higher than 20%. In 1995, four regions had an unemployment rate higher than 20%. Since the end of January 1999 the unemployment rate in the SR has risen by 0.7 points, reaching the level of 16.33%. The highest unemployment rates are found in the districts of Rimavska Sobota (33.54%), Revuca (32.83%), and Velky Krtis (30.51%). The lowest rates of unemployment have been recorded in the districts of Bratislava IV (3.12%), Bratislava III (3.71%) and Bratislava II (4.17%) (*Selected Figures about Regions in the SR for 1997; Inter-regional Comparison in the SR for 1994*).

- a high number of applicants for each available job. At the beginning of 1994 there were 46 job applicants for each available job; toward the end of 1995 there were 22 applicants (Radicová 1997).

- a high unemployment rate among school graduates, especially among people with a reduced capacity to work and among groups that are not fully socially integrated (in particular, the Roma). There is a considerable disparity between the qualifications required of people filling available jobs and the qualification structure of job applicants. In December 1995 only 11% of available positions were for unqualified and unskilled laborers, yet the proportion of the unemployed who were untrained (those with only elementary education) was 33% (*Report on Social Situation of the SR Population in 1995* 1995).

- a high and ever-increasing number of long-term unemployed. At the end of 1994 the average duration of unemployment, as recorded in the labor office, was 372 days, as compared to December 31, 1993, when unemployment averaged 277 days (*Statistical Bulletin* 1:1996, 2:1996).

The proportion of people unemployed for a long time (over a year) increased by 13.7% between 1993 and 1995, to 53.7%. A close look at long-term unemployment suggests that the causes of this adverse development can be found in the problems faced by certain groups of the population in the labor market. The worst handicap in the labor market is a low level of education; more than 80% of the long-term unemployed are people either with incomplete education or with completed elementary and secondary school education but without a final, leaving exam (*Social Policy in SR in 1996* 1997).

Unemployment among school-leavers is a specific problem. Young people (24 and under) are the second largest group among the long-term unemployed. The largest group is people aged 30 to 39 (who are, in fact, at their most productive age). Besides the direct economic loss that results from an idle workforce, the specific loss of this age group's human capital does considerable damage (Radicová 1996).

A decrease in the number of long-term unemployed requires an increase in the intensity of requalification and a decrease in interregional differences in economic activity. However, the proportion of requalified people among the unemployed remains low (for instance, in the first half of 1995 only 3% of registered job applicants were requalified) (*Report on Social Situation of the SR Population in 1995* 1995). In 1995 government expenditures to help the unemployed were distributed to socially purposeful workplaces, to public beneficiary activities, and to requalification programs in the following respective proportions: 71.1%, 20.8%, and 4.3%. Each year the proportion of expenditures dedicated to requalification programs is reduced (thus a year before, in 1994, it had been 5.7%).

However, the long-term significance of requalification as part of an active employment policy is not great. This is because there are simply not enough jobs (existing and new jobs are already covered by "normally" qualified workers). It is also because the most problematic group (in terms of long-term unemployment) is the unqualified, and for this group requalification is not effective; either long-term education or training is needed. Lastly, because requalification programs are organized at the regional level, where there is often a very low, vague, and uncertain demand for skills, they are generally accompanied by very weak processes of needs assessment, and the need for particular skills is often overestimated (Radicová 1996).

The biggest sums paid by social assistance are benefits determined by the social situation of the unemployed and their families. There were 147,101 job applicants who were social assistance benefit recipients in December 1995, a decline of 12.7% from 1994. In 1995 job applicants registered in labor offices accounted for 83% of all those receiving social assistance benefits because of social dependence (*Social Policy in SR in 1996* 1997). It should be noted that a job applicant is not considered to be a social dependent if, after being removed from the register, he does not work, even if his income is below level of the subsistence minimum. This means that if an unemployed person is taken off of the register because, for instance, of her noncooperation with the labor office, the payment of the social assistance benefits, to which she would be entitled as a social dependent, is stopped. This potentially leads to a group of people living below the subsistence minimum level.

In 1995 job applicants were paid SK4,057.6 million in social assistance benefits and SK2,181.5 million from the Employment Fund's resources for passive labor market policy. This means that the state budget contributed 86% more to the financial security of job applicants than did the Slovakian Employment Fund. Generally stated, SK6,239.1 million was devoted to payments to the unemployed in 1995, 12.8% more than in 1994 (*Slovak Statistics* 1995).

Gender Risks

Today gender does not play an important role in the character of poverty, low-income families, families with dependent children, people in need, and unemployment. As already noted (and because standard-of-living estimates are based on two-income families), one-parent families with dependent children are among the social groups in need. Usually, a one-parent family is a female-parent family. However, if a man is in the same situation he faces the same problems as a woman. In other words, impoverishment is not caused by gender itself but by the social reality encountered by one-parent families.

Gender differences are connected to the labor market. As Table 6.8 shows, women and men are concentrated in different economic sectors.

Two-thirds of women are employed in 10 (out of 54) economic sectors. The majority of women are employed in the sectors that have the lowest incomes or that have below-average incomes.

As a consequence of this, there are income differences between men and women. Women's incomes are, on average, 10–15% lower than men's. This concentration of women in typically "female" sectors and professions is inherited from the former regime and is the effect of the different cultural and value systems of Slovakian women.

The rate of 46.4% of women who are economically active is higher than, for example, the rate in Austria and Germany and lower than in Finland or Sweden. A total of 78.8% of women are in part -time jobs. The main reasons for women to work part-time are their health, child care, an employer's initiative, and their own personal decision (*Women about Themselves* 1997).

The Risk of Becoming and Remaining Homeless

Expenditures on housing play a critical part in the household budget. However, there remains no correlation between increasing rents and real costs. The Slovak government continues to postpone the implementation of a new system of rents based on economic principles (these were initially prepared in March 1994 but, even after their last "due date" of August 1995, had not come into force), and the state offers no support for housing construction (*Actualized Proposal of State Residential Policy Conception* 1995–1996). Yet socially dependent households at today's incomes and without state support cannot provide housing for themselves.

The statistical office of the Slovak Republic did a survey in 1995 and found that 7% of households had not been able to pay rent several times during the last 12 months and that 4% of households had not been able to pay rent once in the last year. Six percent of households had been unable to pay for electricity and heating several times in the year, and 4% had been unable to pay for these amenities on one occasion in the year. If there is the possibility of buying an apartment from the state, 36.3% of households can pursue it only using loans. To the extent that support from the state is not directly the result of, or regulated by, laws, it is practically dependent on the state budget. This budget is insufficient to cover the actual need (or requests) for housing support (*Information Bulletin Názory* 1996).

Minority Risk—Foreigners and Ethnic Minorities

Foreigners have a right to be employed in Slovakia if they have permanent residence, refugee status, or long-term residence (with a work visa and permission to work). Permission to work is given by the district labor office. By the end of 1995, granted over the course of 1995, there were 3,784 applicants and 2,686 people who were granted permission to work in the Slovak Republic (0.12% of the total number employed) (Radicová 1997).

Slovakia's population was originally heterogeneous in terms of both nationality and religion. Apart from the majority Slovak population, there are a large number of Hungarians and Roma and about 10 other nationalities in smaller numbers. The majority are Catholic, but there are also Protestants, Greek

Catholics, an Orthodox population, and other believers, as well as a large share of the population who describe themselves as "without religion."

The Roma are in an unfavorable social situation. By the end of 1995 they accounted for 24.4% of recorded job applicants, up from 12.4% at the end of 1994 (*Report on Social Situation of the SR Population in 1995* 1995).

Roma youth are particularly affected by the problem of long-term unemployment. Approximately 60% of young unemployed Roma (14–24-year-olds) have been seeking jobs for almost a year, and the remainder, for over a year (the proportion of Roma among the unemployed is about 13%). The reasons for high Roma unemployment are lower qualifications and education and a high proportion of Roma who have limited work abilities. The Roma population suffers from the coexistence of a number of characteristics that increase the risk of long-term unemployment and impoverishment (e.g., low levels of qualification and high rates of disability).

THE "ROMA PROBLEM"

The social situation of the Roma is deteriorating, and many of them now fall into the category of the absolutely poor.[1] The social distance of the rest of the population from Roma is very high, and cases of discrimination, as well as open racism, remain common. Moreover, the majority of Slovak citizens refuse to act in solidarity with Roma.

Sociological surveys that have monitored attitudes toward national minorities have found that the social distance felt toward the Roma is the greatest. Hostility toward Roma is spread, with equal intensity, through all strata of Slovak society and has not changed over time. According to a FOCUS survey (FOCUS 1994), Roma are not "appropriate" neighbors for four-fifths of Slovaks. According to an Institute for Public Opinion (ÚVVM) survey (ÚVVM 1995), 77% of Slovaks evaluate their attitudes toward Roma as "very bad." In addition, 52% of those interviewed by ÚVVM agree that more severe legislation should be adopted to deal with the Roma, and 66% agree that the majority population should be separated from the Roma.

The Slovak Republic and its state bodies have been criticized by the European Union, the Council of Europe, and the United States for their approach toward national minorities. After the parliamentary elections of 1994 this criticism is fair. However, the situation of all minorities (including political and social minorities) is also deteriorating—the general political situation has become unbearable, the political polarization of society has increased, and very serious deficits of democracy have appeared. The situation of the Roma is seriously affected by this development—deficiencies in solutions to the so-called Roma problem come from deficiencies in the application of democratic principles.

The Situation of the Roma in Slovakia until 1989

In the postwar period the state authorities refused to accept the Roma as a distinct nationality. They supposed that the Roma could overcome their "backwardness" only if they gave up their way of life and assimilated, as much as possible, with the majority population. In practice this meant that no Roma folk music ensembles or youth or sport clubs could be established, no Romany songs could be sung at schools, no Romany books or magazines were published, and there were no Romany fairy tales for children on television. Neither the name Roma nor Gypsy was used; the state authorities called them "citizens of Gypsy origin."

The efforts of the state were aimed at solving the housing problems, low employment, and poor school attendance of the Roma. Although these intentions were good, solutions were enforced without sensitivity, without sufficient expertise, and with more or less violence. The process of settling down nomadic Vlachika Roma continued in a similar vein. Politicians believed that it was better to live in houses than as nomads and, without consulting the relevant group of nomadic Roma, passed a law in 1958 that "settled them down." Soon horses and carriage wheels were confiscated. Likewise, the solution to the housing problem was primitive. Many families were violently taken to the Czech districts, where they were ordered to settle down. Other Roma families were moved into new blocks of flats but were unable to adapt to the new conditions. Many Roma felt alone and out of touch with their relatives in these newly designated places of residence and began returning to their home settlements.

Similar procedures were used in the program to educate Roma children. Many ordinances were adopted that forced Roma parents to send children to schools. However, Roma mothers usually did not understand the necessity of educating their children and felt that they were suffering at school. State authorities did not try to know the Roma or to understand their opinions about life but instead enforced their own ideas of what was good and used large financial resources in doing so. Afterward they blamed the Roma for the lack of success of the policies that they had unilaterally imposed on them (Vašecka 1995).

1989—Turning Point for the Roma in Slovakia

The year 1989 was a turning point for the Roma for many reasons. Shortly after the November 1989 changes, the first Roma political party was established—the Romany Civil Initiative. After this many other parties and cultural associations appeared. In 1990 Roma were, for the first time, elected to the Parliament, and their representatives got into important positions in, for instance, the Office of the Government of the Slovak Republic, the Ministry of Culture, and the Ministry of Education. However, the Roma political scene remains too shattered to be effective. There are 38 Roma political parties registered at the Ministry of Interior, but only three of them are national—the Romany Civil Initiative, Romany Intelligence for the Coexistence, and the Party for the Protection of Romanies.

In the area of culture and education, the Roma weekly *Romano il* (Romany Letter) was started, as was a monthly magazine, *Roma*. In 1993 the professional Roma theater Romathan was established in Kosice, and there are now regular programs on the radio and television devoted to the Roma. At the Pedagogical School in Nitra a new Department of Roma Culture was established to educate teachers going to teach in primary schools with a high proportion of Roma children. Present teachers of Roma children have joined to form the "0 classes club," discussing ways to make school more attractive to Roma pupils. In addition, the Art High School, oriented to Roma culture, was started in 1995 in Kosice. In 1993 the children's textbook *Romano Hangoro* and the reader *Genibarica* were published.

On the other hand, the social transformation initiated in 1989 brought high unemployment to the Roma and thus caused additional impoverishment. High unemployment is among the factors that have resulted in the Roma being unprepared for social change and their refusing to adapt. The pseudo-universalistic system of welfare existent before 1989 provided the Roma with social benefits but did not allow them a say. However, many Roma liked and got used to these benefits.[2] Low levels of education and insufficient qualifications make it difficult for Roma to be successful in the labor market. Many give up, losing the motivation necessary to find solutions to their own social problems. Instead, they become reliant on the unemployment benefits and social security that they receive from the government. In 1995 labor offices tried to reduce the number of unemployed by deleting from their registers those who rejected a job offer as "reluctant to cooperate."

A Description of Roma Legislation

There is no "special Roma legislation" in Slovakia. However, the rights of all ethnic minorities are protected by the Slovak Constitution (Articles 33 and 34). According to the constitution, the Roma are guaranteed the right to develop their own culture, the right to education in their mother tongue, and the right to be involved in matters relating to ethnic minorities. However, under different Slovak governments since 1989, the lower legislative body has initiated and accepted three regulations that relate to Roma. The Slovak government accepted the first postrevolution Initiative on a Rapprochement with the Roma in 1991 (No. 153). Turbulent changes in the Slovak political scene and different government priorities meant that the initiative was not implemented.

The new, 1996 Initiative on a Rapprochement with Citizens Requiring Special Care (No. 310) was based on the earlier one and was provoked by the brutal skinhead attack and homicide in Ziar nad Hronom in 1995. The Governmental Department of the Commissioner for People Requiring Special Care was created as a consequence of this initiative. For more than two years different experts worked on the new governmental initiative, and in November 1997 the new Initiative on Government Rapprochement with the Roma (No. 796) was accepted. Although the material in this initiative is prepared very accurately, there are three problematic aspects to it:

- The material does not allocate any financial resources from the state budget for 1998.

- The material does not offer outlines of institutional competencies and personal responsibilities.
- The material deals with the problems of all Roma (on ethnic lines) but offers solutions exclusively to "people requiring special care."

Conflict Involving the Roma and Problems of Racism in Slovakia

The atmosphere of conflict encompassing the Roma has worsened since 1989. Extremists offering quick-fix solutions to the Roma problem are also given public space in the new democratic environment. Politicians and political parties known for their racism toward the Roma are represented in Parliament and in government (e.g., the Slovak National Party, which is part of the Slovak governing coalition).

The Roma are the most negatively perceived ethnic group. The residents of Slovakia are much more hostile to the Roma than to any other ethnic group, including immigrants of other races. Attacks against Roma are increasingly frequent and are becoming more violent. In July 1995 the first obviously racially motivated homicide was committed in Ziar nad Hronom. During an attack on Roma a group of skinheads beat a 17-year-old Roma boy, Mário Goral. The skinheads poured gasoline on him and set him on fire. Mário Goral died in the hospital 10 days later. Eleven days after the incident the government and the president made a statement about the crime.

After the Ziar nad Hronom incident Roma demanded that the position of an ombudsman or commissioner for Romany issues be created. In response, the government created a commissioner for "citizens requiring special care"; however, the candidate for this position suggested by Roma parties was not appointed. Instead, a non-Roma was appointed to the position.

Since 1989 the social distance between the majority population and Roma has been increasing. Their present form of cohabitation could be characterized as living next to each other, but not together. In the region of eastern Slovakia the process of noninstitutionalized racial segregation has begun (e.g., there are signs in restaurants stating, "Roma are prohibited from entering"). In villages the first attempts to institutionalize this segregation have appeared, with referenda about the separation of Romany settlements from the village (e.g., in the village of Zehra) and decrees prohibiting Roma from going out at night (e.g., in Spisské Podhradie) (Vašecka 1995).

The Status of Roma in Slovakia

The status of the Roma in the Slovak Republic is, in short, bad. Roma are virtually unable to protect their own rights. The following factors may have had an effect on this situation (Vašecka 1995):

1. The Roma are a minority almost without an elite. The layer of Roma intelligentsia in Slovakia is very thin.
2. The Roma are a minority without political representation. The absence of relevant political representation is closely related to the thinness of the Roma intelligentsia. However, it may be that the dispersion of the Romany political space is of even

more consequence here.

3. The Roma are a marginalized minority. They are not used to participating equally in dialogues with the rest of society.

4. The Roma are a minority that overlaps with the bottom layers of society. Roma living standards in Slovakia are generally very low. This is caused by their low educational levels and consequent high rates of unemployment. Roma are the first to lose jobs and find it very hard to get new ones.

5. The Roma are a minority toward which a majority population extends a lot of social distance.

6. The Roma are a minority deprived of its historical roots. Since the era of Maria Theresa few assimilation processes have been initiated in Central Europe. However, even during the last 40 years the Roma in Slovakia have been forced to live according to the rules of the majority. Communist social engineers, in their efforts to create "a new human being," prevented the Roma from continuing as nomads or as blacksmiths and have created a group both marginalized and, in some respects, unable to adapt to life in modern society.

The Ethnicity of the Roma

Ethnicity definitely became more salient in the period after 1989 than it was during communism. Not only is this true for Slovakia, but it is a natural reaction to the proclaimed international character and reality of a closed society that existed under the communist regime. It is also a reaction to unsolved problems that were frozen for more than 40 years and that then emerged, leading to the creation of the independent Slovak state. Furthermore, the recent political changes have brought some ethnic groups the chance to proclaim their ethnicity for the first time—for instance, Roma, who were perceived only as "citizens of Gypsy origin" before 1989, could after 1989 claim their ethnicity. However, the question of Roma national pride is complicated by the social distance of the majority population and negative Roma self-perception. Roma in camps try to hide their ethnic background and want to integrate into the society and consciously neglect Roma culture and traditions.

Roma ethnicity is difficult to define, although the question of who is a Roma may be obvious to nonexperts. Anthropological features tend to be overused as markers of Roma ethnicity, and some Slovak experts, reacting against this approach, have started to define Roma using markers of "enforced identity." However, other than skin color, no methods of identification have been found, and most Slovak researchers do not work on the issue.

Slovak research institutions (such as FOCUS, GFK, the Statistical Institute, AISA Slovakia, and the Slovak Academy of Science Kosice) have been doing research on ethnicity since 1989. However, the only research to focus on Roma ethnicity and Roma self-perception is the 1995 Statistical Institute's "Romanies in 1994." Major findings of this research are:

- The Roma do not want to revive their culture.
- Roma identity has become a private issue; in public Roma intend to assimilate into the majority population.

The low level of Roma ethnic self-identification can be seen in the willingness (or, in this case, lack of willingness) of the Roma to explore their constitutional right to use their own language in an educational setting and cultural context (see Figure 6.1, Appendix). The preference for the Roma language to be used diminishes as respondents are asked about higher levels of education. Furthermore, the majority of Roma oppose the use of the Roma language in all educational settings.

Figure 6.2, charting Roma responses to questions about the use of the Roma language in different parts of the media, also shows a low level of Roma national consciousness.

The low level of ethnic self-identification among Roma can also be seen in the lapsing of Roma traditional practice (Figure 6.3). Almost half of the Roma included in the Statistical Office's sample state that Roma should both adopt the best from the lifestyle of the majority population and simultaneously keep up their own culture. Nineteen percent wanted to maintain old Roma traditions exclusively and 28% hold the opposite opinion, that Roma should adapt to the life of the majority population completely.

According to this research, two-thirds of Roma households keep up all or some Roma traditions. Old traditions are largely maintained by the Roma with the lowest socioeconomic status, those who live in shelters. Roma traditions are most intensively rooted in Roma households based in isolated Roma camps. The Slovak Statistical Office also discovered that 87% of Roma do not want to live a nomadic way of life, and only 40% of those interviewed consider the *vajda* (natural leader of Roma in the region) institution to be necessary.

Poverty and the Roma

Generally speaking, all national minorities in Slovakia have the same standard of living. The exception to this are the Roma, who are overrepresented among the poor. Some experts argue that Ruthenians and some Hungarians are also overrepresented among the very poor, but this phenomenon is tied to issues of the "marginalized regions" of Slovakia, not to ethnicity. There are no statistics available that allow comparison of the poverty of the Roma, Ruthenians, and Hungarians. However, inferences about the poverty of Ruthenians and Hungarians are possible from statistics giving the rates by region of the registered unemployed (on December 31, 1997). Of the 79 districts in Slovakia, 17 have a rate of unemployment of over 18%. All of these districts are among the "marginalized regions" of Slovakia, and Hungarians, Ruthenians, and the Roma are overrepresented in all of them (*Chosen Figures about Regions in the SR for 1997* 1997).

Roma are so overrepresented among the poor that they have become a symbol of poverty and backwardness. However, it is very important to distinguish Roma in the cities from Roma in the villages and camps. These three groups have little in common. The Roma who live in cities experienced the process of assimilation and were relatively well integrated into the majority population. Roma from villages live together with the majority population but have not been assimilated into it. Neither of these two groups of Roma displays any significant features of ethnic poverty. However, Roma who live in Roma camps are very different. These people live in unbearable conditions, and it is not difficult to substantiate the hypothesis that ethnicity is the source of their poverty. Their situation is generally made worse by the fact that Roma camps are usually located in marginalized regions or in regions with high rates of unemployment.

The Roma from Roma camps may be defined as an underclass. However, this issue is complicated by the internal division of the community and the persistence of the caste system. For instance, Vlachike Roma exclude themselves from the Roma community, and the social distance between them and other Roma is even greater than between the Roma and the majority population. The position of the Vlachike Roma is that of an undercaste and has its roots in violence that occurred in the late 1950s (when Vlachike Roma were the only group of Roma who continued to live a nomadic way of life).

Whether there is an underclass in Slovakia is a provocative question. The institutional networks of social policy cover all of the citizens of Slovakia; practically nobody can be institutionally excluded from the society in the way that is possible in the United States. However, this issue rests on a theoretical debate that is both ongoing and controversial.

CONCLUSION

The global figures on expenses paid for the social package, which this state has to push ahead, represent approximately 14% of GDP, which is 4% more than in the developed Western countries. The size of the social package is considerable, having an influence on the competitiveness of the economy.

A serious problem concerning the income differentiation is represented by the fact that 76% of households fall within the range from half of the average net income per person to 1.5 times the net monthly income per person (in the United States, 54%), and 85% of households up to twofold the average net income per person.

The comparison to the United States is significant: GDP per capita in constant prices in 1995 was USD26,016; in Slovakia, USD3,240. Average annual income per person in the United States in 1995 was USD17,227; in Slovakia, USD1,389. Average monthly nominal wage in the United States was USD1,500; in Slovakia, USD242.

The crucial aspect of the social situation is the overall low income level and, most of all, the insolvent middle strata with poor income. The insolvency of the middle strata is consequently reflected, by way of tax and insurance payments, in all areas of social policy (in social welfare, health care, housing policy, education policy, and labor market policy).

Owing to redistribution principles, 46% of the economically active citizens and 44% of the unemployed appear to be in the same income range—half of the net average income per person. For the economically active citizens in this income category, the question remains whether it makes sense to remain employed at all. The system of social security, derived from redistribution, is always connected with the risk of work demotivation. In a situation when, for the majority of the population, work is not a gate to a better standard of living, as a considerable part of production is dispensed not in the principle of solidarity but in the principle of redistribution, the demotivation effect is increasing, and the principle of individual responsibility is weakening. An extensive welfare state becomes a tool of status quo reproduction (its limitation means decline of the overall standard of living), and at the same time it is an obstacle to any advancement or growth. If until 1989 the social incomes were the factor of differentiation in the society, today they are the factor of homogenization of the society. In this respect, the most discriminated social group is the economically active citizens. The social policy thus can fulfil only its regulatory function; however, it has no chance for prevention. It solves urgent problems produced by the employment policy and the general macroeconomic situation. Without recovery of the economy and restructuring of economic sources, the social policy will remain in the position of ad hoc solutions and socialistic redistribution mechanisms, the result of which will be an officially low standard of living.

The view of the general social situation of households in the SR and the comparison with the situation in other transforming countries generate one basic conclusion—the social policy measures do not offer a solution. Extending the already strong welfare state is, in terms of resources, not only endangered but even potentially endangers the further creation of resources. In the long run, under the current conditions, more and more redistribution means will have to be incurred in order to maintain the current level of social income. Unless a fundamental, significant change occurs in economic policy, which would reinforce, most of all, the middle class, the social policy will be able to fulfil its regulatory function only with vital problems. Minor changes in individual benefits, or changes of competencies of individual persons, are not the option. The current principle of redistribution should therefore be replaced by the principle of solidarity for the groups with specific needs. Guided by this type of principle, social policy might prevent social threats instead of simply extinguishing existing problems.

APPENDIX

Table 6.1
Percent of Households at Social and Subsistence Minimum Levels

Year	% of households in category of social minimum level	% of households in category of subsistence minimum level
1958	21%	n/a
1980	13%	1.54%
1985	10.4%	1.60%
1988	9.56%	1.13%

Table 6.2
Average Monthly Income per Person (SK)

Year	1970	1980	1988	1992	1996
Cash	892	1,364	1,699	2,155	3,471
In kind	69	46	68	91	75
Total	961	1,410	1,767	2,246	3,546

Table 6.3

Households by Social Activity of the Household Head and by Net Cash Income per Person in 1996

	% Econ. Active[1]	% Unem[2]	% Econ. inactive with own source of subsist.[3]	% House-wives[4]	Retired[5]	Total[6]
Up to the subsistence level (SL) (inclusive) SK 1,736	9.3	46.7	25.8	66.7	3.7	8.8
From SL up to average	45.7	44.2	12.2	28.6	38.7	37.7
Average SK 3,472	5.3	1.3	0.0	0.0	9.8	6.7
Up to 1.5 times the average SK 5,208	26.5	5.8	11.4	0.0	42.9	31.3
Up to 2 times the average SK 6,944	4.2	1.8	14.1	0.0	4.0	9.5
2 times of the average and more	9.0	0.1	35.7	0.0	0.9	5.92
Total[1]	100 %	100%	100 %	100 %	100 %	100 %

1. The economically active are those people who, at the time of the survey, were employed or were in a similar relationship with an organization, association, private person, or other legal entity; employers; and the self-employed (private farmers, craftsmen, tradesmen, etc.), regardless of the length of their service. Included in the group are also people in basic military service or in civil military service, people in custody or those serving a sentence, working pensioners, and women on maternity leave.
2. The unemployed (work applicants), include all people seeking work, regardless of whether they are receiving benefits: people made redundant following firm closures or organizational changes; school graduates who have never been in a work relationship; released prisoners, unable to find work after their incarceration; citizens presently between jobs; women who, following maternity leave, are unable to return to their original place of work.
3. The economically inactive with their own sources of subsistence are people who live on the income from property.
4. Housewives are women without a work relationship. This category does not include women who are at home involuntarily (e.g., women who were dismissed from work following organizational changes or the company's closure) or women on maternity leave.
5. The retired are citizens whose main source of income is a pension (retirement, disability, widow's or widower's).
6. Variations from 100 % were caused as a result of rounding in initial information.

Source: Authors' calculations based on Microcensus 1997, Institute of Statistics of the SR 1997.

Table 6.4
Households by Level of Net Monthly Cash Income per Person in 1992 and 1996

Total	1996		1992	Difference in 1996
Up to the level of SL (inclusive) SK1,736	8.8 %	Up to the level of SL (inclusive) SK1,078	2.8 %	+ 6 %
From SL to average	37.7 %	From SL to average	41.7 %	- 4 %
Average SK3,472	6.7 %	Average SK2,155	6.2 %	+ 0.5 %
Up to 1.5 times average SK5,208	31.3 %	Up to 1.5 times average SK3,233	39.6 %	- 8.3 %
Up to 2 times average SK6,944	9.5 %	Up to 2 times average SK4,310	6.7 %	+ 2.8 %
2 times average and more	5.9 %	2 times average and more	3 %	+ 2.9 %
Sum	100 %		100 %	

Source: Authors' own calculations of Microcensus 1992.

Table 6.5
Household Income Structure by Net Monthly Income per Person in 1996 and 1992

	Work 1996 1992 differ.		Social 1996 1992 differ.		Other 1996 1992 differ.		Total
Up to SL (inclusive)	42.5 % 32.6 %	+ 9.9	53.2 % 66.3 %	- 13.1	4.3 % 1.1 %	+ 3.2	100 %
From SL to average	60.5 % 58.1 %	+ 2.4	36 % 41.2 %	- 5.2	3.5 % 0.7 %	+ 2.8	100 %
Average	58.8 % 57.2 %	+ 1.6	37.3 % 42.2 %	- 4.9	3.9 % 0.6 %	+ 3.3	100 %
Up to 1.5 times average	66.2 % 64.4 %	+ 1.8	29.5 % 35.1 %	- 5.6	4.3 % 0.5 %	+ 3.8	100 %
Up to 2 times average	84.6 % 81.8 %	+ 2.8	10.2 % 16.9 %	- 6.7	5.2 % 1.3 %	+ 3.9	100 %
2 times average and more	87.1 % 88.5 %	- 1.4	5.7 % 7.1 %	- 1.4	7.2 % 4.5 %	+ 2.7	100 %
Total	66.8% 63.6 %	+ 3.2	28.5 % 35.4 %	- 6.9	4.7 % 1.0 %	+ 3.7	100 %

Table 6. 6

Household Income Structure by Level of Social Activity of Household Head

	Work income	Social	Other	Total
Economically active	83.7 %	11.8 %	4.5 %	100 %
Unemployed	37.4 %	56.0 %	6.6 %	100 %
Econ. inactive with own source of subsistence	41.0 %	8.9 %	50.1 %	100 %
Housewife	25.6 %	67.9 %	6.5 %	100 %
Old pensioner	20.6 %	74.6 %	3.9 %	100 %
Total	66.8 %	28.5 %	4.7 %	100 %

Sources: Authors' own calculations based on Microcensus 1997; Institute of Statistics of the SR 1997.

Table 6.7

Household Income Structure by Level of Net Income per Person Based on Social Activity of Household Head

	Work		Social		Other	
	Econ. active	Unem.	Econ. active	Unem.	Econ. active	Unem.
Up to SL (incl.)	59.9 %	20.4 %	35.9 %	76.5 %	4.2 %	3.1 %
From SL to average	77.3 %	41.4 %	19.3 %	52.0 %	3.4 %	6.9 %
Average	83.6 %	60.2 %	12.4 %	18.2 %	4.0 %	21.6 %
Up to 1.5 times average	87.1 %	69.0 %	9.0 %	20.5 %	3.9 %	10.5 %
Up to 2 times average	89.5 %	52.8 %	5.7 %	16.2 %	4.8 %	30.9 %
2 multiple times and more	89.2 %	0.0 %	4.3 %	0.0 %	6.5 %	100 %
Together	83.7 %	34.4 %	11.8 %	56.0 %	4.5 %	6.6 %

Source: Authors' own calculations based on Microcensus 1997; Institute of Statistics of the SR 1997.

Table 6.8
Employment Share of Women and Men by Sectors

Sector	Women	Men	Sum
Trade	60%	40%	100%
Education	76.9%	23.1%	100%
Healthcare	79.8%	20.2%	100%
Textile industry	75.6%	24.2%	100%
Clothing industry	91%	9%	100%
Leather industry	68.3%	31.7%	100%
Hotels, restaurants	63.2%	36.8%	100%
Communication	61.9%	38.1%	100%
Monetary/insurance	75%	25%	100%

Source: Slovak Statistics 1995.

Figure 6.1
Opinion of Romanies about Usage of Roma Language in Education Process (%)

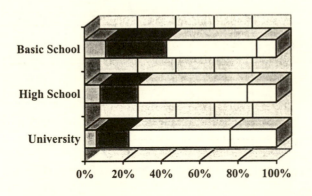

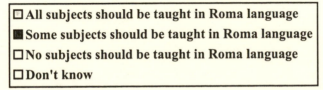

Source: Statistical Figures and Charts, 1995.

Figure 6.2
Opinion on Exercising the Roma Language (%)

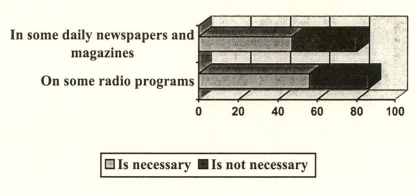

Source: Statistical Figures and Charts, 1995.

Figure 6.3
Maintaining National Traditions in the Household (%)

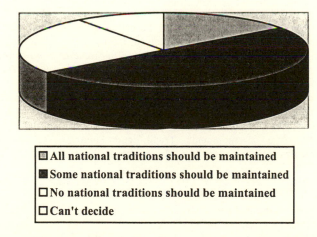

Source: Statistical Figures and Charts, 1995.

NOTES

1. However, the process of differentiation is also taking place among the Roma.

2. The forced full employment that existed under the communist regime was not always positive or as universal as it initially appeared. Often the rate of Roma employment was not very high because many Roma were retired as disabled following local doctors' diagnoses—a practice that "solved" the problem of hidden unemployment.

REFERENCES

Actualized Proposal of State Residential Policy Conception, Ministry of Residential Development and Public-beneficiary Works, January 1996, October 1995, Bratislava.

Analýza struktury chudého obyvatelstva v Ceskoslovensku v roce 1998 (Analysis of the Structure of Poor Inhabitants of Czechoslovakia in 1998). Bratislava: VÚPSVaR, 1999.

Basic Figures in the Field of Social Security in the Development Series 1957–1994 (Základné údaje z oblasti sociálneho zabezpecenia vo vývojových radoch 1957–1994). Bratislava: Ministry of Labor, Social Affairs, and Family, 1995.

Bútora, M., and Huncík, P. (eds.). *Slovensko 1995* (Slovakia 1995). Bratislava: IVO - Institute of Public Affairs, 1996.

The Constitution of the SR. Bratislava, 1992.

Chudoba ako sociálny problém (Poverty as a Social Problem). Volume, BICFS, MPSVaR, Statistický úrad SR, Bratislava, 1995.

Dostál, O. "Minorities." In *Global Report on Slovakia*, edited by M. Bútora. Bratislava: Institute of Public Affairs, 1997.

FOCUS. *Aktuálne problémy Slovenska* (Actual Problems of Slovakia—Sociological Survey). Bratislava: Centrum pre sociálnu analýzu, 1994.

Feglová, V., Kusá, Z., Radicová, I., and Simunková K. *Conceptualization of Poverty in Slovakia—Discussion on Methodological Issues and Measurement*. Budapest: MWA–Max Weber Foundation, 1995.

GFK. *Problémy tolerance a intolerance v CR a SR* (The Problems of Tolerance and Intolerance in Czech and Slovak Republics). Praha: Institut pro výzkum trhu., 1995.

Gurán, P., and Filadelfiová, J. *Hlavné demografické trendy a rodina, Svet—Európa—Slovensko* (The Main Demographic Trends and Family, World—Europe—Slovakia). Bratislava: BICFS—Bratislava International Centre for Family Studies, 1995.

A Helsinki Watch Report: Struggling for Ethnic Identity. Czechoslovakia's Endangered Gypsies. New York: Human Rights Watch, 1992.

Indicators of Economic Development of the SR (Indikátory ekonomického vývoja SR). Bratislava: Statistics Institute of the SR, 1996.

Information Bulletin Názory. Bratislava: Statistics Institute of the SR 7, 1996.

Inter-regional Comparison in the SR for 1994 (Medziokresné porovnania v SR za rok 1994). Bratislava: Statistics Institute of the SR, 1994.

Kolektív autorov. *Etnické mensiny na Slovensku* (The Ethnic Minorities in Slovakia). Kosice, Spolocenský ústav SAV, 1991.

Koncepcné zámery vlády SR na riesenie problémov Rómov v súcasných spolocensko-ekonomických podmienkach (vládny materiál, zodpovedný BALÁZ, B.). Bratislava, 1998.

Kusá, Z. (ed.). *Past and Present Poverty*. Bratislava: SPACE, 1997.

Mann, A. B. Utrpenie Rómov pocas druhej svetovej vojny (The Roma Suffering during World War II). Detva, Dom kultúry A. Sládkovica Detva, 1991.

Mann, A. B. (ed.). Neznámi Rómovia (Unknown Romanies). Národopisný ústav SAV, Bratislava, Ister Science Press, 1992.

Práca a sociálna politika (Work and Social Policy) No. 1:1996, 2:1996, 3:1996, 4:1996, 5:1996, 6:1996.

Radicová, I. Human Dignity and Social Exclusion, Council of Europe, Brussel, HDSE project (97) 17.

Radicová, I. (ed.). Pre ludí a ludoch (For People and about People). Bratislava: SPACE, 1995.

Radicová, I. "Statism, Egalitarism and Transition: The Case of Slovakia." International Review on Comparative Public Policy 7, 1996.

Radicová, I. Sumár rizikových faktorov sociálnej politiky (Sum of Risk Factors of Social Policy), IS SAS, Sociológia 6, Bratislava, 1996.

Radicová, I. and Woleková, H. "Sociálna politiky a sociálna situácia" (Social Policy and Social Situation). In Slovakia 1997. Bratislava: IVO, 1998.

Report on Social Situation of the SR Population in 1995. Ministry of Labor, Social Affairs, and Family, Bratislava, 1995.

Slovenská statistika a demografi (Slovak Statistics and Demography). Bratislava: Statistics Institute of the SR, 1993, 1995, 1996.

Social Policy in SR in 1996. Bratislava: Ministry of Labor, Social Affairs, and Family, 1997.

Statistical Analysis and Information in 1995. Complete series. Bratislava: Slovak Statistics Institute (SSI).

Statistical Bulletin, 1:1996, 2:1996, Statistics Institute of the SR, Bratislava.

Statistical Figures and Charts. Complete series. Bratislava: SSI, 1995, 1996.

Statistical Review of the Slovak Republic, 4:1994, 1:1995, 2:1995.

Sveton, J. Vývoj obyvatelstva na Slovensku (Development of the Population in Slovakia). Bratislava: Epocha, 1969.

Ústav pre výskum verejnej mienky pri Statistickom Urade SR. Rómovia v roku 1994 (Správa zo sociologického výskumu) (The Romanies in 1994—Sociological Survey). Bratislava: Statistický Úrad SR, 1994.

Ústav pre výskum verejnej mienky pri Statistickom Úrade SR. Rasizmus, xenofóbia, antisemitizmus a intolerancia vo vedomí obyvatelov Slovenskej republiky (Správa zo sociologického výskumu). (Racism, Xenophoby, Anti-Semitism and Intolerance in the Counsciousness of Slovak Inhabitants—Sociological Survey). Bratislava: Statistický Úrad SR, 1995.

Vašecka, M. Spolocenské problémy a podmienky ich riesenia na lokálnej úrovni v procese revitalizácie obecného spolocenstva (Magisterská práca) (The Social Problems and Conditions of Their Solving on the Local Level in the Process of Civic Society Revitalization—M.A. Thesis). Brno, Katedra sociologie Filozoficke Fakulty Masarykovy Univerzity, 1995.

Vybrané údaje o regiónoch za rok 1997 (Selected Figures about Regions in the SR for 1997). Bratislava: Statistic Institute of the SR, 1998.

Women about Themselves. Research report. Bratislava: BICFS, 1997.

7

Conclusions: Spectres of the Underclass

Michael Stewart

From the Black Sea to near the Black Forest the aftermath of 40 years of a "planned" economy and the inability of restoration capitalism to clear away the inherited social and economic mess in Central and Eastern Europe with anything like reassuring speed render ever more credible the suggestion that we are witnessing the emergence of a more chronic and devastating poverty than any seen since the 1930s.

Iván Szelényi, Rebecca Emigh, and Eva Fodor's introduction to this volume (Chapter 1) establishes beyond doubt that, in some countries at least, we are seeing people being locked into a prison of long-term unemployment from which neither their own nor even their children's prospects of escape are at all certain. In this sense, they argue, there is an underclass emerging in several countries of the region. The editors are careful to distinguish their use of the term "underclass" in an objective, statistical sense (focusing on the eminently measurable features of structural unemployment and poor school results) from that of ideologues who talk of the "welfare-dependent." In order to do so, they return to what appears to be the original, sociological meaning of the term. At the same time the authors are fully aware of the importance of "classificatory struggles" in shaping the nature, experience, and trajectory of poverty. Since in these classificatory struggles the meaning of "underclass" is up for grabs, I propose to ask here what it would mean to admit or concede that there is, throughout the postcommunist zone, an emergent underclass. The foregoing chapters have begun to sketch a sociological picture of potentially long-term immiserization; here the processes of categorization that shape research projects, social policy, and government-directed reform initiatives are considered.

The term "underclass," in popular and journalistic speech at least, derives its force, it seems to me, from the sense in which it suggests a difference from familiar patterns of class differentiation. Whereas in the (various) classical models social classes were constituted by their relations one with another, the underclass is formed by its absence of relations with others. Of course here the term "underclass" links up with that other, even more widely used term "social exclusion." When sociologists and journalists alike talk of social exclusion, we imagine a series of interrelated, more or less pathological behaviors resulting from lack of access to the institutions and practices that constitute neighborliness and citizenship. If a household does not have the money to go on holiday when its neighbors are so fortunate, if adult persons have no sense of the value of their vote, if parents feel that the local school is a no-go zone in which they are likely to be humiliated in front of their own child, if a family's necessary economic activities place it on the edge of the law, then in all these (and numerous other imaginable ways) the household involved no longer feels part of society but feels excluded, reduced to relating only to others in its own condition—as if part of an unwanted ethnic group. This is, of course, not primarily a matter of feeling and perception. If members of a household have no daily contact with the outside world, if they have lost the institutional forms of welfare protection and other means of self-preservation (e.g., access to nonexploitative rates of interest), then they are really excluded from the forms of sociality that enable more fortunate people to experience a sense of belonging.

While this use of the term "underclass" accurately pinpoints a distinctive social phenomenon, I question some of the baggage with which it tends to be associated. First is the link with unemployment, for it is commonly assumed that loss of work in the long-term will, in and of itself, create underclass-type phenomena. But it is also possible that the long-term unemployed, though in a difficult structural position in a modern society, do not constitute an underclass. As a thought experiment, consider the possibility that there exists in a given country a body of people who by ill chance have formed a cohort of long-term unemployed. These are not people who are unemployed between jobs or while they seek a new career; they are unlikely to find, or at least will have great difficulty ever finding, permanent, waged work again. These are, of course, people with all kinds of social, interpersonal, and technical skills, but in the statistics at least they will appear evermore as "the unemployed." Given their preexistent skills and the fact that the loss of the status "waged" does not eliminate those skills, it is hardly surprising to find, some years later, that many, if not most, of these people have found informal, unregistered, occasionally semi- or fully illicit activities in which they put their abilities to use to make some extra money. In fact, in many cases this "extra" money becomes rather substantial, certainly enough to support holidays at the level they used to have when formally employed, enough to clothe their school-age children and themselves well enough not to appear "shameful" when going to a parents' evening, and so on. Yet, on paper, these people appear as so many digits with an increasing number of months' unemployment behind them. When journalists and others look at the statistics, they assume that there must be attendant social problems. When these same commentators come across cases of organized criminality in the economy, indiscipline in the schoolroom, violence among football standees, attacks on the police, it seems to make sense to move from correlation to cause, to construct a terrifying narrative of social breakdown. But is it not possible in this situation that the two narratives have become *arbitrarily* linked, that "scare stories" about the end of civilized values as we know them are "explained" lazily by the (in reality quite independent) fact that there are large numbers of long-term unemployed?

Critical readers may object that the preceding thought experiment merely repeats platitudes derived from the first principles of neoliberal economists and the politicians whom they have inspired. To the contrary, I would argue, there is now compelling ethnographic evidence that, at least in some cases where outside commentators have adopted the language of social exclusion and moral degeneration of the unemployed, the established picture is largely, if not wholly, false. In a pioneering study on the Naples poor, a locus classicus, one might think, for models of social exclusion (since one finds the combined and long-term effects of national, regional, and local class marginalization on a section of the population), Italo Pardo has shown that the absolutely fixed stereotypes that have fed newspaper stories across Europe of a criminal Neapolitan subclass that is not only incapable of self-improvement but also prevents economic development are wholly misplaced. The *popolino* of Naples are typically seen— not just by journalists but by politicians and reformers as well—as a *misera plebs*, "an underclass—a grasping and backward lumpenproletariat that, dragged down by its culture and beliefs, is irredeemably caught into negative reciprocity [theft] and resigned to marginality and deprivation" (1996:2). By gaining access to the daily lives of the long-term unemployed, Pardo was able to form an original view of the specificity of *popolino* integration into the Italian economy: "success" for the *popolino*, material and spiritual, depended on the ability to combine different resources and domains of existence, transgressing the boundaries that more "respectable" citizens left intact. What Pardo demonstrates at length is the remarkable skill of these poor citizens in blurring boundaries between different sorts of work, trade, and apparently noneconomic networks and activities. While outsiders see in this mixing of categories the traces of criminality and antisocial behavior, to Pardo this reflects a basic misapprehension. From the point of view of the formal categories of industrialism *popolino* behavior does seem perverse, illogical, and precarious. Equally, the marketistic model of entrepreneurial activity makes *popolino* trade seem at times irrational and always grounded in thoroughly "distorted" markets. But managing existence in the gray zone involves skills unfamiliar to those securely footed in the white zone and cannot be framed within, or explained by, the conventional rhetoric of self-justification to which those more securely placed have access. Pardo entitled his book *Managing Existence in Naples* in order to stress the fact that for the *popolino* there is no categorical division of their social networks or activities into economic, political, religious, domestic. All intermingle in a seamless web of getting by. Pardo's point is not, of course, the sociological commonplace that the categorical distinctions that analysts and university faculties make do not hold water in real life, but rather it is the more interesting suggestion that the *popolino* themselves do not make the kinds of separations that their more respectable fellow Neapolitans try to sustain. This, he argues, is the secret of their success.

Note the test of the pudding, as it were. If one of the fundamental meanings of "underclass" is social exclusion, in the sense of having no access to the forums of wider society, of lacking daily contact with people who are not "your own", then, according to Pardo's evidence, the *popolino* of Naples are resoundingly not an "underclass." It seems to me—though to argue this through in these pages would take us too far from the topic—that the problem lies with traditional, mainstream ideas of the place of "work" in making us human and the horror that such ideas generate around the notion of "unemployment." The notion that we are *homo faber* has so many roots and forms in our culture— Christian, peasant-farmer, proletarian socialist, all of which focus around an idea of "productive labour"—that those who make their living otherwise, especially the poor, have difficulty justifying the worth of what they do. To take an analogy that may strike some as far-fetched, "our" unemployed might be like the blacksmith "castes" found in parts of sub-Saharan Africa, people whose means of gaining a livelihood is locally construed as so odd, so abnormal as to be polluting, as so pathological as to lead inevitably to asocial and antisocial behavior. To an outsider it seems clear that the African blacksmiths are barely distinguishable members of their own societies, but insiders treat them as if members of a different species, or at least a different ethnic group—rather as, in Europe, some imagine the seething hordes of an underclass "breeding" the conditions of its own reproduction!

One of the implications of Pardo's analysis is that in the Neapolitan subclass one finds a remarkable degree of cultural energy and creativity as people discover and invent new and surprising ways to manage their existence. Pardo's perspective, like that of many others of his (our) generation, differs in this way from much of the classic sociological literature on "underclass" and the popular view fed in the print media of essentially passive, responsive strata that lack the means to turn the tables on their own conditions and whose way of life can be seen as a mere collection of constrained responses to lack of waged labour, poor housing, financial uncertainty, and so on. The classic statement of this position is to be found in Oscar Lewis' (1966) pioneering work on the "culture of poverty."[1] For Lewis, a culture of poverty emerged at points of protoproletarianisation, when already wretched peasants made the first moves into modernity. The main features of this "culture" were gregarious behavior, informal credit among neighbors, alcoholism, the use of violence to settle quarrels, consensual unions, male desertion, a tendency to live in matrifocal families, and an abiding interest in short-term achievements over and above the long-term (Lewis 1968).

Lewis' work has been justly criticized for many failings (see, e.g., Hannerz 1969; Bourgois 1995:16–18), but the problem that I want to draw attention to here is the notion that there might be a single, coherent, cultural response to poverty, at least to long-term poverty. Leaving aside theoretical objections to any kind of economic reductionism, the model implies that the poor are wholly constrained in searching for adaptive strategies that enable them to "get by" until better times come. If part of the explanatory force of Lewis' argument derives from suggesting that the "culture of poverty" is a rational response to immiserization, rhetorical power is also added by arguing that this "design for living" enables the poor to manage better than they would otherwise.

Both these positions are, however, undermined by empirical research on what actually happens among poor people in ghettos. Whereas Lewis based his most successful and pathbreaking work on the longitudinal study of one extended family, Ulf Hannerz managed to paint a far broader picture of the Washington ghetto (1969), where a number of overlapping and, in part, opposed lifestyles—"mainstream," "swinger," and "street-corner"—were found (1969:38–56). Both in their own but different ways could be explained as a response to poverty and marginalization, but since the styles were different, it was clear that some to-and-fro, at least, was involved between macropolitical and economic constraint and cultural form. None of the local designs for living could be explained simply as a passive response to outside forces. Moreover, the existence of any one style could not logically be explained by its presumed functional fit with the local context—none were optimal, only different. Finally, to a significant extent these different "designs for living" were constituted, in important part, in dialogue one with another and with white, mainstream ideas observed in the wider society.[2]

Despite such limitations, Lewis' work did contain important insights into a widespread cultural syndrome. One of the most important is that, albeit it in a descriptive, nontheorized way, Lewis observed an important contrast between the people whom he was discussing and classic proletarians. In his foreword to the second edition of *La Vida*, in which he tried to elaborate the notion of a culture of poverty, he stated baldly that "when the poor become class conscious, or active members of trade union organisations, or when they adopt an internationalist outlook on the world, they are no longer part of the culture of poverty, although they may still be desperately poor" (1968:xliv). This particular insight has been lost in later writing because critics and supporters alike have mistakenly conflated Lewis' observations with studies of more traditional working-class communities.[3] They were helped in this confusion because Lewis himself considered ideas and ideologies to be mechanistic reflections of economic positions, such as poverty. His critics merely had to show that some poor people did not try to live in the present in order to undermine the whole correlation.

More recent, lesser-known work on the long-term unemployed in northern Ireland has taken Lewis' and Hannerz's ideas a stage further. Leo Howe (1990) describes communities where work was the foundation of most other statuses that married men held. All these were lost with long-term unemployment. In the face of an official, welfare state discourse that has aimed to distinguish the "scrounger" and "cheat" from "real job-seekers", most unemployed men represent themselves as "would-be willing workers" and their dependence on welfare payments as a means to sustain them in their search for productive activity. Howe worked in both Protestant and Catholic communities, and he provides tantalising evidence of ambivalent attitudes to official discourse among the latter. Among Catholics, unemployment is more readily seen as a structural feature of the system rather than a failure of individuals, and many men adopt an ambitious stance vis-a-vis potential payments from the social security office. The Catholics are less afraid to appear as "scroungers" before representatives of a state for which they have little attachment. In the Protestant community, better incorporated materially and ideologically within the British nation state, the rhetoric of the "deserving" and "undeserving" poor is more effective at preventing any activity that could be represented as "scrounging." What Howe's data demonstrate so clearly is that the historical relationship with the state (and thereby also work providers) decisively differentiates strategies in communities of the long-term unemployed, despite the formal, structural, and statistical similarity between them.

What can we learn from such diversity of responses to poverty when we try to understand the variety of postcommunist adaptations that we encounter in this volume? Anthropological research by Frances Pine conducted over the past 20 years in different regions of Poland provides compelling evidence of the contrasting responses to poverty among people who statistically look rather similar. Pine began her research in the socialist period among poor mountain farmers from southern Poland, the so-called Gorale of the Podhale region (1988). Since 1991 she has also investigated textile workers' families (now unemployed) from the Lodz region of northern Poland. In terms of factory closures, rates of unemployment, mortality rates, and other measurable indices of poverty (not to mention the effect of postcommunist political changes such as laws forbidding abortion), both these regions today look rather similar.

The responses of the two communities to postcommunism, however, could not have been more different. When down in the plains, the mountain farmers behave, it seems, rather like successful Roma businessmen and have adapted to the world of wheeling and dealing like ducks to water. The acceptability of the idea of displacing part or all of the household for shorter or longer periods means that Gorale are fully able to exploit new opportunities and not just pine for the lost old ones. While one finds some of the Gorale men rebuilding the city of Berlin (their grandfathers and great-grandfathers built large parts of Budapest and Chicago), and some of the women have found a burgeoning market for au pairs in Athens, many of the Lodz worker-farmers by contrast say that they would never consider leaving the area and that the only things they are good at are weaving and farming. Even those who have tried to establish private enterprises in the past few years have stayed within their chosen fields of textiles or agriculture. Others are still waiting for someone to come to them with jobs/welfare/money.[4]

What might explain such a radical difference in the whole way that people respond to rather similar circumstances? Pine finds the answer in the details of historical difference that shaped the culture, the designs for living found in the two regions. The Gorale have long been outsiders—in the Austro-Hungarian Empire and in modern Poland, a border mountainous people who represent both the core of what it is to be a "traditional" Pole and also something quite foreign. Partly forced away by poverty, partly forced out by rules of partible inheritance, and partly preadapted by traditions of mountain shepherding (and long-distance transhumance), the Gorale have long been accustomed to temporarily seeking their fortune in distant lands. Their position as mountain peoples, far from the centers of power in premodern Europe, and as border people whose loyalty is often doubted further distanced them from an unhealthy respect for authority, rather as the northern Irish Catholics, according to Leo Howe, are freer than their Protestant counterparts in dealings with the welfare state. This kind of liberty is surely one of the sine qua nons for survival as entrepreneurs at the bottom of the social pile. Working with tiny margins of profit, and a regard for bureaucratic formalities, a fear of stepping outside the letter of the law would cripple their ability to make any money at all in our heavily regulated economies.

The difficulties faced by the worker-farmers of Lodz derive in similar measure from their own history. Since the middle of the nineteenth century, when the region was part of the Russian empire, this has been the center of the Polish textile trade—providing at its outset the uniforms for the imperial army. In contrast to the Gorale, where partible inheritance kept women on the land and encouraged male migration, here impartible inheritance threw women onto the local labor market. Under socialism the nationalization of the factories did not transform the health and safety conditions but did mark one further stage in the incorporation of these people by the state. While critical of aspects of the regime, the strong worker culture slotted well into the socialist state's own project. Since the guaranteed security was removed, they have been at a loss, both materially and spiritually, as to how to move on (Pine 1996:140–147). It is striking, for instance, that the inheritance pattern encouraged the emergence of worker-farmers, families who went back to the village to cultivate precious food on small sections of family land. Today, when such resources constitute a small, but nonetheless important, potential, few of the Lodz families that Pine got to know felt comfortable taking produce to market. This would have been too much like *handlowac*, that is, trade. While for the Gorale the Polish word connotes skill and cunning, up in Lodz it is the "dishonest" Gypsies and others who lack a real work ethic who are associated with this term (Pine 1996:140–152).

Again it can be seen that, as in Naples, the ability to juggle, to cross boundaries as do tricksters and other masters of the arts of impersonation and play, and to bring together circles and networks that others would, out of shame, keep apart, enables some of the poor to survive and even, one day, maybe, rise. Often this entrepreneurial spirit may rest on a strong division of the world inside the community and that outside. As Pine has put it, "Trust and morality are implicit at the local level but do not extend to the wider society. Rather, the centre is viewed almost as a field of opportunity, in which gaps can be located to pursue entrepreneurial dealings; these dealings are imbued with little or no sense of moral obligation, and there is little sense of shared identity with the centre" (1998:121). Though the center may view the practice of those from the periphery as akin to that of a Mafia, this is not how matters look from the bottom up.

This seems a highly appropriate place to say a few words about the racialization of poverty, in particular the way in which the Roma of Eastern Europe—who are often seen as a source of Mafia-type behavior—are in danger of being classified as an underclass. From the sociological point of view, which aims to find an accurate historical representation of the historical tendencies in Eastern Europe over the past 50 years, the Roma provide a particularly important case. As Southern Europe and Eastern Europe have become fashionable places to carry out research, and the region has begun to be flooded by pundits with ready-made problems and prepacked solutions, it has become increasingly common to hear that the plight of the Roma is the exemplary case of the ravages wrought by capitalist restoration on a defenseless people. While it is hard to fault the good intentions of the authors and activists in question, what is so often missed in these laments is a sense of the historical circumstances created by the socialist regimes that so crippled *sections* of the Roma community that it is hard at the moment to see how they will recover. It is in this sense strictly impossible to understand the present, let alone predict the future without a good understanding of the past.

Above all, it seems to me, what we have to remember is that although in some respects (especially when one makes a contrast with the prewar treatment of Roma), the Roma were "beneficiaries" of the planned economy—for instance, like other citizens they were guaranteed job security (though 20 years after everyone else)—very many of the welfare policies that appeared to be intended to ameliorate their conditions were, first, designed with very little knowledge of what the Roma might need or want and, second, implemented in such a way that, on the one hand, the Roma felt discriminated against and, on the other hand, the "majority society" felt the Roma were being unfairly privileged! (Stewart 1997). Such an ability to annoy everyone at once was perhaps a peculiar skill of the communist regimes. What is essential to hold on to, though, is that from the perspective of an outsider (both literal outsiders such as myself working in the region at that time but also those like the dissident sociologists working in Eastern Europe in the 1970s and 1980s) the position of the Roma remained what used to be called "multiply disadvantaged," which is to say that in housing, educational, welfare, and employment terms even at the best of socialist times the Roma had it worse, far worse than the average non-Roma (*pace* formalist claims that all citizens of these countries have been covered by the same institutional networks). In this sense the exaggerated deprivation of the Roma under postcommunism is but another legacy of the communist ancestors.

The authors in Chapter 1 ask under what conditions the emergence of a racialized underclass is likely. They draw attention to the historically specific circumstances that shape the conflicts around racialization, contrasting Hungary with its largely monoethnic minority "problem"; Romania, where Roma are only one of several minorities, not all of which suffer economically; and Bulgaria, where all minorities seem to fare rather badly.[5] One of the implications of their argument, which deserves teasing out a little further, is that researchers should be paying more attention to the *struggles* around racialization, the different contests that are taking place in the region between those who would racialize poverty in various ways and those who resist.

Considering the fact that in the field of underclass studies those conducted in the United States have a disproportionate weight, this consideration becomes all the more serious. As anyone who is familiar with this literature will know, in the United States today one is confronted by a racialization of poverty that, thank goodness, still looks like a nightmare from this side of the Atlantic. Reading such modern classics as Macleod's *Ain't No Makin' It* or Bourgois' *In Search of Respect* as well as Wacquant's lesser-known work on Chicago, I was struck by the apartheid-like conditions reigning in this supposed land of liberty. (In fact, of course, real apartheid was in many ways a lot less segregatory in practice than real America is.) Consider the fact that the French sociologist Wacquant reckons that he was the only white person many of his informants had regular dealings with and that he was certainly the only white person who had ever had friendly relations with many of them (1993)—and this in the context of a full panoply of equal opportunities legislation and all the noise around civil rights. In any of the communities of Gypsies that I know personally in Romania, Hungary, Slovakia, and even the Czech Republic, despite the absence of legal safeguards, daily life is not as segregated as across the Atlantic.

I cite Wacquant's work here because he makes a telling point in his publications by contrasting the black belts of the Northeast and Midwest of the United States with his other fieldwork experience in urban France. In the so-called red belt around the big French connurbations one finds many of the same macroeconomic problems as in American inner-city ghettos: a declining population with an imbalanced age, class, and race structure (young, poor, and dark) (1993:368). In both countries the practical difficulties as well as the symbolic stigma of poverty are similar—living in neighborhoods that feel like a kind of internal exile from the rest of society (1993:369). But although there is in France a vociferous far-right wing, even a quasi-fascist party that tries to racialize the "crisis" of poverty, public opinion and organs of the state remain convinced that the real problem is one of "youth." In other words, despite the efforts of some politicians with fairly easy access to media mouthpieces (if due only to the "newsworthy," "scandalous" content of their message) to racialize poverty in France, they have been nowhere nearly as successful as generations of apparently far more moderate U.S. politicians. The experience of segregation and discrimination of these two impoverished communities is correspondingly different. The *beurs* of the red belt know that territorial segregation runs flatly counter to a state ideology that is widely trumpeted; and they are also less likely to succumb to the rhetoric of individualistic achievement and blame the victim theories than their American counterparts; finally, they are able when outside their own neighbourhood to "pass" without being noticed *so long as their address is not known* and can thus participate, if only often fleetingly and in a sense vicariously in the life of the city, living out what Wacquant calls a "fantasy of inclusion" (1993:372–373). Those who dwell in black ghettos have no such passport to temporary freedom.

I find this last example of Wacquant's particularly telling since his experience in France corresponds, rather surprisingly, with my own ethnographic experience in parts of Eastern Europe. Although segregation is more marked in Hungary than in France (and is perhaps increasingly so), even in the late 1980s Roma youth in the town I know best could successfully pass as non-Gypsies, or at least not be treated as *cigany* for shorter or longer periods of time. In this town it was often precisely by concealing one's address that this was achieved. If one did not live on one of the Gypsy settlements in the town, it could be assumed (at least temporarily, depending on adherence to the correct dress code) that, for all intents and purposes, one was not a Gypsy. Of course, a situation in which Roma could be "proud to be Roma" in their daily encounters with non-Roma would be preferable, but in the meantime being able to avoid racism in daily life is a more practical and possibly less self-destructive option than always having to confront it head-on.

This rather minor phenomenon of daily life has a much more important and significant corollary: the persistent cycle of emergence and disappearance of large sections of Roma in censuses in the region. Chapter 3 in this volume touches on some of the most important aspects of this phenomenon. Here I would just stress the way that not declaring oneself as Gypsy, to some extent at least, constitutes an acceptable claim to non-Gypsies. To understand the significance of this social fact one has only to recall the literature on America where the colour bar is more or less absolute. To be nonblack in the States, one has to be "pure" white. There is, famously, no American mestizo population, for, both historically and in the present, to be part black is to be black. Such has not been and still is not the case in the former communist countries.

Of course, if we pause for a moment and look back, the reason for such differences is not hard to find. The history of race, of blacks, in America differs so profoundly from that of Algerians or Africans in France or Roma in Eastern Europe that it is hardly surprising that the current features of race relations should be so different. In none of the European countries did a racial minority form a slave caste in the last century,[6] and in none did the denial of civil rights take the dramatic forms it did in the United States until quite recently.

The implications of these differences for an understanding of "underclass" formation and the appropriate mechanism to fight racialization of poverty are, I believe, profound. First, the existence of racial differences in and of themselves does not generate a racialized underclass. Second, those who *struggle to racialize* poverty will do so within the local understandings of ethnic difference peculiar to their own part of the world. Therefore, third, although there is much to be said for the vigorous pursuit of incontrovertible entitlements and for the uncompromising legal clarity of the U.S. civil rights tradition, it may not necessarily provide the best safeguard against the formation of a real underclass in the region. It may be that local remedies and regional responses will have more to contribute than some of the new missionaries would have us believe.

CONCLUDING COMMENTS

About one hundred and twenty years ago, in a flurry of pamphlets, articles, and book-length monographs, an early theory of the underclass was articulated by the doctors, the poor law commissioners, and the social reformers who worked with or visited among the poor of London. This theory, which for a decade or so won widespread assent in genteel metropolitan circles, asserted that a cancer of demoralisation and degeneration was taking hold among the city's poor, a destructive growth of habits of mind and body that would lead to the inevitable extirpation of this new urban race. The historian of this phenomenon, Gareth Stedman Jones, quotes a typical report: "Finding himself at a disadvantage. . . . [the Londoner] goes through many stages before he is finally eliminated. Irregular labour, odd jobs, sweater's dens, prostitution, subsistence on charity, agitation, 'demonstrations,' and riot are only some of the struggles of the dying Londoner before he pays the debt of nature, whose laws he has no power to obey" (Freeman–Williams 1890, cited in Stedman Jones 1984). There was, naturally, a clutch of interrelated features of this theory that sprang from the particular intellectual context of mid-nineteenth-century England: the notion that moral and physical decline was due to urban conditions; the attention given to the physical, bodily expression of degeneration; the social Darwinian (Spencerian) vision of the impending extinction of species; the idea that immigration from the rural regions was to be the mechanism of selection, both as the cause of further immiserization via competition and as the final solution of the problem of urban poverty via physical elimination of the weaker (urban) party. Yet, despite these distinctive nineteenth-century markers, the historiography of this period inevitably reminds me of current discussions of underclass formation, East and West. We find the same fear that what the prospering, propertied classes see below them is an irreversible decline in economic standards of life, an unstoppable degeneration of moral fiber, a self-reproducing descent into criminality, and, most generally, forms of social exclusion (for instance, from the educational system) that will make any return journey "back" to normality and civility for the generation to come all but impossible. The obvious point to make here, that the history of middle-class ideas repeats itself rather precisely, is too simple and misses the more interesting point. For, paradoxically, it could be argued that this very similarity in the rhetoric of social differentiation gives rise to the hope that the same fate that befell "Outcast Londoners" lies ahead for the new poor of Eastern and Southern Europe: their disappearance, their extinction. This surprising outcome did not take place in London through Darwinian selection and physical extermination but instead occurred through a transformation of the economic and social environment. The London of Nicholas Nickleby and Oliver Twist was all but eliminated in the decade and a half after the end of World War I. The chronic poverty, the backwardness, and the illiteracy that had seemed to condemn teeming swathes of the population were being dramatically eliminated by the mid-1930s (Stedman Jones 1984:348–9).

Of course, we cannot hope that all the poor of postcommunism will fare as well as the London poor 70 years ago. Janos Ladanyi argues convincingly in Chapter 3 in this volume that the crisis of "gypsification" of total villages lies, above all, in the denial to those Roma of all forms of social inspiration from contact with "others" and all forms of economic opportunity to prosper within the community. It is indeed hard to see how residents of these peripheral villages will make good without mass migration to more prosperous regions. But not all Roma live in such desperate conditions, and for those with a foothold in the cities the London example may well prove appropriate.

The historiography of 1920s and 1930s London speaks of industrialization as the motor of change, the disproportionate increase in factory employment in London, and the consequent rise in real wages in that area. But, of course, this focus derives, in part, from the archive sources available. For the most part the resourcefulness of the former "outcasts," their own ability to make use of the "good times" (and remember these were hardly boom years), is lost from the record. But that is no reason today to pass over the likely importance of such "adaptive fitness." In our time, if a similar transformation of poverty is to occur in parts of Eastern and Southern Europe, it will not be achieved by industrialization but will be more in line with the service economy and flexible forms of economic activity that have emerged in parts of the advanced capitalist zone in the past 20 years. In principle at least, if what I have argued for the flexibility and adaptability of the poor of Europe holds good at all, some of those slated for inclusion in the underclass may confound their labellers and find themselves well suited to this brave new world.

NOTES

1. Lewis' name is now rather widely reviled in the Anglo-Saxon world because of the way his ideas were used by later generations of United States-based, policy-oriented sociologists to justify cuts in welfare programs, arguing that since poverty was sustained by "a culture of poverty," there was nothing that the government could do to alleviate conditions. It would be better to let those poor who were culturally "committed" to poverty go to the wall. Readers from Eastern Europe will notice a resemblance in such arguments to- some populist approaches to "the Gypsy question."

2. In this sense many influential Hungarian writers on the culture of poverty remained trapped within the excessive functionalism suggested by Lewis. See, for example, Solt 1976, reprinted 1998.

3. Authors like Charles Valentine and, later, Janice Perlman argued that the urban poor of Latin America were different from their bourgeois countrymen only in the level of their wealth. Such writers accused Lewis of taking situational responses to poverty as expressions of deep-seated cultural values. In contrast to Lewis, Perlman concludes her study by saying that residents of the *favelas* ("slums") in urban Brazil "have the aspirations of the bourgeoisie, the perseverance of pioneers and the values of patriots. What they do not have is an opportunity to fulfil these aspirations" (1976:213). This may have been true of some slum dwellers in urban Brazil, but the implication that there is no distinctive culture among any of the world's poor, just the mechanistic effects of poverty that wealth will remove, seems unwarranted.

4. In more recent work Pine suggests that the Lodz workers are beginning to talk more of lack of money that lack of work, suggesting the shape of an emerging adaptation (1998).

5. See, however, Biro and Biro (1997) for evidence of impoverishment in Szeklerland, Transylvania.

6. In Romania there was a form of unfree Gypsy labor, but it is not at all clear what form of "slavery" this constituted—though it was certainly not plantation slavery—or how many Gypsies were enslaved. As Patrick Williams argues, it is hard to square the vigorous resourcefulness of those Roma who are supposed to have fled Romanian slavery with what we know of postslave populations (personal communication).

REFERENCES

Biro Z. A., and Biro, A. (eds.). 1997. *Igy elunk: Elszegenyedesi folyamatok a Szekelyfoldon*, Regionalis es Antropologiai Kutatasok Kozpontja, Csikszereda: Pro-Prink Konyvkiado.

Bourgois, P. 1995. *In Search of Respect: Selling Crack in El Barrio*. Cambridge: Cambridge University Press.

Hannerz, U. 1969. *Soulside: Enquiries into Ghetto Culture and Community*. New York and London: Columbia University Press.

Howe, L. 1990. *Being Unemployed in Northern Ireland: An Ethnographic Study.* Cambridge: Cambridge University Press.

Lewis, O. 1966. "The culture of poverty." *Scientific American* 210, 10–25.

———. 1968. *La Vida.* (2d ed.). New York: Knopf.

Macleod, J. 1987. *Ain't No Makin' It: Aspirations and Attainment in a Low-Income Neighborhood.* Boulder, CO: Westview Press.

Pardo, I. 1996. *Managing Existence in Naples: Morality, Action, and Structure.* Cambridge: Cambridge University Press.

Perlman, J. E. 1976. *The Myth of Marginality: Urban Poverty and Politics in Rio de Janero.* Berkeley: University of California Press.

Pine, F. 1988. "Kinship, Marriage and Social Change in a Polish Highland Village." Unpublished Ph.D. dissertation, University of London.

———. 1996. "Redefining Women's Work in Poland." Pp.115–132 in R. Abrahams (ed.), *After Socialism: Land Reform and Social Change in Eastern Europe.* Providence and Oxford: Berghahn Books.

———. 1998. "Dealing with Fragmentation: The Consequences of Privatisation for Rural Women in Central and Southern Poland." In S. Bridger and F. Pine (eds.), *Surviving Post-Socialism: Local Strategies and Regional Responses in Post-Socialist Eastern Europe and the Former Soviet Union.* London: Routledge.

Solt, O. 1998 (1976). A Hetvenes Evek Budapest Szegenyei, in Profil (Samizdat 1976). Reprinted in *Meltosagot Mindenkinek, Osszegyujtott irasok, Elso Kotet.*

Stedman Jones, G. 1984 (1971). *Outcast London: A Study in the Relationship between Classes in Victorian Society.* Harmondsworth: Penguin.

Stewart, Michael. 1997. *The Time of the Gypsies.* Boulder: Westview.

Wacquant, L. J. D. 1993. "Urban Outcasts: Stigma and Division in the Black American Ghetto and the French Urban Periphery." *International Journal of Urban and Regional Research* 17, no. 3, 366–383.

Index

About the Contributors

REBECCA JEAN EMIGH is Assistant Professor of Sociology at the University of California, Los Angeles (UCLA). Her research focuses on transitions to capitalism, both contemporary and historical.

EVA FODOR is Assistant Professor of Sociology at Dartmouth College. She works on social inequality, gender, and communist and postcommunist societies.

LIUBENA KONSTANTINOVA is a researcher at the National Centre for Public Opinion Research in Bulgaria. She conducts research on public opinion and the sociology of women.

JÁNOS LADÁNYI is Associate Professor of Sociology at the University of Economic Sciences in Budapest. He is an expert in urban sociology and the sociology of education. His recent work focused on the question of ethnicity and poverty, with particular emphasis on Roma.

NÁNDOR L. MAGYARI is Lecturer of Sociology at Babes-Bolyai University in Cluj, Romania. His research is mainly focused on interethnic relations in Transylvania.

ENIKÖ MAGYARI-VINCZE is Associate Professor at the Faculty of European Studies, Babes-Bolyai University, Cluj, Romania. Her current teaching and research interests include anthropology of complex societies, political anthropology, politics of identity, the anthropology of nationalism, and anthropology of gender.

PETAR-EMIL MITEV is the head of the Studies of Ideologies, Faculty of Philosophy, Sofia University. He is working on problems of East European transition and questions of ethnicity. He has published widely on questions of ideology, ethnicity, and transition.

LIVIA POPESCU is Associate Professor at the Department of Social Work, Faculty of History and Philosophy, Babes-Bolyai University. She specializes in the analysis of social policy and social stratification.

IVETA RADICOVÁ is an Associate Professor of Political Science at Comenius University in Bratislava. Her main research interest is in social policy and social consequences of the transition in Central and Eastern Europe.

TROIAN ROTARIU is Chair of Sociology at Babes-Bolyai University in Cluj, Romania, and one of the leading experts on survey research in Romania.

MICHAEL STEWART is Lecturer of Anthropology at the University of London and the leading expert on East European Roma.

IVÁN SZELÉNYI is Professor and Chair of Sociology at Yale University. He is an authority on social stratification in Eastern Europe.

ELZBIETA TARKOWSKA is Professor of Sociology at the Institute of Philosophy and Sociology, Polish Academy of Sciences. She has published widely on problems of sociology of time, lifestyles, and poverty.

ILONA TOMOVA is a researcher at the Institute of Sociology at the Bulgarian Academy of Sciences. Her work focuses on ethnic communities (Bulgarian Muslims, Turks, and Roma) and their interrelations.

MICHAL VAŠECKA is a researcher at the Open Society Foundation. His work focuses on public policy, national minorities, anti-Semitism, and media discourse in Slovakia.